THE CONSTITUTIONAL HISTORY
OF THE LOUISIANA PURCHASE
1803-1812

THE
CONSTITUTIONAL HISTORY

OF THE

LOUISIANA PURCHASE

1803 - 1812

BY

EVERETT S. BROWN

[1920]

AUGUSTUS M. KELLEY · PUBLISHERS
CLIFTON 1972

First Edition 1920

(Berkeley: University of California Press, 1920)

Reprinted 1972 by
Augustus M. Kelley Publishers
REPRINTS OF ECONOMIC CLASSICS
Clifton New Jersey 07012

. . . .

I S B N 0-678-00742-X
L C N 68-55492

. . . .

PRINTED IN THE UNITED STATES OF AMERICA
by SENTRY PRESS, NEW YORK, N. Y. 10013

PREFACE

One of the most striking features of the history of the United States is the gradual extension of its boundaries westward and the successful operation of a colonial, or territorial, system of government. Hardly had the Constitution, which contained no specific grant of power to acquire territory, been put into effect when the first step in the acquisition of foreign territory was made. The purpose of this monograph is to discuss the most important of the constitutional questions which arose as a consequence of the purchase of Louisiana, and to show how the statesmen and legislators in charge of affairs at that time interpreted the Constitution in answering those questions. Much has been written on the Louisiana Purchase but no connected narrative of its constitutional aspects has hitherto appeared.

The writer believes that he has added many important details to the printed accounts of United States history. For instance, he has given, for the first time, the detailed story of the Senate debate on the Breckinridge Bill. Then, too, there is much to be learned of the struggle between correct theory and actual practice in government from tracing Jefferson's plans for the settlement and government of Louisiana. The status of the inhabitants of territories—so fruitful a theme for controversy even to the present day; the control of slavery and the slave-trade by Congress, set forth with startling bitterness in the Senate debate on the Breckinridge Bill; and the Indian and land questions, always incidental to American westward expansion, all have new light shed upon them.

A certain limitation should here be made. This study has been confined principally to the lower part of the province purchased from France, that which was organized as Orleans

v

Territory and which later entered the Union as the state of Louisiana. Occasional reference is made to Upper Louisiana but to have traced the constitutional history of the entire area known as Louisiana would have involved entering a field almost limitless in extent. The writer hopes, however, to make further investigation of the constitutional history of the territorial expansion of the United States.

In writing this monograph, much hitherto unpublished manuscript material has been utilized. Personal investigation was conducted in the following places: the University of California Library; the Bancroft Library; the Cabildo (home of the Louisiana Historical Society), and the City Hall, New Orleans; the Library of Congress, especially the Manuscript Division; the Bureau of Rolls and Library of the State Department, Washington, D. C.; the Boston Public Library; the Massachusetts Historical Society Library; the Athenaeum; Harvard University Library; the American Antiquarian Society Library, Worcester, Mass.; the New Hampshire Historical Society Library, and the New Hampshire State Library, both located at Concord; and the New York Public Library.

Much new information was obtained from the William Plumer manuscripts, a mine of hitherto little-consulted material. William Plumer was born at Newburyport, Massachusetts, in 1759, but moved with his parents to Epping, New Hampshire, in 1768. He was given a liberal education, following which he engaged in the practice of law. Entering the political field, he served for a number of years in the state legislature, and rose to the position of presiding officer of the house of representatives and, later, of the senate. He was a member of the state constitutional convention in 1791–1792; served as United States senator from New Hampshire from December 6, 1802, to March 3, 1807; was governor of his state for the terms of 1812–1813 and 1816–1819; and, as presidential elector in 1820, cast the single vote against James Monroe. Plumer devoted the later years of his life to literature. He died in 1850.

Having decided early in life to write a history of the United States, Plumer made use of every opportunity to collect materials to that end. His ambition as a historical writer was not gratified, but he left a vast quantity of manuscripts, invaluable for the history of his period. A small part of this collection was used by William Plumer Jr. in his *Life of William Plumer*. In that book, however, the younger Plumer practically ignored the very valuable memorandum which Senator Plumer kept of the debates in the United States Senate from 1803 to 1807. This memorandum gives detailed information on government matters seemingly nowhere else obtainable. Neither the Government nor the newspapers at that time kept a full report of the debates in Congress. Especially was this true of those of the Senate.

A part of this "Memorandum" was contributed by the present writer to the *American Historical Review*, XXII (1917), 340–364. No other writer, so far as I can ascertain, has extensively used the Plumer "Memorandum." In the monograph a differentiation in citation is made between the "Memorandum" and Plumer's letters, the latter being referred to as *MSS*. Plumer's papers have not been arranged in any more definite order than that in which he left them, which makes citation of them rather difficult.

Other important manuscripts used were the *Claiborne Papers*, consisting of six volumes entitled "Claiborne's Correspondence relative to Orleans Territory," and one volume, "Orleans Territory, Miscellaneous." These volumes in the Bureau of Rolls and Library in the Department of State in Washington, contain Governor Claiborne's reports of the territorial government of Louisiana, or, to be more exact, of Orleans Territory, from

December, 1803, when the province was turned over to the American commissioners, until the admission, in 1812, of Orleans Territory into the Union as the state of Louisiana. The volume of miscellaneous papers contains a few items of as late date as 1815. An idea of the number of letters in the Claiborne collection and the subject matter contained in them. can be obtained by consulting David W. Parker, *Calendar of papers in Washington relating to the territories of the United States,* Washington, D. C., 1911 (Publication number 148 of the Carnegie Institution). Copies of Claiborne's letters and papers have been preserved in Jackson, Mississippi.*

From the Jefferson, Madison, and Monroe papers were gleaned many items not contained in the published writings of these statesmen. Especially was this true of letters which had been available only in part in printed form. The following bibliographical aids were of much assistance in the examination of the voluminous collections just cited:

Calendar of the Correspondence of Thomas Jefferson, Part I, *Letters from Jefferson.* Bulletin No. 6 of the Bureau of Rolls and Library of the Department of State, Washington, 1894.

Ibid., Part. II, *Letters to Jefferson.* Bulletin No. 8 of the same department. Washington, 1895.

Ibid., Part III, *Supplementary.* Bulletin No. 10 of the same department. Washington, 1903. (Calendar of papers received after the publication of Bulletin No. 8.)

---

* See the *Third Annual Report of the Director of the Department of Archives and History of the State of Mississippi from October 1, 1903, to October 1, 1904,* Dunbar Rowland, director. Nashville, Tenn., 1905. Also *Eleventh and Twelfth Reports of the Director of the Department of Archives and History of the State of Mississippi from November 1, 1911, to October 31, 1912. An Official Guide to the Historical Materials in the Mississippi Department of Archives and History,* Dunbar Rowland, LL.D., director. Nashville, Tenn., 1914.

At the time when this monograph was being written, the *Official Letter Books of W. C. C. Claiborne, 1801–1816,* edited by Dunbar Rowland (6 vols. Jackson, Miss., 1917) had not yet appeared. Many of the Claiborne letters cited in manuscript form are now available in print.

Preface

Calendar of the Correspondence of James Monroe. Bulletin No. 2 of the same department. Washington, 1893.

Calendar of the Correspondence of James Madison. Bulletin No. 4 of the same department. Washington, 1894.

Arrangement of the Papers of Madison, Jefferson, Hamilton, Monroe, and Franklin. Bulletin No. 5 of the same department. Washington, 1894.

A number of unpublished letters bearing on the subject of Louisiana were found in the *Pickering Papers,* in the library of the Massachusetts Historical Society. Consultation of the Pickering collection also afforded the opportunity of correcting or verifying dates and names used erroneously or doubtfully by editors of the printed works of some of Pickering's correspondents. *The Historical Index to the Pickering Papers* in the Massachusetts Historical Society, *Collections,* Sixth Series, III, Boston, 1896, was of great assistance in the use of these papers.

Occasional important letters were picked up in odd places. An excellent example is the Nahum Mitchell letter, quoted in Chapter VIII, which was found among the *Robbins Papers.* The present writer is unaware of its ever having been previously used.

Needless to say, the published writings of the statesmen already mentioned, as well as many others, were carefully consulted. A full list is given in the bibliography.

The controversial side of the Louisiana question is well illustrated by contemporaneous printed pamphlets and newspapers. On the publications of this type, the citations in the monograph and the bibliography afford sufficient comment.

Secondary authorities were used only to substantiate a statement already obtained from primary sources, or when the author of the book cited was himself quoting primary authorities. In this respect the books most used were those of Henry Adams and Charles Gayarré.

The writer wishes to thank all those librarians and archivists who made possible his search for materials. In particular, in this respect, does he owe much to the never-failing kindness of Mr. John C. Fitzpatrick of the Manuscript Division of the Library of Congress. Acknowledgments are also due to Professor Frederick J. Teggart of the University of California for suggestive criticism; and to Professor Herbert E. Bolton and the editorial committee of the University of California Press for the editing of the monograph. The writer's wife was especially helpful in the arduous task of copying manuscripts and in reading proof. Finally, the writer desires to express his appreciation of the kindly and scholarly assistance of Dr. Eugene Irving McCormac of the University of California, under whose guidance this study was made.

EVERETT SOMERVILLE BROWN.

WASHINGTON, D.C., December 18, 1918.

CONTENTS

xi

CHAPTER I

EVENTS LEADING TO THE PURCHASE

The early years of the nineteenth century were crucial ones for the new government of the United States. The "critical period" under the Articles of Confederation had led to the demand for a more effective plan of government, and the Constitution was the result. The ratification of this instrument was, however, but the beginning of another period of experiment; or better, perhaps, another chapter in the history of the old experiment. The danger of disunion and consequent disintegration had become apparent to all thinking citizens of the young nation. Such dangers must in future be avoided or independence threatened to become a curse rather than a blessing. Did the Constitution offer the solution of these perplexing problems? It was a well known fact that the Constitution was the result of compromises and that it had been ratified by the people in the states only after a long campaign and in the face of strong opposition. The Constitution had merely laid down a framework of government; a framework which had to be elaborated into a working system. The powers of the Federal Government must be made strong enough to meet the needs of the country as a whole, but could this be done without infringing upon the constitutional rights claimed by the states? What were the rights of the "original partners" to the compact? Could their relative importance in the councils of state be altered without their consent, given by their legislatures or by conventions called for that purpose?

Only fourteen years after the ratification of the Constitution a tremendous new problem was thrust upon the infant government for settlement. This was the acquisition of Louisiana, a vast, undeveloped, foreign country, equal in size to the entire

United States of that day.   What would be its effect on the destinies of the Republic?

Undoubtedly the purchase of Louisiana was one of the most momentous steps in the history of our country.   In its broader aspects, viewed from the present time, it insured to the American people the opportunity of westward expansion, and through the ownership of a vast public domain helped in the upbuilding of a broader national feeling and occasioned the downfall of the policy of strict construction of the Constitution.[1]   In its own day the acquisition, after the establishment of independence and the Constitution, was hailed as "the greatest political blessing ever conferred on these states."[2]

Yet the purchase of Louisiana incidentally raised many constitutional points, the settlement of which has been of the utmost significance in the constitutional history of the United States. In the words of Professor Frederick J. Turner: "When the whole sweep of American history and the present tendencies of our life are taken into view, it would be possible to argue that the doctrines of the Louisiana Purchase were farther-reaching in their effect upon the Constitution than even the measures of Alexander Hamilton or the decisions of John Marshall."[3] To this strong statement may be added that of a well known expositor of the Constitution, who asserts that the purchase of Louisiana from France "gave such direction to the subsequent thought of the people and led to such marshaling of political forces, that nearly all the leading events of later American history were either traceable to or in some measure shaped or determined by it."[4]

---

[1] Turner, "Significance of the Frontier in American History," in American Historical Association, *Annual Report, 1903,* 218.

[2] David Ramsay, *An Oration on the Cession of Louisiana to the United States,...May 12, 1804,...* Charleston, S. C.

[3] Turner, "Significance of the Louisiana Purchase," in *Review of Reviews,* XXVII, 584.

[4] Cooley, "The Acquisition of Louisiana," in Indiana Historical Society, *Publications,* II, 65.

What did the men who helped to frame the Constitution think of the questions involved in the acquisition and government of Louisiana? What interpretation of that instrument was made by members of Congress when the question of the right to acquire and govern foreign territory came before them? The writings of the statesmen concerned, and the debates in Congress show the great interest displayed in the problems which arose; and the settlement of these problems has served as the basis for similar decision in later cases. Details might vary, but in the broader aspects of constitutional interpretation arising from the acquisition of foreign territory by the United States, the Louisiana Purchase served as the great precedent.

The events leading to the purchase of Louisiana may be treated briefly. The necessity for the control of a place of deposit for merchandise on the lower Mississippi had been recognized by a large part of the people of the United States. A widespread alarm was therefore aroused when, through the cession of the Louisiana territory by Spain to France, a stronger power came into contact with the United States in that region. President Jefferson in his second annual message to Congress, December 15, 1802, declared: "The cession of the Spanish Province of Louisiana to France, which took place in the course of the late war, will if carried into effect, make a change in the aspect of our foreign relations which will doubtless have just weight in any deliberation of the Legislature connected with that subject."[5]

Upon the first rumors of such a transfer of Louisiana from Spain to France, Secretary of State Madison had written to Robert R. Livingston, United States minister to France, asking him to find out whether or not these rumors were true; and if so, to ascertain whether France could not be induced to transfer the Floridas to the United States, provided they were included

[5] Richardson, *Messages and Papers of the Presidents*, I, 343.

in the cession.] At the very least, West Florida was to be
obtained, if possible. If the Floridas were not included in the
transfer, Livingston was to make every effort to obtain the
consent of France and Spain to their cession to the United
States. Should he learn that the Floridas were still in the
hands of Spain, Livingston was to act in harmony with Charles
Pinckney at Madrid in an attempt to procure them.[6] Livingston
immediately opened negotiations with the French Minister of
Exterior Relations.[7] Spain insisted that the Floridas were not
included in the cession, while France held that they were.[8] Livingston continued negotiations. In answer to a question from
Joseph Bonaparte whether the United States would prefer the
Floridas to Louisiana, Livingston replied that his Government
had no wish to extend its boundary across the Mississippi. All
that was sought was security, not extension of territory.[9]

While these negotiations were being carried on under the
direction of the President, Congress was not idle. On January
4, 1803, Roger Griswold of Connecticut read the part of the
President's message of December 15 relating to the cession of
Louisiana to the French and made the following motion:

> *Resolved,* That the President of the United States be requested to direct
> the proper officer to lay before the House copies of such official documents
> as have been received by this Government, announcing the cession of Louis-
> iana to France, together with a report explaining the stipulations, circum-
> stances, and conditions, under which that province is to be delivered up;
> unless such documents and reports will, in the opinion of the President,
> divulge to the House particular transactions not proper at this time to be
> communicated.

Griswold stated that although he did not desire from the President papers that might be improper at the time, nevertheless

---

[6] Madison to Livingston, September 28, 1801, in *Annals of Congress,*
7 Cong., 2 Sess. (1802–1803), Appendix, 1014–1016.

[7] *Ibid.,* 1022–1023.

[8] *Ibid.,* 1052.

[9] Livingston to the President, October 28, 1802, in *ibid.,* 1055.

he considered the subject very important, and one that might require from the Legislature further protection for the frontier facing the ceded province.[10]

When the question came up for discussion on the following day, John Randolph of Virginia moved to commit the resolution to the Committee of the Whole on the state of the Union.[11] This was opposed by Griswold, who claimed for the House all the information in the power of the Executive to give. Referring the resolution to the committee would be putting it to sleep and the Legislature would be deprived of information it ought to possess.[12] Rutledge of South Carolina declared that "did he consider that the giving publicity to any information on this subject would in the least interfere with the Constitutional functions of the President, he would be the last man to support the resolution" of Griswold. He could see no impropriety, however, in asking the President for information relative to that which he had stated as a fact; that is, as much information as the president considered it expedient to give.[13]

Samuel Smith of Maryland turned to the case of the British Treaty of 1794 (Jay's Treaty) as a precedent. At that time, he said, one party in the House had called for the papers on the principle that the negotiations having been terminated, the House

---

10 *Annals of Congress*, 7 Cong., 2 Sess. (1802–1803), 312.

11 *Ibid.*, 314.

12 *Ibid.*, 314–315.

13 *Ibid.*, 316. Compare the stand taken by Representative Shackleford of Missouri, March 7, 1916, on the McLemore resolutions when he said he favored a resolution warning citizens of the United States against traveling on ships of the belligerent powers, but if agitation for one had disturbed the President's diplomatic negotiations, he was ready to vote against it. In this connection the report of the House Committee on Foreign Affairs on these same resolutions is worth noting. In recommending that the resolutions be laid on the table (March 3), the committee said in part, "Under the Constitution the practice and precedents in this country, the conduct of diplomatic negotiations has been left to the President and with this practice the committee does not think it proper for the House of Representatives to interfere."

had a right to obtain information before granting ·money under a treaty. This party, however, acknowledged a call for information to be improper during a pending negotiation.[14] Huger of South Carolina did not consider the present case similar to that arising out of the British Treaty. In the latter instance, one party in the House claimed the right to demand the information of the Executive, and he was obliged to deliver it; while the other party did not acknowledge the right of the House to demand, or the obligation of the President to obey. In the present case nothing was asked except what the Executive should think proper to furnish. If proper for Congress to know the contents of the Convention he thought they ought to have the documents; if not proper, the reason should be given.[15] Smilie of Pennsylvania claimed that in the debate on the British Treaty the resolution proposed had not been peremptory but had been qualified by an exception of such papers as the President might consider it improper to furnish. He confirmed his remark by quoting from the House Journals.[16]

Griswold said the ground of opposition in 1796, under the British Treaty, had been that the resolution had claimed the right of the House to decide upon a treaty, and to establish this point papers had been called for. On the decision of the question of granting or refusing the application, had depended the establishment of the right of the House to participate in the treaty-making power. Those who had voted against the call had denied this right. In the case of the Louisiana convention, continued Griswold, there was no difference of opinion as to the power of the House. The President having expressly stated in his message that the cession would have weight in the delibera-

---

[14] *Annals of Congress,* 7 Cong., 2 Sess. (1802–1803), 316.

[15] *Ibid.,* 318.

[16] *Ibid.*

tions of the Legislature, information was necessary.[17] Despite Griswold's objection, Randolph's motion to refer the motion to a Committee of the Whole on the state of the Union carried by a vote of forty-nine to thirty-nine.[18]

In the debate on Randolph's motion, various views were expressed regarding the relation of the branches of the Government to one another. Dana of Connecticut held it to be not only proper but the duty of the House to request any information from the President which would assist in the proceedings. The President, he said, was designated by the Constitution as the proper person from whom information on such subjects as the one under discussion was to be obtained.[19]

Randolph's answer to Dana opened the way for a broader interpretation of executive powers:

> But, sir, it seems that this unfortunate resolution betrays so entire an ignorance of the distribution of the powers of our Government as to clothe the Executive with an authority not only not devolved upon it by the Constitution, but which is the peculiar province of this and the other branch

---

[17] *Ibid.*, 319. For Washington's refusal to comply with the request of the House, see his message of March 30, 1796, in Richardson, *Messages and Papers of the Presidents*, I, 194–196.

Because he as President was called upon to take a stand on the question of the participation of the House in treaty-making, Jefferson's statements on the treaty-making power at the time of the Jay Treaty are of significance. In a letter to William B. Giles, December 31, 1795, he said it was "the true theory of our constitution, that when a treaty is made, involving matters confided by the constitution to the three branches of the legislature conjointly, the representatives are as free as the President & Senate were to consider whether the national interest requires or forbids their giving the forms & force of law to the articles over which they have a power." Jefferson, *Writings* (Ford, ed.), VII, 41.

On March 21, 1796, Jefferson wrote to Monroe that although the President and Senate had the general power of making treaties, yet all articles contained in a treaty necessitating an act of legislation must be submitted to the House, which as one branch of the Legislature "are perfectly free to pass the act or refuse it, governing themselves by their own judgment whether it is for the good of their constituents to let the treaty go into effect or not. On the precedent now to be set will depend the future construction of our constitution, and whether the powers of legislation shall be transferred from the P. Senate & H. of R. to P. Senate & Piarningo or any Indian, Algerine or any other chief." *Ibid.*, VII, 67–68.

[18] *Annals of Congress*, 7 Cong., 2 Sess. (1802–1803), 321.

[19] *Ibid.*, 353.

of the Legislature. The gentleman [Mr. Dana] denies the power of the Executive to redress injuries received from foreign nations.... Have I, indeed, so far mistaken, and, contrary to my own avowed principles, am so disposed to augment the Executive powers at the expense of the other departments of the Government? Suppose, on the representations of the Court of Spain, that Court, which is more than probable, should restore the rights of navigation and deposit, disavow the conduct of their officers in violating those rights, and, moreover, punish them for it? Would any person deny that, through the agency of the Executive, constitutionally exercised, the injury was redressed?...

By the Constitution of the United States, the Executive is the representative of the United States to foreign nations. It is furnished with organs by which to receive their propositions, and to communicate their own. The Constitution, therefore, presumes that to this department may be entirely confided our negotiations with foreign States.... Until it could be shown that some specific act of the Executive had rendered that department unworthy of our confidence, we might consistently express it: and, even if proof of such misconduct could be established, it would not alter the tenor of the Constitution, however the individual might be affected by it. For your Constitution, sir, is not of that precarious nature which depends on the fluctuating characters of particular men.[20]

John Randolph's phrase, "fluctuating character," might well be applied to himself for it is doubtful if a more unique man ever sat in Congress. A sturdy defender of the states' rights theory, and one strongly opposed to the centralizing tendencies of the National Government, he was at the time of this debate one of the leaders of his party in supporting the acts of the Jefferson administration, which was now about to do so much toward strengthening the federal power. The open break with his party had not yet come and Randolph was a man whose influence was steadily growing. To be sure, he did not completely close his eyes to the dangers which he considered threatening to the rights of the states and his voice was often heard in protest against certain of the measures introduced by the administration.

The exigencies of the situation seemed to Jefferson to demand that prompt action be taken to secure the interests of the United

---

[20] *Ibid.*, 360–361.

States. With that object in view he nominated Robert R. Livingston to be minister plenipotentiary and James Monroe minister extraordinary and plenipotentiary, to enter into a treaty or convention with the First Consul of France for the securing of the rights of the Americans on the Mississippi. To facilitate negotiations with Spain, since the possession of the territory along the Mississippi was still in her hands, Charles Pinckney was nominated minister plenipotentiary to that country, and James Monroe was given the same position with regard to Spain as in his appointment to France.[21]

There was considerable objection to the appointment of Monroe, due, Senator Plumer says, to the fact that Monroe, when recalled by Washington, was friendly with the men whom Napoleon Bonaparte considered as Jacobins and enemies to him. Good policy, in Plumer's opinion, would have dictated the sending of a man who would be well received by the government to whom he was sent. The appointment was confirmed by the close vote of fifteen to twelve.[22]

News of Monroe's appointment was sent to Livingston by Secretary of State Madison, January 18, 1803. The object of the negotiations was stated to be the procurement of New Orleans and the Floridas; and consequently the establishment of the Mississippi as the boundary line between the United States and Louisiana. Toward this end a sum of money would be offered the French Government; also, such regulations of the commerce

---

21 Richardson, *Messages and Papers of the Presidents*, I, 350–351, Message to the Senate, January 11, 1803. On this matter Manasseh Cutler wrote to Dr. Joseph Torrey, January 15, 1803: ''The object is to make a purchase of the Province [New Orleans]. This is certainly the best thing that can be done. It will save us from the expenses, hazard, and evils of a war.... The whole business is now left with the Executive, and Monroe, late Governor of Virginia, is the minister, it is said, who is sent on this business.'' Cutler and Cutler, *Life, Journals and Correspondence of Rev. Manasseh Cutler*, II, 122.

22 Plumer to Livermore, January 13, 1803; Plumer to Daniel Plumer, January 15, 1803, in *Plumer MSS*. See also Plumer to John Taylor Gilman, January 18, 1803, in Plumer, *Life of William Plumer*, 249.

of the Mississippi and of the other rivers entering the Gulf of Mexico as ought to prove satisfactory to France.[23]

In order to assist the President in his negotiations for a place of deposit on the Mississippi, the House of Representatives took under consideration, January 12, 1803, the report of a committee on the following resolution:

> *Resolved,* that a sum of two millions of dollars, in addition to the provision heretofore made, be appropriated to defray any expenses which may be incurred in relation to the intercourse between the United States and foreign nations, to be paid out of any money that may be in the Treasury, not otherwise appropriated, and be applied under the direction of the President of the United States, who, if necessary, is hereby authorized to borrow the whole or any part thereof; an account whereof, as soon as may be shall be laid before Congress.

The committee stated the object of the resolution to be to enable the Executive to commence, with more effect, a negotiation with the French and Spanish governments relative to the purchase from them of the island of New Orleans and the two Floridas. The need for a place of deposit was pointed out, as also for an outlet from Mississippi through West Florida. The acquisition of East Florida was considered advisable, if not a necessity. Increase of territory was not the object sought; although "if we look forward to the free use of the Mississippi, the Mobile, the Apalachicola, and the other rivers of the West, by ourselves and our posterity, New Orleans and the Floridas must become a part of the United States, either by purchase or by conquest." The committee reported favorably on the resolution.[24]

On February 15, 1803, a confidential message from the House was received by the Senate, transmitting a bill which had

---

[23] *Annals of Congress,* 7 Cong., 2 Sess. (1802–1803), Appendix, 1063–1064.

[24] *Ibid.,* 370–374.

passed the House, entitled "An act making further provision for the expenses attending the intercourse between the United States and foreign nations," in which the concurrence of the Senate was requested.[25]

There were those in the Senate who believed in forcible occupation of the desired territory. Ross of Pennsylvania claimed the indisputable right to free navigation of the Mississippi and to a place of deposit, and introduced resolutions authorizing the President to take immediate possession of such place or places as he saw fit for this purpose. The President was also to be authorized to call into service the militia of the neighboring states and the Mississippi Territory, not exceeding fifty thousand, and to employ them together with the military and naval forces of the Union for effecting the desired objects. The sum of five millions of dollars was to be appropriated to the carrying into effect of these resolutions.[26]

Although Ross' resolutions were struck out, the constitutional questions involved were not so quickly passed by. The danger of armed action on the part of the Executive was pointed out by Clinton of New York, who said that the measure would tend toward upsetting the balance of the Government by giving extensive powers to the Executive: it was an inevitable consequence of war in free countries that the power which wielded the force always rose above the power that expressed the will of the people. The state governments would be greatly weakened. "Those stately pillars which support the magnificent dome of our National Government will totter under the increased weight of the superincumbent pressure."[27]

---

[25] *Ibid.*, 90.

[26] *Ibid.*, 95–96. By friends of the administration Ross was suspected of representing a group of men ready to plunge the country into war and ruin to gratify party ends. For this view, see the *National Intelligencer*, February 16, 1803.

[27] *Annals of Congress*, 7 Cong., 2 Sess. (1802–1803), 132.

Gouverneur Morris of New York expressed the opinion that the western regions were peculiarly the heritage of the American people and must be held open to the westward migration of the overflowing population of the eastern states. For this reason New Orleans and the Floridas must not be separated from the United States.[28] Other senators held more strictly than Morris to the constitutionality of the measure proposed. Stevens T. Mason of Virginia demanded:

> Does the gentleman not know that the militia cannot be sent on the service of invasion into the territory of their neighbors? Does he not know that we are destitute of any authority to send them? The Constitution gives Congress the power over the militia to 'suppress insurrections, and repel invasions,' but nothing further.... Gentlemen tell us that they are willing to entrust to the Executive the power of gong to war, or not, at his discretion.... Who gave them the authority to vest in any other authority than in Congress the right of declaring war?... He could not, as one, without treason to the Constitution, consent ever to relinquish the right of declaring war to any man, or men, besides Congress.[29]

Mason looked into the future when he declared that Gouverneur Morris's statement that immediate possession of the Floridas must be secured, showed that the deposit at New Orleans was not the real object which Morris had in mind. "Presently we shall be told we must have Louisiana; then the gold mines of Mexico—these would be good things if come by honestly—then Potosi—then St. Domingo, with their sugar, coffee, and all the rest."[30]

The House bill "making further provision for the expenses attending the intercourse between the United States and foreign nations" passed the Senate by the close vote of fourteen to

---

[28] *Annals of Congress,* 7 Cong., 2 Sess. (1802–1803), 195.

[29] *Ibid.,* 216.

[30] *Ibid.,* 218–219. The movement of Americans into Spanish territory is confirmed a little later by John Smith in his letter to Jefferson, August 30, 1803, from West Florida. A rumor having reached him that Louisiana was to be exchanged for Florida, Smith advised against it. Florida could soon be obtained at a low price. It was rapidly being settled by Americans. *Jefferson Papers,* "Letters received at Washington, 2d Series," LXXVI (46).

twelve.[31] When Senator Plumer, as chairman of the Committee on Enrolled Bills, presented the act to Jefferson, on February 26, the President said that a great point had now been gained, a new precedent established in our Government, namely, the passage of an important act of Congress in *secret session*.[32]

It does not fall within the province of this discussion to follow in detail the story of the purchase of Louisiana.[33] It is the history of the constitutional problems arising out of that acquisition which will be taken up. Livingston and Monroe wrote from Paris, May 13, 1803, announcing the purchase.[34] Madison in reply stated that the President approved of the action taken by the negotiators, despite the lack of instructions, such action having been justified by the reasons given by the two ministers.[35]

The reception of the treaty in Congress is described by Jefferson in his letter to Livingston, November 4, 1803, in which he wrote that the treaty was generally approved except by the Federalists, whose numbers were so greatly reduced that they counted for little.[36] Writing to Captain Meriwether Lewis, November 16, Jefferson said, "The votes of both Houses on ratifying and carrying the treaties into execution, have been precisely party votes, except that General Dayton has separated from his friends on these questions, and voted for the treaties."[37]

---

[31] *Annals of Congress,* 7 Cong., 2 Sess. (1802–1803), 104.

[32] Plumer, *Life of William Plumer,* 255–256.

[33] See Henry Adams, *History of the United States,* I, 423–446, II, 25–50.

[34] *Annals of Congress,* 7 Cong., 2 Sess. (1802–1803), Appendix, 1145–1150.

[35] *Ibid.,* 1166, Letter of July 29, 1803.

[36] Jefferson, *Writings* (Washington, ed.), IV, 510.

[37] Jefferson, *Writings* (Memorial ed.), X, 434. A similar statement appears in Plumer's "Memorandum," under date of October 20, 1803. Plumer defended his own vote against ratification of the treaty on the ground that he considered it as a direct violation of the Constitution. The admission of such a vast territory into the Union would tend to divide the United States into separate empires. It would destroy the influence of the "Eastern States" in Congress. Plumer to Daniel Plumer, November 22, 1803, in *Plumer Mss.* This was the stock New England argument against the purchase.

CHAPTER II

THE CONSTITUTIONAL RIGHT TO ACQUIRE TERRITORY: CONTEMPORARY OPINION

One of the first constitutional questions to be discussed as a result of the purchase of Louisiana was: did a constitutional right to acquire territory exist?

No specific grant of such power was to be found in the Constitution. Article four, section three, declares:

> New States may be admitted by the Congress into this Union; but no new State shall be formed or erected within the jurisdiction of any other State; nor any State be formed by the Junction of two or more States, or Parts of States, without the consent of the Legislatures of the States concerned as well as of Congress.

> The Congress shall have power to dispose of and make all needful Rules and Regulations respecting the Territory or other Property belonging to the United States; and nothing in this Constitution shall be so construed as to Prejudice any claims of the United States, or of any particular State.

Was the authorization of power to acquire territory to be found in these provisions?[1] This was a disputed question.

Article eleven of the Articles of Confederation contained the provision: "Canada, acceding to this Confederation, and joining in the measures of the United States, shall be admitted into, and entitled to, all the advantages of this union; but no other colony shall be admitted into the same unless such admission be agreed to by nine states."[2]

In Edmund Randolph's "Propositions" in the Federal Convention, commonly known as the Virginia Plan, we find under

---

[1] No such interpretation was made by Madison in his explanation of these sections of the Constitution in the *Federalist*. See No. 42 (Ford, ed. 1898); also Ford's footnote, 284–285.

[2] Elliot, *Debates on the Federal Constitution*, I, 84.

number ten: *"Resolved,* That provision ought to be made for the admission of states, lawfully arising *within the limits of the United States,* whether from a voluntary junction of government or territory, or otherwise, with the consent of a number of voices in the *national legislature less than the whole."*[3] This proposal would seem to apply only to territory then owned by the United States.

Patterson's proposals, or the New Jersey Plan, merely declared "that provision ought to be made for the admission of new states into the Union."[4] The restrictions of the Randolph plan were not included. Hamilton's plan contained a provision similar to that of the Patterson plan.[5] The Charles Pinckney draft provided for the admission of new states into the Union by the Legislature on the same terms with the original states, if two-thirds of the members present in both Houses should agree thereto.[6]

A definite restriction appears in the report of the Committee of Detail where it is stipulated that new states soliciting admission into the Union "must be within the *present* limits of the United States."[7] In a later report the important word *present* was omitted.[8]

The draft of a Constitution as reported by the Committee of Five, August 6, 1787, contained the following article:

Article 17. New states, lawfully constituted or established *within the limits of the United States,* may be admitted by the legislature into this government; but to such admission *the consent of two-thirds of the members present in each house shall be necessary.* If a new state shall arise

---

[3] Elliot, *Debates,* I, 144–145; Farrand, *Records of the Federal Convention,* I, 22. Italics mine.

[4] Elliot, *Debates,* I, 177; Farrand, *Records of the Federal Convention,* I, 245.

[5] Farrand, *Records of the Federal Convention,* III, 629–630.

[6] Elliot, *Debates,* I, 149; Farrand, *Records of the Federal Convention,* III, 601, Appendix D.

[7] Farrand, *Records of the Federal Convention,* II, 147. Italics mine.

[8] *Ibid.,* II, 173.

within the limits of any of the present states, the consent of the legislature of such states shall be also necessary to the admission. If the admission be consented to, the new states shall be admitted on the same terms with the original states.[9]

No agreement was reached as to the meaning of these proposals, and thus the way was opened for differences of opinion in later interpretation of the disputed points. According to Gouverneur Morris this clause of the Constitution had been purposely left vague.[10]

Other provisions of the Constitution afforded justification to many for the acquisition of territory. These were the power given to Congress to declare war,[11] and the treaty-making power of the President and Senate.[12] The consequent power of the Government to acquire territory, either by conquest or by treaty, was advanced at the time of the purchase of Louisiana. This view received the legal sanction of the Supreme Court a little later.[13]

The acquisition of territory was defended by others on the ground that the United States as a sovereign state could adopt all the methods of extending its possessions recognized by international usage. With the expansion of the United States this last interpretation has come more and more to be generally accepted.

To what extent these various interpretations were supported and denied in relation to Louisiana it will now be our purpose to investigate.

---

[9] Elliot, *Debates*, I, 229–230. Italics mine.

[10] Sparks, *Life of Gouverneur Morris*, III, 192; Farrand, *Records of the Federal Convention*, III, 404. See below.

It is interesting to note that when a portion of the citizens of the United States at a later date had an opportunity of drawing up a new constitution, a specific provision for the acquisition of new territory was made. See article 4, section 3, clause 3, of the constitution of the Confederate States.

[11] Article I, section 8, clause 11.

[12] Article II, section 2, clause 2.

[13] See below.

The news of the purchase of the whole of Louisiana caused Jefferson some surprise but it cannot be said that he had never contemplated the extension of American control westward. As early as 1786 the report of discontent in Kentucky and the threat that this region might separate itself from the Confederacy, caused him to remark that this would be a "calametous event." He believed an increase of votes in Congress would be a good thing in helping to keep down the little divisions existing there.[14] The Confederacy "must be viewed as the nest from which all America, North & South is to be peopled." The territory while in possession of Spain, he continued, was in good hands and care must be taken not to press too soon on the Spaniards. The only danger lay in the fact that the Spaniards might be too feeble to hold the territory until the Americans were ready to take it piece by piece. At the time of writing, the navigation of the Mississippi was regarded as absolutely necessary. That was all the Americans were *as yet* ready to receive.[15]

Again, in 1791, Jefferson, in discussing the invitation of Governor Quesada to settlers to come into Florida, remarked that he wished a hundred thousand Americans would go. "It will be the means of delivering to us peaceably, what may otherwise cost us a war. In the meantime we may complain of this seduction of our inhabitants just enough to make them [the Spaniards] believe we think it very wise policy for them, and confirm them in it."[16]

Constitutional difficulties which might arise from such acquisition of territory do not seem to have entered Jefferson's head, but when the decision was made in January, 1803, to send Mon-

---

[14] On August 17, 1821, in referring to the admission of Missouri into the Union Jefferson wrote to Henry Dearborn: "I still believe that the Westward extension of our confederacy will ensure its duration, by overruling local factions, which might shake a smaller association." Jefferson, *Writings* (Federal ed.), XII, 206.

[15] Jefferson, *Writings* (Ford, ed.), II, 188–189. Italics mine.

[16] *Ibid.*, V, 316.

roe to negotiate for the purchase of New Orleans and Florida, the question of the constitutionality of the purchase was raised. Attorney General Levi Lincoln foresaw the storm of opposition which might be expected, and worked out a novel and unique scheme to avert the attack. His plan is disclosed in a letter to Jefferson, January 10, 1803. The importance of New Orleans and the Floridas, with the unimpeded navigation of the Mississippi to the United States, in his opinion justified almost any risk for their attainment. The mode of attainment while substantially securing the object sought for, would, perhaps, free it from "formidable difficulties."

> The idea is [he continued] that for the common advantage of having great, fixed, and natural boundaries between the territory of France and the United States, and to secure to the latter, the full and unimpeded navigation of, maritime & commercial rights important, and naturally appurtenant to a country bordering on navigable rivers, in the neighborhood of a sea coast, and from the interior of which country, navigable rivers empty themselves into a neighboring sea, France agrees to extend the boundaries of the Mississippi Territory, and of the State of Georgia [to the Mississippi River and the Gulf, including all the desired territory]. By this indirect mode, if it is feasible, would not the General Govt avoid some constitutional, and some political embarrassments, which a direct acquisition of a foreign territory by the Govt of the United States might occasion?
>
> For instance, would not the territory added to the respective states by the enlargement of their boundaries, as an incident immediately by the act of accretion, assimilate to the principal, and merging in them, be subject to their authority, and of course to the authority of the United States?
>
> If the proposed acquired property, or territory, can be thus melted down, and consolidated, instead of being federated with the States already united, their laws would extend to it, in common with other parts of the enlarged States, without risking the doubtful attempt, so to amend the Constitution, as to embrace the object; or hazarding the ratification of the treaty, from an opposition to such an amendment—or being exposed to the consequences of such an amendment being refused—The Inhabitants thus added, and who would have been citizens of the enlarged state, had the acquired territory originally been a part of such state, would of course be considered as citizens; and others get naturalized under the existing laws. This

mode of naturalization would keep one door closed against future controversy, and dangerous divisions, in our country, and on a principle somewhat similar to the one sanctioned by Jay's treaty.

If the opinion is correct, that the Genl Govt when formed, was predicated on the then existing *United* States, and such as could grow out of *them*, & out of *them* only, and that its authority, is, constitutionally, limited to the people composing the several political State Societies in that union, & such as might be formed out of them; would not a direct independent purchase, be extending the executive power further, and be more alarming and [illegible] by the opposition and the Eastern States, than the proposed indirect mode? Is there not danger, that, The Eastern States, including even Rhode Island & Vermont, if not New York, & other states further South, would object to the ratification of a treaty directly introducing a state of things, involving the idea of adding to the weight of the Southern States in one branch of the Govt of which there is already too great a jealousy & dread, while they would acquiesce in that increase of the other branch consequent on the enlargement of the boundaries of a State?

It is foreseen that the opposition and the eastern States will take a distinction, between securing the free navigation of the Mississippi, with a convenient deposit for merchandise, and a measure and the principles of a measure, which may add one or more States to the Union, and thereby change that relative influence between different parts of the United States, on which the general Govt. was predicated. No plan of necessity, of commercial utility, or national security, will have weight with a violent party, or be any security against their hostile efforts & opposition clamor....

The principles, and the precedent, of an independent purchase of territory, it will be said, may be extended to the East or West Indies, and that some future executive, will extend them, to the purchase of Louisiana, or still further south, & become the Executive of the United States of North & South America....

The mode of acquiring new territory by extending the boundaries of existing States, will foreclose these objections, as well as supersede the necessity of amend[ing] the Constitution, and perhaps prevent the rejection of the acquisition treaty, if such a one should be made.

The consequences deducible from the principles & the precedent, in the present case, if predicated on the advantages & necessity of having great natural boundaries for national ones, and the river navigation naturally belonging to the country; would necessarily be limited by the object, and if extended, to the utmost could never be injuriously applied in future. The only case, in which the principle could possibly be applied hereafter, would be in extending the boundaries of some of the northern States to the river St. Lawrence.

This mode of acquiring property by the U. S. in adding to the territory of particular States, would require their consent. In the proposed instance they would not object, Georgia ought to give the money we owe her, on account of her late cession for this acquisition New Orleans & W Florida being of the territory of Mississippi, may in future be made a State, if it shall be found to be useful, without altering the constitution. From this accession of inhabitants to the territorial Govt. it would soon arrive to its second grade, and increase the value & sale of lands belonging to the U. S.''[17]

It is not necessary to point out the obvious weakness in Lincoln's plan. The best possible reply is that of Gallatin, to whom Jefferson submitted Lincoln's letter. Gallatin laid down a clear statement of broad construction of the Constitution. He could see no difference ''between a power to acquire territory for the United States and the power to extend by treaty the territory of the United States.'' Annexation of new territory to a state was no more acceptable than the plan to extend the boundaries. If the Legislature and Executive could not acquire territory under the Constitution for the use of the Union, certainly, contended Gallatin, they could not acquire it for the use of one state. Was there any constitutional objection to the acquisition of territory? Gallatin's answer to the question is worth following in detail:

The 3d Section of the 4th Article of the Constitution provides: 1st. That new States may be admitted by Congress into this Union. 2d. That Congress shall have power to dispose of and make all needful rules and regulations respecting the territory and other property belonging to the United States.

Mr. Lincoln, in order to support his objections, is compelled to suppose, 1st, that the new States therein alluded to must be carved either out of other States, or out of the territory belonging to the United States; and, 2d, that the power given to Congress of making regulations respecting the territory belonging to the United States is expressly confined to the territory *then* belonging to the Union.

A general and perhaps sufficient answer is that the whole rests on a supposition, there being no words in the section which confine the authority

---

[17] *Jefferson Papers,* ''Letters Received at Washington, 2d. Series,'' LII (25). See also Henry Adams, *History of the United States,* II, 78–79.

given to Congress to those specific objects; whilst, on the contrary, the existence of the United States as a nation presupposes the power enjoyed by every nation of extending their territory by treaties, and the general power given to the President and Senate of making treaties designates the organ through which the acquisition may be made, whilst this section provides the proper authority (viz. Congress) for either admitting in the Union or governing as subjects the territory thus acquired. It may be further observed in relation to the power of admitting new States in the Union, that this section was substituted to the 11th Article of Confederation, which was in these words: 'Canada acceding, etc; shall be admitted into, etc., but no other colony shall be admitted into the same, unless such admission be agreed to by nine (9) States.' As the power was there explicitly given to nine (9) States, and as the other powers given in the Articles of Confederation to nine (9) States were by the Constitution transferred to Congress, there is no reason to believe, as the words relative to the power of admission are, in the Constitution, general, that it was not the true intention of that Constitution to give the powers generally and without restriction.

As to the other clause, that which gives the power of governing the territory of the United States, the limited construction of Mr. Lincoln is still less tenable; for if that power is limited to the territory belonging to the United States at the time when the Constitution was adopted, it would have precluded the United States from governing any territory acquired, since the adoption of the Constitution, by cession of one of the States, which, however, has been done in the case of the cessions of North Carolina and Georgia; and, as the words ''other property'' follow, and must be embraced by the same construction which will apply to the territory, it would result from Mr. L's opinion, that the United States could not, after the Constitution, either acquire or dispose of any personal property. To me it would appear:

1st. That the United States as a nation have an inherent right to acquire territory.

2d. That whenever that acquisition is by treaty, the same constituted authorities in whom the treaty-making power is vested have a constitutional right to sanction the acquisition.

3d. That whenever the territory has been acquired, Congress have the power either of admitting into the Union as a new State, or of annexing to a State with the consent of that State, or by making regulations for the government of such territory.

The only possible objection must be derived from the 12th[18] Amendment, which declares that powers not delegated to the United States, nor prohibited by it to the States, are reserved to the States or to the people.

---

[18] Tenth.

As the States are expressly prohibited from making treaties, it is evident that, if the power of acquiring by treaty is not considered within the meaning of the Amendment as delegated to the United States, it must be reserved to the people. If that be the true construction of the Constitution, it substantially amounts to this; that the United States are precluded from, and renounce altogether, the enlargement of territory, a provision sufficiently important and singular to have deserved to be expressly enacted. Is it not a more natural construction to say that the power of acquiring territory is delegated to the United States by the several provisions which authorize the several branches of government to make war, to make treaties, and to govern the territory of the Union?

After this clear-cut, logical exposition of broad construction of the Constitution, which would have done credit to any Federalist, Gallatin weakened and added, ''I must, however, confess that after all I do not feel myself perfectly satisfied; the subject must be thoroughly examined; and the above observations must be considered as hasty and incomplete.''[19]

Gallatin's arguments had weight with Jefferson. This is shown in his reply to Gallatin: ''... You are right, in my opinion, as to Mr. L's proposition: there is no constitutional difficulty as to the acquisition of territory, and whether, when acquired, it may be taken into the Union by the Constitution as it now stands, will become a question of expediency. I think it will be safer not to permit the enlargement of the Union but by amendment of the Constitution.''[20]

Although Jefferson was influenced somewhat by Gallatin's interpretation, his constitutional scruples as to incorporation of new states formed from territory acquired since the ratification of the Constitution were not yet overcome. The arrival of the treaty of cession July 14, 1803, and the short period allowed for

---

[19] Gallatin, *Writings* (Adams, ed.), I, 111–114. Adams dates this letter January 13, but no date appears on the original received by Jefferson other than the note in Jefferson's handwriting, ''Departmt of Treasy rece'd Jan. 13, 1803.'' For Gallatin's later view regarding the need of an amendment in this matter, see below.

[20] *Ibid.*, I, 115; Jefferson, *Writings* (Ford, ed.), VIII, 241 (footnote). This statement has received various interpretations; see *Insular Cases*, 125–126, 152–153, 292–293.

ratification, limited to October 30, obliged Jefferson to convene Congress earlier than usual.[21] The date decided upon was October 17. Jefferson felt it to be important that Congress should be supplied with all the available information respecting the treaty. Congress would be "obliged to ask the people for an amendment of the Constitution, authorizing their receiving the province into the Union, and providing for its government; and the limitations of power which shall be given by that amendment, will be unalterable but by the same authority...."[22]

On July 18, Jefferson informed Benjamin Austin, by letter, of the arrival of the treaty and conventions, and, after giving a brief statement of their provisions, he added: "They will of course require an amendment of the Constitution adapted to the case which will leave the inhabitants & territory for some time in a situation difficult to be defined, but the acquisition has decided the painful question whether we are to be a peaceable or a warring nation...."[23]

The need of a constitutional amendment to authorize the acquisition was again stated in a letter which Jefferson wrote to John Dickinson, August 9, 1803:

But there is a difficulty in this acquisition which presents a handle to the malcontents among us, though they have not yet discovered it. Our confederation is certainly confined to the limits established by the revolution. The general government has no powers but such as the constitution has given it; and it has not given it a power of holding foreign territory, and still less of incorporating it into the Union. An amendment of the Constitution seems necessary for this. In the meantime we must ratify & pay our money, as we have treated, for a thing beyond the constitution, and rely on the nation to sanction an act done for its great good, without its previous authority. With respect to the disposal of the country, we must take the island of New Orleans and west side of the river as high up as

21 Th. J[efferson] to T[homas] R[andolph], July 15, [18]03, in *Jefferson Papers,* Coolidge Collection, Massachusetts Historical Society Library.

22 Jefferson to Wm. Dunbar, July 17, 1803, in Jefferson, *Writings* (Ford, ed.), VIII, 254–255 (footnote).

23 *Jefferson Papers,* "Letters from Jefferson, 1st Series, 1802–1803," IX (112).

Point Coupee, containing nearly the whole inhabitants, say about 50,000, and erect it into a state, or annex it to the Mississippi territory; and shut up all the rest from settlement for a long time to come, endeavoring to exchange some of the country there unoccupied by Indians for the lands held by the Indians on this side of the Mississippi, who will be glad to cede us their country here for an equivalent there: and we may sell our lands here and pay the whole debt before it comes due.[24]

Although Jefferson frequently spoke of closing the territory across the Mississippi to settlement,[25] it was not his idea that the land there should remain permanently in the hands of the Indians. Land offices were to be opened east of the river and settlers established there. When the eastern side had been filled, a range of states was to be laid off on the opposite bank from the head to the mouth of the river. This policy was to be followed, range after range, advancing compactly as population increased.[26]

Constitutional difficulties and expediency, the good of his country, were conflicting in Jefferson's mind. He laid bare his thoughts in this matter to Breckinridge:

This treaty must of course be laid before both Houses, because both have important functions to exercise respecting it. They, I presume, will see their duty to their country in ratifying & paying for it, so as to secure a good which would otherwise probably be never again in their power. But I suppose they must then appeal to the nation for an additional article to the Constitution, approving & confirming an act which the nation had not previously authorized. The Constitution has made no provision for our

---

[24] Jefferson, *Writings* (Ford, ed.), VIII, 262–263. Jefferson had given considerable thought to the control of emigration to the ceded territory. Robert Smith assured him that this could be accomplished by constitutional prohibition that Congress should not establish a new state or territorial government in the acquired territory north of latitude thirty-two degrees, and that no grant or title to any of the territory should be given to any persons except Indians. Jefferson, *Writings* (Ford., ed.), VIII, 241–242. Henry Adams, *History of the United States*, II, 83–84. For Jefferson's policy with regard to the removal of the Indians into Louisiana, see Miss Annie Heloise Abel, ''The History of Events resulting in Indian Consolidation west of the Mississippi,'' in American Historical Association, *Annual Report, 1906*, I, 241–249.

[25] See below.

[26] Jefferson to Breckinridge, August 18, 1803, in Jefferson, *Writings* (Ford, ed.), VIII, 244 (footnote); (Washington, ed.), IV, 500–501.

holding foreign territory, still less for incorporating foreign nations into our Union. The Executive in seizing the fugitive occurrence which so much advances the good of their country, have done an act beyond the Constitution. The Legislature in casting behind them metaphysical subtleties, and risking themselves like faithful servants, must ratify & pay for it, and throw themselves on their country for doing for them unauthorized, what we know they would have done for themselves had they been in a position to do it. It is the case of a guardian, investing the money of his ward in purchasing an adjacent territory; and saying to him when of age, I did this for your good; you may disavow me, and I must get out of the scrape as I can: I thought it my duty to risk myself for you. But we shall not be disavowed by the nation, and their act of indemnity will confirm and not weaken the Constitution, by more strongly marking out its lines.[27]

It is very interesting to follow Jefferson in his perplexity. Fear of a change of mind on the part of Napoleon led him to write to his friends enjoining silence concerning the constitutional difficulties arising out of the acquisition of Louisiana.[28] An inkling of the expected struggle along party lines is seen in the admonition to Breckinridge to impress the necessity of the presence of western Senators on the first day of the session as

---

[27] *Ibid.* The need of an amendment was admitted by Jefferson to Senator Plumer. See Plumer, *Life of William Plumer*, 362–363. Judge Cooley considered it difficult to conceive of any doctrine more dangerous to the fundamental ideas of the American Union than that the Constitution could be ''shut up'' temporarily in order that the Government might accomplish something not warranted by it. ''The practical settlement of the question of Constitutional power,'' says Cooley, ''did not heal the wound the Constitution received when the chief officer holding office under it advised the temporary putting it aside, and secured the approval of his advice by a numerical majority of the people. The poison was in the doctrine which took from the Constitution all sacredness, and made subject to the will and caprice of the hour that which, in the intent of the founders, was above parties, and majorities, and presidents, and congresses, and was meant to hold them all in close subordination. After this time the proposal to exercise unwarranted powers on a plea of necessity might be safely advanced without exciting the detestation it deserved; and the sentiment of loyalty to the Constitution was so far weakened that it easily gave way under the pressure of political expediency.'' Thomas M. Cooley, ''The Acquisition of Louisiana,'' in Indiana Historical Society, *Publications*, II, no. 3 (1887), 81–88. See also Lodge, *Life and Letters of George Cabot*, 333–334.

[28] Jefferson to Thomas Paine, August 18, 1803, in Jefferson, *Writings* (Ford, ed.), VIII, 245 (footnote); Jefferson to Breckinridge, *ibid.*, 244–245; Jefferson to Secretary of State [Madison], *ibid.*, 245.

every friend of the treaty was needed.[29] To Gallatin Jefferson
wrote that it would be well to say as little as possible about the
constitutional difficulty, and have Congress act on it without
talking; and yet in this same letter he presented an amendment
to cover the case.[30]

Jefferson's idea of an amendment to the Constitution was one
which gave general powers, with specific exceptions. He submitted the substance of such an amendment to Madison:

> Louisiana as ceded by France to the U. S., is made a part of the U. S.
> Its white inhabitants shall be citizens, and stand, as their rights & obliga-
> tions, on the same footing with other citizens of the U. S. in analogous
> situations. Save only that as to the portion thereof lying north of the
> latitude of the mouth of the Arkansa river, no new State shall be estab-
> lished, nor any grants of land made therein, other than to Indians, in
> exchange for equivalent portions of land occupied by them, until amend-
> ment to the Constitution shall be made for those purposes.

Looking once more to the future Jefferson added: ''Florida
also, whenever it may be rightfully obtained, shall become a part
of the U. S. Its white inhabitants shall thereupon be citizens, on
the same footing with other citizens of the U. S. in analogous
circumstances.''[31]

The constitutionality of the treaty and of its provisions was
a topic of conversation between Jefferson and his friends, who
urged him to take a broad view of the powers granted to the
Federal Government under the Constitution. Wilson Cary
Nicholas, senator from Virginia, in a letter to Jefferson, September 3, 1803, admitted having reflected much on the subject of
the power of the United States to acquire territory, and to admit
new states into the Union:

> Upon an examination of the constitution, [writes Nicholas] I find the
> power as broad as it could well be made (3d par. 4 art.), except that new

29 Jefferson to Breckinridge, August 18, 1803, *ibid.*, VII, 244–245.

30 Gallatin, *Writings* (Adams, ed.), I, 144–145 (August 23, 1803). See
also Jefferson to Levi Lincoln, August 30, 1803, in Jefferson, *Writings*
(Ford, ed.), VIII, 246–247; (Washington, ed.), IV, 504–505.

31 Jefferson, *Writings* (Ford, ed.), VIII, 241–245 (August 25, 1803);
(Washngton, ed.), IV, 503; Gallatin, *Writings* (Adams, ed.), I, 145.

States cannot be formed out of the old ones without the consent of the *State* to be dismembered; and the exception is a proof to my mind that it was not intended to confine the congress in the admission of new States to what was then the territory of the U. S. Nor do I see anything in the constitution that limits the treaty-making power, except the general limitation of the power given to the government, and the evident object for which the government was instituted. If it is determined that Congress possess exclusively, all the powers that are to be found in the enumeration of powers given to that body, it will be deciding that there does not exist in the U. S. a power competent to make a treaty, for I will venture to assert, that a treaty cannot be formed, without the exercise of one or more of those powers by the president and the Senate, particularly a commercial treaty—nor does it seem to me that the sanction of Congress wou'd cure the defect, & that wou'd be to give them substantially the power of ratification, or rejection. Nor do I believe we could ever expect any Nation to form a treaty with us under such construction of our constitution; for I do not see what wou'd prevent subsequent legislatures from repealing the laws upon which the validity of a treaty depended; and indeed making laws in direct violation of such a treaty, if it was admitted that it derived all its power from a law. I am aware that this is to us delicate ground, and perhaps my opinions may clash with the opinions given by our friends during the discussion of the British treaty.[32] Upon due consideration, it really appears to me that a different construction of the constitution, from that which I have given it, would be to transfer the treaty making powers to congress, or to deprive the govt of the U. S. of the capacity of making treaties. I should be wanting in the sincerity and candour with which you have always permitted me to give you my opinion if I was to forbear to recommend to you to avoid giving an opinion as to the competence of the treaty making power, to make such a treaty as that lately entered into with France, by giving an opinion before the Senate act upon it, you wou'd take the whole responsibility of that opinion upon yourself in the public estimation, whereas if the Senate act before your opinion is known they will at least divide the responsibility with you. I shou'd think it very probable if the treaty shou'd be by you declared to exceed the constitutional authority of the treaty making power, that it would be rejected by the Senate, and if that should not happen, that great use wou'd be made with the people, of a wilful breach of the constitution.[33]

Jefferson's reply is a clear statement of his stand on the interpretation of the Constitution. After remarking on the danger of delay and the necessity for rapid action on the

---

[32] Jay's Treaty.

[33] *Jefferson Papers*, "Letters to Jefferson, 2d. Series," LXIII, (47); Henry Adams, *History of the United States*, II, 87–88.

part of Congress, he turned his attention to the constitutional questions involved. Reverting to strict construction Jefferson declared it as his belief that Congress did not have the power of admitting new states into the Union outside the territory owned at the time of the adoption of the Constitution. Continuing he said:

When an instrument admits two constructions, the one safe, the other dangerous, the one precise, the other indefinite, I prefer that which is safe & precise. I had rather ask an enlargement of power from the nation, when it is found necessary, than to assume by a construction which would make our powers boundless. Our peculiar security is in the possession of a written Constitution. Let us not make it a blank paper by construction. I say the same as to the opinion of those who consider the grant of the treaty making power as boundless. If it is, then we have no Constitution. If it has bounds they can be no others than the definitions of the powers which that instrument gives. It specifies and delineates the operations permitted to the federal government, and gives all the powers necessary to carry these into execution. Whatever of these enumerated objects is proper for a law, Congress may make the law; whatever is proper to be executed by a treaty, the President & Senate may enter into the treaty; whatever is to be done by a judicial sentence, the judges may pass the sentence. Nothing is more likely than their enumeration of powers is defective. . . . Let us go then perfecting it, by adding, by way of the Constitution, those powers which time & trial show are still wanting. . . . I confess, then, I think it important, in the present case, to set an example against broad construction by appealing for new power to the people.

But here again Jefferson shows that strict construction can give way to what is considered essential to the common good: ''If, however, our friends shall think differently, certainly I acquiesce with satisfaction; confiding, that the good sense of our country will correct the evil of construction when it shall produce ill effects.''[34]

Jefferson was apparently won over to the side of broad construction for he no longer held out for an amendment to

---

[34] Jefferson to Wilson C. Nicholas, September 7, 1803, in Jefferson, *Writings* (Ford, ed.), VIII, 247–248 (footnote); (Washington, ed.), IV, 505–507.

the Constitution. What was necessary to be done he left to Congress.[35] Doubtless such an amendment as Jefferson desired could have been carried without great difficulty, but it was not proposed, and an important precedent for future action in regard to the acquisition of territory was established. How far Jefferson was influenced by the European situation it is not necessary here to discuss.[36]

The President was not alone in his appreciation of the constitutional questions involved in the purchase of Louisiana. Although party lines decided the attitude of the majority of the leaders, nevertheless an examination of contemporary opinion throws much light on the interpretation of the Constitution. Fisher Ames denounced the whole affair in no uncertain terms. The less territory the better was his declaration. By adding the territory beyond the Mississippi, ''we rush like a comet into infinite space. In our wild career, we may jostle some other world out of its orbit, but we shall, in every event, quench the light of our own.''[37] Yet, dropping his party bias, Ames could not bring himself to assent to the argument of the Federalists, now the party of strict construction, that ''our government is merely an affair of special pleading, and to be interpreted in every case as if everything was written down in a book.'' Certain powers he considered inseparable from the fact of a society being formed, and incident to its being. Then he rather pessimistically concludes: ''Besides, as party interprets and amends

---

[35] Here it must be remarked that Gallatin, who had argued so strongly for broad construction, in commenting on the President's message observed ''that not even Congress can prevent some constitutional irregularity in the proceedings relative to occupying and governing that country before an amendment to the Constitution shall take place.'' Gallatin, *Writings* (Adams, ed.), I, 158; remarks on the President's message [Received Oct. 4, 1803].

[36] On this point see Adams, *History of the United States*, II, 92–93.

[37] Ames to Christopher Gore, October 3, 1803, in Ames, *Works*, I, 323–324. See also a letter of Ames to Thomas Dwight, October 31, 1803, *ibid.*, 329–330.

the Constitution, and as we the people care not a pin's point for
it, all arguments from that source, however solid, would avail
nothing.''[38]

John Quincy Adams was a sturdy defender of strict construction of the Constitution in the Louisiana affair. At a later
date he criticized Jefferson for getting into office under the
banners of states' rights and state sovereignty, and the pretense
that the Government of the Union had no powers except those
expressly delegated by the Constitution, and immediately purchasing Louisiana, ''an assumption of implied power greater in
itself and more comprehensive in its consequences, than all the
assumptions of implied power in the twelve years of the Washington and Adams Administrations put together.''[39]

In an argument with Attorney General Wirt over the constitutionality of the Louisiana purchase, Adams inquired where
in the Constitution the power to purchase territory was located.
Wirt answered that there was a power to make treaties. This
did not satisfy Adams, who vehemently denounced the purchase
as in substance a dissolution and recomposition of the Union:

> It made a Union totally different from that for which the Constitution
> had been formed. It gives despotic power over territories purchased. It
> naturalizes foreign nations in a mass. It makes French and Spanish laws
> a large part of the laws of the Union. It introduced whole systems of
> legislation abhorrent to the spirit and character of our institutions, and all
> this done by an administration which came in blowing a trumpet against
> implied power. After this, to nibble at a bank, a road, a canal, the mere
> mint and cummin of the law was but glorious inconsistency.

Upon Wirt's statement that the people had sanctioned the
purchase through their representatives in Congress, Adams
replied that this doctrine was too bold for him.[40]

Adams believed that an amendment to the Constitution was
necessary for the carrying through of the Louisiana Treaty, and

---

[38] Ames to Thomas Dwight, *ibid.*, I, 334.
[39] John Quincy Adams, *Memoirs*, V, 364–365 (October 20, 1821).
[40] *Ibid.*, V, 401 (November 17, 1821).

told Madison that unless some one else did so he would consider it his duty to move such an amendment. Madison answered that "he did not know that it was universally agreed that it required an amendment."[41] During the debate in the Senate upon the bill to enable the President to take possession of Louisiana, Adams moved an amendment to the last House amendment of the Senate bill which had come back from the House, by adding the words, "consistently with the Constitution of the United States." This was ruled out.[42]

In the autumn of 1803 when the constitutionality of the recent purchase of Louisiana was causing considerable agitation, Henry W. Livingston wrote to Gouverneur Morris asking him to find out what was the intention of the framers of the Constitution on this point. Morris replied:

... It is not possible for me to recollect with precision all that passed in the Convention, while we were framing the Constitution; and if I could, it is most probable that a meaning would have been conceived from incidental expressions, different from that which they were intended to convey, and very different from the fixed opinions of the speaker. This happens daily.

I am certain that I had it not in contemplation to insert a decree in *de coercendo imperio* in the Constitution of America. Without examining whether a limitation of territory be or be not essential to the preservation of republican government, I am certain that the country between the Mississippi and the Atlantic exceeds by far the limits, which prudence would assign, if in effect any limitation be required. Another reason of equal weight must have prevented me from thinking of such a clause. I knew as well then as I do now, that all North America must at length be annexed to us. Happy, indeed, if the lust for dominion stops there. It would, therefore, have been perfectly Utopian to oppose a paper restriction to the violence of popular sentiment in a popular government.[43]

---

[41] *Ibid.*, I, 267–268 (October 28, 1803).

[42] *Ibid.*, I, 268 (October 29, 1803).

[43] Sparks, *Life of Gouverneur Morris*, III, 185; Farrand, *Records of the Federal Convention*, III, 401. For a difference in the rendering of this letter, see Anne Cary Morris, *Diary and Letters of Gouverneur Morris*, II, 441–442. The Sparks edition seems to make the better sense and has been generally accepted.

Just how much importance and significance can be attached to Morris's statement it would be difficult to determine, since the reasons advanced may have been made to fit the accomplished deed. It is worth noting, however, that a definite attempt was made to ascertain what the men who framed the Constitution themselves understood by its provisions. Could Morris but see the wide extent of the possessions of the United States at the present day he might find justification for his statement that "paper restrictions" would avail little in the face of American expansion. While not all of North America has been annexed, the "lust for dominion" has not stopped here but has included island possessions a great distance from the original states of the Union.

Morris was not alone in his statement concerning "paper restrictions." George Cabot feared that the influence of New England would be diminished by the acquisition of territory in the south. He thought a paper Constitution "too feeble a barrier to obstruct a triumphant majority in their course," and was apprehensive of any alteration they felt it necessary to make.[44]

---

[44] Cabot to Pickering, December 10, 1803, in *Pickering Papers*, "Letters from Correspondents, 1800–1803," XXVI, 336 (Mass. Hist. Soc.); Lodge, *Life and Letters of George Cabot*, 333–334.

The persistence of the idea here expressed by Cabot is seen in his biographer's account of Jefferson's action. Granting that Jefferson was right in purchasing peace, Lodge nevertheless insists that in carrying out his policy, Jefferson violated the Constitution. "Thus," he says, "the first example was given of both the will and desire to violate the Constitution, if the popular feeling would sustain the executive and the legislature in so doing; and in this fact lies the pernicious and crying evil of the Louisiana purchase. It was the first lesson that taught Americans that a numerical majority was superior to the Constitution, was a safe protection against it when violated, and that when policy approved the necessity of change, it was easier to break than to legally and regularly amend the provisions of our charter." Lodge, *Life and Letters of George Cabot*, 434–435. Cf. the statement of Judge Cooley already quoted.

Alleged ulterior motives for Jefferson's action are found in Quincy's *Life of Josiah Quincy*, 90–91, where Jefferson and his partisans are accused of deliberately seizing the opportunity of giving Congress authority to multiply new states in foreign territories without any appeal to the states, their object being to add slave states to the Union. There is no ground for such a charge.

Manasseh Cutler was of practically the same opinion as Cabot. Besides declaring that the treaty was a "flagrant violation of the principles of the Constitution," he repeated the much-held New England opinion that the admission into the Union of a new state formed from this territory would throw the balance of political power to the southern states, and in all probability "will lay the foundation for a separation of the States."[45]

Although not referring to the Louisiana country, the position of the United States with regard to the acquisition of foreign territory was stated by Robert R. Livingston in a conversation reported by Barbé Marbois. In answer to Marbois's statement that many French politicians were afraid that the United States would eventually conquer the French West Indies, Livingston denied that this would ever take place. Although the whites there required to be protected against the slave population,

it would be contrary to our institutions and even our interests to undertake this charge.... Should these colonies hereafter wish to belong to us and to enter into the Union, we could not receive them; we could still less have them as dependent and subject possessions. I do not foresee what will happen if, in their emergencies, they should resort to our generosity and protection. But do not fear that we shall ever make the conquest of that which we would not wish to accept even as a gift.[46]

Substituting Spanish insular possessions for French, Livingston's "emergencies" have arisen. We have made the conquest and they have been made "dependent and subject possessions." Whether they will remain so is one of the interesting problems for the future to solve.

One of the strongest defenders of the purchase of Louisiana, and on constitutional grounds at that, was found among the leaders of the Federalist party at the very time when party

---

[45] Cutler to Dr. Torrey, October 31, 1803, in Cutler and Cutler, *Life, Journals and Correspondence of Manasseh Cutler*, II, 138.

[46] Barbé Marbois, *History of Louisiana*, 299.

spirit was beginning to run high in New England. This was John Adams, who, writing to Josiah Quincy, February 9, 1811, gave one of the best arguments possible in support of the act of the Jefferson administration:

The Union appears to me to be the rock of our salvation, and every reasonable measure for its preservation is expedient. Upon this principle, I own I was pleased with the purchase of Louisiana, because, without it, we could never have secured and commanded the navigation of the Mississippi. The western country would infallibly have revolted from the Union. Those States would have united with England, or Spain, or France, or set up an independence, or done anything else to obtain the free use of that river. I wish the Constitution had been more explicit, or that the States had been consulted; but it seems Congress have not entertained any doubts of their authority, and I cannot say that they are destitute of plausible arguments to support their opinion....

But I was saying a word upon the Constitution. You appear to be fully convinced that the Convention had it not in contemplation to admit any State or States into our Confederation, then situated without the limits of the thirteen States. In this point I am not so clear. The Constitution, it is true, must speak for itself, and be interpreted by its own phraseology; yet the history and state of things at the time may be consulted to elucidate the meaning of words, and determine the *bona fide* intention of the Convention. Suppose we should admit for argument's sake, that no member of the Convention foresaw the purchase of Louisiana! It will not follow that many of them did not foresee the necessity of conquering, some time or other, the Floridas and New Orleans, and other territories on this side of the Mississippi; the state of things between this country and Spain in 1787, was such as to render the apprehensions of a war with that power by no means improbable, the boundaries were not settled, the navigation of the river was threatened, and Spain was known to be tampering, and England too.

You think it impossible the Convention could have a thought of war with Great Britain, and the conquest of Canada. In this point I differ from you very widely. The conduct of Great Britain, and the conduct of our States, too, was such as to keep up very serious apprehensions between the two powers. The treaty of peace was not fulfilled on either side. The English had carried away the negroes, in direct violation of a most express stipulation; they held possession by strong garrisons of a long train of posts within our territory, commanding many nations of Indians, among whom they excited dispositions hostile to us; the limits were not settled against Nova Scotia, and many turbulences between the inhabitants arose.

On the other side the old debts were not paid, and positive laws existed in many, if not most, of the States, against their recovery. I therefore think it highly probable that the Convention meant to authorize Congress in future to admit Canada and Nova Scotia into the Union, in case we should have a war, and be obliged to conquer them by kindness or force.[47]

One staunch supporter of the Jefferson administration took the stand that the cession of Louisiana gave additional security to the free form of the Constitution. Had the French remained in possession of that country and colonized it, the United States would have been forced to maintain a large standing army. The result would have been heavy taxes for the maintenance of this army, and an expensive patronage. Republican forms of government would have been undermined and the way paved for the concentration of power in the hands of an hereditary monarch.[48]

Any doubts as to the constitutional right of the United States Government to acquire territory were laid to rest by Chief Justice Marshall in 1828 when he declared: "The Constitution confers absolutely on the Government of the Union the powers of making war, and of making treaties; consequently, that Government possesses the power of acquiring territory, either by conquest or by treaty."[49]

---

[47] John Adams, *Works*, IX, 631–632. This strong statement does not appear to have been used in the arguments from precedent and from the opinions of early statesmen cited in the Insular Cases.

[48] David Ramsay, *An Oration on the Cession of Louisiana to the United States* (1804), 14.

[49] *American Insurance Co. vs. Canter*, I Peters, 511.

CHAPTER III

THE STATUS OF THE ACQUIRED TERRITORY: CONTEMPORARY OPINION

What was to be the status of the acquired territory? From the standpoint of constitutional interpretation this question proved a difficult one to answer. Many and divergent were the answers proposed. There might be practically a consensus of opinion in favor of the acquisition of territory: that seemed in harmony with the ideas held by a large majority of the people of the United States as to the power of a sovereign nation. Could, however, such acquired territory be formed into states and be admitted into the Union on an equal footing with the original states? If so, by whose authority? Would not the "balance of power" among the old states be upset? Was not the consent of each of the parties to the original contract under the Constitution a necessary prerequisite to the admission of new states into the Union? On the other hand, could the United States hold territory not destined at some future day to become a state? Contemporary opinion on these questions throws much light on the interpretation of the Constitution by men who lived near to the time when that instrument of government was framed.

The relation Louisiana would bear to the rest of the United States aroused comment at the time of the acquisition. One contemporary writer stated the questions for the Government to decide as follows:

1. Whether this territory, under the peculiar limitations of the Federal Constitution can immediately be admitted into the Union with the States?
2. Whether it is considered under those subordinate relations to the United States, that characterize the Indiana and Mississippi territories? or,

3. Whether the cession by treaty attaches itself to the empire as a *fief*, to be held upon the same principles as the Scotch and Irish Unions, and the island of Jamaica and Canada, by the crown of England?[1]

Another writer who styles himself "Sylvestris" questioned whether, if a portion of West Florida could be obtained from Spain, it might not be worthy of an amendment of the Constitution to incorporate that territory, together with the territory of New Orleans, with the present government on the Mississippi, and admit the whole into the Union as a new state, as soon as the population entitled it to such admission.[2]

Still another considered it farcical to pretend that the Louisiana territory could not be erected into separate establishments, all associated under one federal compact. Such a confederation could as well be maintained between *twenty* as between *seventeen* independent states. Furthermore, the interchange of commercial commodities would not fail to convince both the North and South of the special advantages of each, and bind them more closely to one another.[3]

In making plans for the acceptance of Louisiana, Jefferson felt it necessary to come to a decision as to the footing on which the new territory was to be placed, and to put this plan in the hands of friends in Congress. Considering an amendment to the Constitution as the proper mode, he sketched one to be

---

[1] Allan B. Magruder, *Political, Commercial and Moral Reflections, on the late cession of Lousiana to the United States* (1803), 95. Magruder did not think the expansion of territory could produce any dangerous effect. While it was true that when a new state was formed in Louisiana, the Federal circle would be expanded, the state governments merely receded in point of "geographical mensuration" from the general seat of government. Louisiana's remote situation would not give either more power to itself or diminish the influence of the Federal Government. *Ibid.*, 73.

Magruder was a native of Kentucky but had moved to Louisiana. He took an active part in politics, being a state representative, and serving as United States senator from Louisiana from November 18, 1812, to March 3, 1813.

[2] Sylvestris, *pseud.*, *Reflections on the Cession of Louisiana to the United States* (1803), 26–27.

[3] David A. Leonard, *An Oration . . . on the late acquisition of Louisiana* (1804), 20.

proposed by Congress to the states as soon as Congress should meet. This amendment he submitted to members of the Cabinet for suggestions or approval.[4]

The amendment was in harmony with Jefferson's idea of strict construction of the Constitution, for practically every conceivable contingency was provided for and legislative action was stringently circumscribed. The text of the proposed amendment was as follows:

The province of Louisiana is incorporated with the U. S. and made part thereof. The rights of occupancy in the soil, and of self-government, are confirmed to the Indian inhabitants, as they now exist. Pre-emption only of the portions rightfully occupied by them & a succession to the occupancy of such as they may abandon, with the full rights of possession as well as of property & sovereignty in whatever is not or shall cease to be so rightfully occupied by them shall belong to the U. S.

The legislature of the Union shall have authority to exchange the right of occupancy in portions where the U. S. have full right for lands possessed by Indians within the U. S. on the East side of the Mississippi: to exchange lands on the East side of the river for those of the white inhabitants on the West side thereof and above the latitude of 31 degrees: to maintain in any part of the province such military posts as may be requisite for peace or safety: to exercise police over all persons therein, not being Indian inhabitants: to work salt springs, or mines of coal, metals and other minerals within the possession of the U. S. or in any others with the consent of the possessors; to regulate trade & intercourse between the Indian inhabitants and all other persons; to explore and ascertain the geography of the province, its productions and other interesting circumstances; to open roads and navigation therein when necessary for beneficial communication; & to establish agencies and factories therein for the cultivation of commerce, peace and good understanding with the Indians residing there.

The legislature shall have no authority to dispose of the lands of the province otherwise than as hereinbefore permitted, until a new Amendment of the constitution shall give that authority. Except as to that portion thereof which lies South of the latitude of 31 degrees; which whenever they deem expedient, they may erect into a territorial Government, either sep-

---

[4] Jefferson to Gallatin, July 9, 1803, in *Jefferson Papers*, ''Letters from Jefferson, 1st Series, 1802–1803,'' IX (96).

arate or as making part with one on the eastern side of the river, vesting the inhabitants thereof with all the rights possessed by other territorial citizens of the U. S.[5]

The weak points in this lengthy plan of amendment were pointed out by Secretary of the Navy Robert Smith, to whom it had been submitted by Jefferson. While agreeing with the general purpose of the proposed amendment, Smith doubted the advisability of attaching so many provisions to the Constitution.[6]

Regarding the Indian question and occupancy of lands, Smith asked if it might not be better to leave this to be settled by legislative provision. He felt that if the Indian rights of occupancy became a part of the Constitution the Government might find itself much entangled, especially in its dealings with hostile Indians.[7]

Jefferson was not alone in laying plans for the acceptance of the territory and arranging for its control. It was taken for granted that the treaty would be ratified by the Senate. As early as July 9, 1803, over three months before Congress met, Gallatin, as Secretary of the Treasury, began considerations of the problem of revenue in Louisiana, particularly that drawn from duties on imports and exports. The amount of exports, especially the articles like cotton, indigo and sugar—the latter most important of all—which paid duty on their importation into the United States was a subject under investigation. The revenue collected by the United States from sugar Gallatin estimated at not less than nine hundred thousand dollars a year. It was therefore important to ascertain the quantity annually exported from New Orleans, in order either to find means of supplying the deficiency of revenue should sugar be imported

---

[5] Jefferson, *Writings* (Ford, ed.), VIII, 241-249.
[6] *Ibid.*
[7] Smith to Jefferson, July 9, [18]03, in Jefferson, *Writings* (Ford, ed.), VIII, 241-242 (footnote).

from there duty free, or to devise a method by which the duty might still be collected.

> My present idea [wrote Gallatin] was that until an amendment to the Constitution had been adopted, all the duties on imports now payable in the United States should be likewise paid on importations to New Orleans. All the duties on exports now payable at New Orleans by Spanish laws should cease, and all articles of the growth of Louisiana which, when imported into the United States, now pay duty, should continue to pay the same, or at least such rates as would, on the whole, not affect the revenue.[8]

Gallatin's letter is significant in several respects. The idea that the Constitution would be amended to allow the treaty of cession to be carried into execution was brought out once more. Of particular interest in the light of the Insular Decisions is Gallatin's opinion concerning the revenue, which was an important phase of the question of the status of the acquired territory. While extending the import duties payable in the United States to Louisiana and dropping duties on exports under Spanish laws, Gallatin, as will be noticed, planned to continue to impose duties on articles imported into the United States from Louisiana. Gallatin's reason, as he himself gives it, was one of expediency—the collection of a revenue. Nevertheless the imposition of these import duties would set Louisiana apart from the rest of the territory of the United States.

On October 31, Gallatin, in accordance with his understanding of the situation, informed Claiborne, who was to take possession of Louisiana, that the existing duties on imports and exports, being levied in that province under Spanish law, should continue until Congress should otherwise provide.[9]

---

[8] Gallatin to Jefferson, July 9, 1803, in Gallatin, *Writings* (Adams, ed.), I, 127.

[9] Gallatin, *Writings* (Adams, ed.), I, 167. Gallatin's opinion in this matter was cited in the *Insular Cases*, 175, 176–178, 316–317.

Compare the statement in Moore, *Digest of International Law*, I, 311: "When Florida was ceded to the United States and possession of it had actually been taken it was held by the Secretary of the Treasury, whose opinion was sanctioned by the Attorney-General, that, under our revenue laws, its ports must be regarded as foreign until they were established as domestic by an act of Congress."

Congress soon made the provision spoken of by Gallatin by an act, approved February 24, 1804, for laying and collecting duties on imports and tonnage within the ceded territory. This act provided that the same duties which were laid on goods imported into the United States should be laid and collected on goods imported into Louisiana.

All laws laying any duties on goods imported into the United States from the ceded territory were repealed. Furthermore, the President was authorized to erect the shore, waters and inlets of the bay and river Mobile into a separate district and establish a port of entry and delivery *"whenever he shall deem it expedient."*[10] The full significance of this last provision became apparent when the West Florida question became acute.[11]

The plan of an amendment which would leave but little initiative in the hands of the Legislature was early given up by Jefferson. Even before the drafting of a second amendment[12] he wrote to Horatio Gates that, "If our legislature dispose of it [the territory] with the wisdom we have a right to expect, they may make it the means of tempting all our Indians on the East side of the Mississippi to remove to the West, and of condensing instead of scattering our population." In the same letter Jefferson drops some hints as to the contemplated government of the territory. He did not think it would be a separate government, but presumed New Orleans and the settled country across the river would be annexed to the Mississippi Territory. The rest would be locked up from American settlement and left to the self-government of the natives.[13]

In his Third Annual Message to Congress, October 17, 1803, Jefferson announced the transfer of Louisiana by France to the United States, adding *that when the transfer had been sanc-*

---

[10] *Laws of the U. States*, III, 569–574. Italics mine.

[11] See below, Chapters X and XI.

[12] For which, see above.

[13] Jefferson to Horatio Gates, July 11, [18]03, in Jefferson, *Writings* (Ford, ed.), VIII, 249–250.

tioned by the Senate, the matter would be laid before the House of Representatives "for the exercise of their functions, as to those conditions which are within the powers vested by the constitution in Congress."[14]

Then comes a clear statement of the powers of Congress over territories:

> With the *wisdom of Congress* it will rest to take those ulterior measures which may be necessary for the immediate occupation and temporary government of the country; *for its incorporation into our Union;* for rendering the change of government a blessing to our newly-adopted brethren; *for securing to them the rights of conscience and of property;* for confirming to the Indian inhabitants their occupancy and self-government, establishing friendly and commercial relations with them, and for ascertaining the geography of the country acquired.[15]

On October 21, 1803, Jefferson submitted a special message on Louisiana to Congress, announcing the exchange of ratifica-

---

[14] Italics mine.

At least one Senator considered the language used in the message improper for a President. "He not only publicly pledges himself to ratify the treaties if the Senate shall advise thereto, but takes it for granted that the Senate will sanction them. As far as his -influence can extend this is destroying the freedom of opinion in the Senate on that subject." Plumer, "Memorandum," October 17, 1803–March 27, 1804, 2–3. Plumer might have stated his objections even more emphatically had he seen the correspondence of Jefferson and his closest friends in which the ratification was not only taken for granted but plans made for the government of the territory, even before Congress met.

Plumer's disapprobation, in substance, was revived during the administration of McKinley when that President was criticized for issuing, on December 21, 1898, prior to the ratification of the treaty with Spain ceding the Philippines, an executive order which contained the following words: "With the signature of the treaty of peace between the United States and Spain by their respective plenipotentiaries at Paris on the 10th instant, and as the result of the victories of American arms, the future control, disposition, and government of the Philippine Islands are ceded to the United States. In fulfilment of the rights of sovereignty thus acquired, etc." The treaty-making power of the United States did not ratify the treaty until February, and the treaty did not go into effect until April 11, 1899. W. W. Willoughby, *The Constitutional Law of the United States,* I, 385, footnote.

[15] Jefferson, *Writings* (Ford, ed.), VIII, 268–269; Richardson, *Messages and Papers of the Presidents,* I, 358–359. Italics mine. Compare the sentiment expressed here with that in the proposed amendment. Jefferson's opinion of the powers of Congress over the territories underwent numerous changes. These will be discussed under the subject of the government of Louisiana.

tions between the President and the First Consul of France. He asked for a consideration of the treaty and conventions by Congress in its legislative capacity. He pointed out that some important provisions could not be carried into execution without the aid of the Legislature, and urged a decision without delay.[16]

What composed the constitutional rights of the House of Representatives in regard to the treaty caused considerable debate.[17]

Other questions of constitutional interpretation, fraught with very great significance to the well-being of the nation, were raised.

Congress [Rufus King wrote] may admit new States, but can the Executive by treaty admit them, or, what is equivalent, enter into engagements binding Congress to do so? As by the Louisiana Treaty, the ceded territory must be formed into States, & admitted into the Union, is it understood that Congress can annex any condition to their admission? if not, as Slavery is authorized & exists in Louisiana, and the treaty engages to protect the *Property* of the inhabitants, will not the present inequality, arising from the Representation of Slaves be increased?

King desired that the representation and taxation might be limited to free inhabitants only.[18]

Pickering, referring to King's letter, claimed that the ruling party did not pretend that the Louisianians were *citizens* of the United States; nor had they ventured to say that the Government had a *constitutional* power to incorporate the new country into the Union. To him it appeared evident that in a few years, when their power had become more confirmed, they would erect states in the territory and incorporate those states into the Union. The future to Pickering had a dark outlook, for the Constitution

---

[16] Jefferson, *Writings* (Ford, ed.), VIII, 274; Richardson, *Messages and Papers of the Presidents*, I, 362–363.

[17] See below.

[18] King to Colonel Pickering, November 4, 1803, in King, *Life and Correspondence of Rufus King*, IV, 324–325, "Letter *probably* to Pickering": doubt removed by examination of the original letter, *Pickering Papers*, "Letters from Correspondents 1800–1803," XXVI, 319 (Mass. Hist. Soc., Library). See Madison's opinion on the question of imposing restrictions on prospective states, p. 48.

would become only a convenient instrument to be shaped, by construction, into any form that would best promote the views of the operators. He concluded with the remark that it might be better if we had no Constitution, for "the leaders of the populace wanting the function of a Constitutional power might then be more cautious in their measures."[19]

Gouverneur Morris declared that he was not sorry that the Louisiana treaty had been ratified and provision made for carrying it into effect in accordance with the wish of the President. He added that by their acts the Democrats had done more to strengthen the Executive than the Federalists had ever dared to contemplate.[20] Reverting to the inquiry made by Henry W. Livingston[21] Morris wrote, December 4, 1803:

> A circumstance, which turned up in conversation yesterday has led me again to read over your letter of the third of November, and my answer of the twenty-eighth. I perceive now, that I mistook the drift of your inquiry, which is substantially whether Congress can admit, as a new State, territory, which did not belong to the United States when the Constitution was made. In my opinion they cannot.
>
> I always thought that, when we should acquire Canada and Louisiana it would be proper to govern them as provinces, and allow them no voice in our councils.[22] In wording the third section of the fourth article, I went as far as circumstances would permit to establish the exclusion. Candor obliges me to add my belief that, had it been more pointedly expressed, a strong opposition would have been made.[23]

It could probably be shown that this policy would have been more dangerous to the Government than the overthrow of the balance of power by the admission of new states, from which the

---

[19] Pickering to Rufus King, March 3, 1804, in *Pickering Papers*, "Letters to his Correspondents, 1801–1813," XIV, 97 (Mass. Hist. Soc. Library).

[20] Sparks, *Life of Gouverneur Morris*, III, 184.

[21] See above.

[22] Morris's opinion does not harmonize with the spirit of article eleven of the Articles of Confederation which made specific provision for the admission of Canada into the Union.

[23] Sparks, *Life of Gouverneur Morris*, III, 192; Farrand, *Records of the Federal Convention*, III, 404.

New Englanders claimed to fear so much. Fortunately for the future of the new Republic this interpretation of the Constitution was not accepted. Morris, however, persisted in the belief that the admission of the inhabitants of the ceded territory into the Union would prove dangerous. He pessimistically remarked that at the rate things were going, "the Constitution cannot last, and an unbalanced monarchy will be established on its ruins."[24]

One of the staunchest supporters of strict construction of the Constitution throughout the struggle over Louisiana was John Quincy Adams. He confessed that the whole subject had caused him sleepless nights.[25] He complained that Pickering, who differed with him on the Louisiana matter, was guided by expediency rather than by constitutional right.[26] The question of taxing the people of Louisiana without their own consent was abhorrent to Adams. He therefore moved in the Senate the adoption of the following resolutions:

Resolved, That the people of the United States, have never, in any manner delegated to this Senate, the power of giving its legislative concurrence to any act for imposing taxes upon the inhabitants of Louisiana, without their consent.

Resolved, That by concurring in any act of legislation for imposing taxes upon the inhabitants of Louisiana without their consent, this Senate would assume a power, unwarranted by the constitution and dangerous to the people of the United States.

Resolved, That the power of originating bills for raising revenue, being exclusively vested in the House of Representatives, these resolutions be carried to them by the Secretary to the Senate: that whenever they think proper they may adopt such measures as to their wisdom may appear necessary and expedient for raising and collecting a revenue from Louisiana.[27]

---

[24] Morris to Jonathan Dayton, January 7, 1804, in Sparks, *Life of Gouverneur Morris*, III, 203.

[25] John Quincy Adams, *Memoirs* (Adams, ed.), I, 285, January 8, 1804.

[26] *Ibid.*, I, 289, January 15, 1804.

[27] John Quincy Adams, *Writings* (Ford, ed.), III, 25–26; *Memoirs*, I, 286 (footnote).

A vote was taken upon each resolution. The first and second were rejected by twenty-one to four. The third was unanimously rejected.[28]

Adams believed that the consent of the people of the United States and of the people of Louisiana was necessary to make Louisiana a part of the American Union. France could only cede her property right to the territory; while the right of sovereignty inherent in the people must be ceded by an act of their own and acquired by some act of the people of the United States.[29]   Considering an amendment to the Constitution necessary, he drafted one and submitted it to Madison and Pickering, neither of whom approved of it. The tenor of the amendment was a grant of general power to Congress to annex new territories to the Union at its discretion.   The exercise of sovereign powers by Congress over the people of Louisiana Adams considered an assumption of power not delegated.   However, this power having been acquiesced in, there was no constitutional obstacle to the admission of Louisiana into the Union as a state.   He did not think it the intention of the framers of the Constitution to limit the admission of new states into the Union to the original territory of the United States.   Such an intention would have probably been expressed.   A comparison of the Articles of Confederation with the Constitution showed, said Adams, that the power to admit new states was substituted for the clause authorizing the admission of Canada.   The power in the Constitution applied to the admission of states within the original territory of the Union, but there was no reason to believe that it was intended to apply so exclusively.

"Manifest destiny" again comes to the fore and Adams concluded:

---

[28] John Quincy Adams, *Memoirs* (Adams, ed.), I, 287, January 10, 1804.

[29] See Adams's speech in the Senate, February 18, 1804, as reported by Plumer, in Chapter VII.

The whole continent of North America appears to be destined by Divine Providence to be peopled by one *nation*, speaking one language, professing one general system of religious and political principles, and accustomed to one general tenor of social usages and customs. For the common happiness of them all, I believe it indispensable that they should be associated in one federal Union.[30]

Pickering expressed himself as in favor of something more practical than the doctrine proposed by Adams. He held that the people were accustomed to such transfers and to being ruled without their inclinations being consulted. He would give individuals no option except quiet obedience or expatriation. He would provide for a gradual amelioration of their laws, in conformity with the principles of our own jurisprudence, winning their affections and assimilating them as fast as possible to the character of citizens of the United States.[31]

To Adams's inquiry by what clause in the Constitution Pickering deemed Congress authorized to tax and govern Louisiana, Pickering answered that Congress in its legislative capacity was often obliged to legislate in cases where correct theory forbade it, negro slavery being an example. Although some stipulations in the treaty, or even the purchase itself, were not warranted by the Constitution; and although the abstract theory of government forbade the taxing, or the imposing of laws on any people without their own consent; yet with regard to Louisiana, it having become in fact a province of the United States the "general welfare" required Congress "to provide" for its government. Pickering expressed himself as willing to coöperate in forming the same regulations for the "general welfare" as would have been proper had Louisiana been in all respects constitutionally acquired.[32]

---

[30] Letter to John Adams, August 31, 1811, in John Quincy Adams, *Writings* (Ford, ed.), IV, 204–210. See also Henry Adams, *Documents relating to New England Federalism*, 52–55.

[31] Pickering to Stephen Higginson, January 14, 1804, in *Pickering Papers*, ''Letters to his Correspondents, 1801–1803,'' XIV, 84.

[32] Pickering to Higginson, January 16, 1804, *ibid.*, XIV, 89.

Echoes of the Louisiana question and its results, directly and indirectly, can be traced far down even into Madison's writings. Perhaps no man was better qualified than he to say what the meaning of the Constitution was. His clear-cut way of going immediately to the heart of any question is well illustrated in this connection. On the admission of Missouri into the Union Madison wrote:

> As to the power of admitting new States into the federal compact, the questions offering themselves are: whether congress can attach conditions, or the new States concur in conditions, which after admission, would abridge or *enlarge* the constitutional rights of legislation common to the other States; whether Congress can by a compact with a new member take power either to or from itself, or place the new member above or below the equal rank and rights possessed by the others; whether all such stipulations, expressed or implied would not be nullities, and so pronounced when brought to a practical test....[33]

"On the whole," said Madison, "the Missouri question, as a constitutional one, amounts to the question whether the condition proposed to be annexed to the admission of Missouri would or would not be void in itself, or become void the moment the territory should enter as a State within the pale of the Constitution."[34] The truth of this statement is borne out by the history of the territorial expansion of the United States.

Constitutional construction was at the bottom of the whole matter of the acquisition of territory with its inhabitants, turning on the right to acquire and to admit when acquired.[35]

---

[33] Madison to Robert Walsh, November 27, 1819, in Madison, *Writings* (Hunt, ed.), IX, 6–7.

[34] *Ibid.*, IX, 12.

[35] Madison to James Robertson, April 20, 1831, in Madison, *Letters and other Writings* (Congressional ed.), IV; 171.

CHAPTER IV

THE DEBATE ON THE TREATY : THE TREATY-MAKING POWER[1]

As soon as the news that the President had signed the treaty became known there arose at once the question of the interpretation of the constitutional provisions concerning treaty-making. Jefferson had been warned of possible difficulties on this score by both Madison and Gallatin. The draft of the President's message of October 17 had been submitted to Madison, who, under date of October 1, commented on it. He thought it well to avoid "what the theory of our constitution does not seem to have met, the influence of deliberations and anticipations of the H. of Reps. on a Treaty depending in the Senate." Delay might arise from the doubtfulness and novelty of a communication of a treaty negotiated by the Executive to both Houses for their respective deliberations.[2]

Gallatin thought the treaty ought not to be laid before both Houses of Congress until after ratification by the Senate. "The House of Representatives," he wrote, "neither can nor ought to act on the treaty until after it is a treaty." Great care, he continued, should be taken against possible encroachment upon the constitutional rights of the Senate. Grants of money or other legislative acts for enabling the Executive to carry on a negotiation could be asked for before the negotiation had been opened or the treaty received. After the negotiation had been

---

[1] For a recent general treatment of this topic see W. W. Willoughby, *The Constitutional Law of the United States*, I, Chapters XXXII–XXXV; also Samuel B. Crandall, *Treaties: Their Making and Enforcement*.

[2] Jefferson, *Writings* (Ford, ed.), VIII, 266 (footnote). That it was not wise for the House to take part in treaty-making was laid down by John Jay in the *Federalist* (Ford, ed.), no. 64. See also no. 75 by Hamilton.

closed and the treaty signed, as in the case at hand, the House need not be consulted until ratification by the President and Senate has been completed.[3]

Just what claims to participation in treaty-making the House would put forth were soon evident. On October 22, 1803, it was reported to the House that the conventions entered into with the Government of France for the cession of Louisiana to the United States had been ratified by the Senate and were laid before the House in its legislative capacity. John Randolph submitted a resolution providing for the carrying into effect of the treaty and conventions. This was submitted to a committee. to which the President's message had been referred.[4]

Two days later, October 24, Gaylord Griswold of New York moved a resolution asking that the President be requested to have laid before the House a copy of the treaty between France and Spain, entered into October 1, 1800, together with a copy of the deed of cession of Louisiana from Spain to France under that treaty, if such deed existed; also copies of any correspondence which might have taken place between the Governments of the United States and Spain which would show the assent or dissent of Spain to the cession of Louisiana to the United States, together with any other documents in possession of the American Government showing that the United States had really acquired title to the possession of Louisiana.[5]

Varying degrees of opinion became evident in the debate which followed the introduction of this resolution. John Randolph opposed the resolution and was answered by Goddard of Connecticut. Smilie of Pennsylvania also opposed the motion, and quoted Washington's reply to the House on the demand for the papers in relation to Jay's Treaty. Elliot of Vermont

---

[3] Gallatin, *Writings* (Adams, ed.), I, 156; remarks received by Jefferson October 4.

[4] *Annals of Congress*, 8 Cong., 1 Sess. (1803–1804), 382.

[5] *Ibid.*, 385.

opposed the call on the Executive for papers, while Thacher of Massachusetts spoke for the resolution. Nicholson of Maryland favored the call for the papers on the treaty but not the recognition of any claim of Spain. Mitchill of New York acknowledged the right of the House to request of the President the copies of the papers mentioned in the resolution under debate; his opposition to the resolution arose from the persuasion he felt, that the papers were unnecessary, and some of them impossible to obtain.[6]

The question was taken on agreeing to the first part of the resolution which requested the President to cause to be laid before the House a copy of the treaty between France and Spain, of October 1, 1800, and was carried by the casting vote of the Speaker. The other parts of the motion were lost. The original motion was amended to read:

Resolved, That the President of the United States be requested to cause to be laid before the House a copy of the treaty between the French Republic and Spain, on the 1st October, 1800, together with a copy of any instrument in possession of the Executive, showing that the Spanish Government has ordered the province of Louisiana to be delivered to the Commissary or other agent of the French Government.

The motion was lost by the close vote of fifty-nine to fifty-seven.[7]

On October 25, the House went into the Committee of the Whole for consideration of measures for carrying the treaty into effect.[8] Gaylord Griswold desired to know where was to be found the constitutional power of the Government to incorporate the territory with its inhabitants into the Union of the United States, with the privileges of the United States. The constitutional right of making treaties, he said, was vested in the President and Senate and a treaty made by them on a subject constitutionally within their treaty-making power, was valid

6 *Ibid.*, 387–402.
7 *Ibid.*, 418–419.
8 *Ibid.*, 432.

without the consent of the House. The House could refuse the necessary means of carrying treaties into effect but this power was not the same as that conferred by the Constitution. Should, however, the treaty-making power be exceeded, it ought not to be carried into effect. Even a beneficial measure, if it violated the Constitution, should be resisted. Quoting the third article of the treaty, Griswold declared:

> Here then is a compact between the French Government and that of the United States, to admit to citizenship persons out of the jurisdiction of the United States, as it now is, and to admit territory out of the United States, to be incorporated into the Union. He did not find in the Constitution such a power vested in the President and Senate. If such a power be not expressly vested, it must be reserved to the people. It was not consistent with the spirit of the Constitution that territory other than that attached to the United States at the time of the adoption of the Constitution should be admitted; because at that time the persons who formed the Constitution of the United States had a particular respect to the then subsisting territory.

Even though the framers of the Constitution had looked forward to a greater population they had not intended that an addition of territory large enough to overbalance all the rest should be made. He did not believe that any such power had been delegated to any department of the Government. If it had been placed anywhere it must rest with the Legislature, for the Constitution states that new states are to be admitted into the Union by Congress.[9] This provision, however, related to the then existing territory of the United States. Power to incorporate new territory did not exist; but if this power did exist the Legislature, and not the Executive, could incorporate the territory into the Union. It was the duty of the House, he concluded, to resist the usurped power exercised by the Executive.[10]

Griswold also took exception to the seventh article of the treaty, which provided that the ships of France and Spain

---

[9] Article 4, section 3.
[10] *Annals of Congress,* 8 Cong., 1 Sess. (1803–1804), 432–433.

should have the same right, under certain conditions and for a term of twelve years, of entering the ports of the ceded territory as those of the United States. The inference was that a favor was being granted to the port of New Orleans over other ports of the United States. Such discrimination was contrary to the ninth section of the first article of the Constitution which states that "no preference shall be given by any regulation of commerce or revenue to the ports of one State over those of another." The treaty becoming a law of the land, had made a commercial regulation, giving the ports of the ceded territory a preference to any other ports. Giving an advantage to the ports in question would be "a fatal blow proposed against the Constitution of the United States, for it would destroy the reciprocity of interest that unites at present the different members of the Union."[11]

John Randolph answered Griswold by stating clearly the treaty-making powers as he interpreted them:

If the Government of the United States possess the Constitutional power to acquire territory from foreign States, the Executive, as the organ by which we communicate with such States, must be the prime agent, in negotiating such an acquisition. Conceding, then, that the power of confirming this act, and annexing to the United States the territory thus acquired, ultimately rests with Congress, where has been the invasion of the privileges of that body? Does not the President of the United States submit this subject to Congress for their sanction? Does he not recognize the principle ... that no treaty is binding until we pass the laws for executing it—that the powers conferred by the Constitution on Congress cannot be modified or abridged, by any treaty whatever—that the subjects of which they have cognizance cannot be taken, in any way, out of their jurisdiction? ... As to the initiative, in a matter like this, it necessarily devolved on the Executive.[12]

Roger Griswold of Connecticut was not altogether satisfied with the interpretation here given. While declaring that the power of making treaties belonged exclusively to the President,

---

11 *Ibid.*, 434.
12 *Ibid.*, 436–437.

with the consent of the Senate, and that a treaty, constitutionally made and ratified, became a law and must be executed, he
still maintained that the treaty must be consistent with the
Constitution in every respect. A treaty repugnant to the Constitution either in subject-matter or in form of ratification could
not be constitutionally considered a treaty. Congress, in such
a case, was bound to support the Constitution and refuse its
consent to laws which would infringe that instrument.[13]

Nicholson took it upon himself to answer the charge that the
President and Senate have no right to pledge the Government
for anything not immediately within their own powers. He
pointed out that the President and Senate have the treaty-
making power but nearly all of the treaties ratified by them
contain stipulations which must be performed by the House, if
performed at all. This had been the case in the last convention
made with Great Britain, in which the President and Senate
pledged the United States to the payment of six hundred thousand pounds sterling, yet no constitutional power to do so was
possessed by them; nor could the money have been paid without
the concurrence of the House. No doubt of the constitutionality
of this stipulation had been held. Furthermore, no question had
been raised over the pledge in the present treaty to pay to France
fifteen million dollars, although the treaty could not be carried
into effect without the coöperation of the House.

Nicholson also discussed the point made by Roger Griswold
that since the treaty embraced objects not in the power of the
General Government, the whole treaty was invalid. This, he
held, was not true. Impossible covenants in a treaty might be
void and not invalidate the rest. There was a distinction between articles of a treaty which were violated by one party, and
articles which from the nature of things, or from previous
engagements, were void. As a precedent he cited the Treaty of
Peace with Great Britain, concluded in 1783, the fourth article

---

[13] *Annals of Congress,* 8 Cong., 1 Sess. (1803–1804), 460.

of which provided that creditors on either side should meet with no lawful impediments to the recovery of debts contracted previous to the war. This was a stipulation impossible for Congress to perform. In the matter of debts the individual states had uncontrolled authority. While the right to make treaties had been given to the General Government by the Articles of Confederation, the assent of the states was necessary before this part of the treaty could be carried out. This article was invalid, and never fulfilled on the part of the United States, yet the whole treaty was not thereby nullified. Nicholson held that even if it should be determined that Congress could not admit the ceded territory into the Union as a state, yet the remainder of the treaty with France would remain valid.[14]

It was not in the House alone that the extent of the treaty-making power was under probe. On November 2, when the Senate resumed the second reading of the bill, entitled, ''An act authorizing the creation of a stock to the amount of eleven millions two hundred and fifty thousand dollars, for the purpose of carrying into effect the convention of the 30th of April, 1803, between the United States of America and the French Republic and making provisions for the payment of the same,'' a debate arose on the question: shall the bill pass?[15] White of Delaware declared that the United States must have possession of New Orleans and such other places on the Mississippi, necessary to secure the complete and uninterrupted navigation of that river. This much was essential to the peace of the United States and to the prosperity of the West. ''But as to Louisiana, this new, immense, unbounded world, if it should ever be incorporated into this Union, which I have no idea can be done but by altering the Constitution, I believe it will be the greatest curse that could at present befall us.''[16]

---

14 *Ibid.*, 468–470.
15 *Ibid.*, 31.
16 *Ibid.*, 33.

The constitutional right to acquire by treaty a small area does not seem to have troubled Senator White: a larger area was another matter. The friends of the bill were not slow in pointing out the weakness of this argument.[17]

The lack of power under the Constitution not only of the treaty-making body, but of any or all departments of government as they existed, was set forth by Senator Pickering of Massachusetts in his classic exposition of the state-compact theory of the formation of the Federal Government:

'The Constitution and the laws of the United States made in pursuance thereof, and all treaties made, or which shall be made, shall be the supreme law of the land.'[18] But a treaty to be obligatory, must not contravene the Constitution, nor contain any stipulations which transcend the powers therein given to the President and Senate. The treaty between the United States and the French Republic, professing to cede Louisiana to the United States, appeared to him to contain an exceptionable stipulation—a stipulation which cannot be executed by any authority now existing. It is declared in the third article, that the inhabitants of the ceded territory shall be incorporated in the Union of the United States. But neither the President and Senate, nor the President and Congress, are competent to such an act of incorporation. He believed that our Administration admitted that this incorporation could not be effected without an amendment of the Constitution, and he conceived that this necessary amendment could not be made in the ordinary mode by the concurrence of two-thirds of both Houses of Congress, and the ratification of the Legislatures of three-fourths of the several States. He believed the assent of each individual State to be necessary for the admission of foreign country as an associate in the Union: in like manner as in a commercial house, the consent of each member would be necessary to admit a new partner into the company.

Pickering, however, "had never doubted the right of the United States to acquire new territory either by purchase or conquest and to govern the territory so acquired as a dependent province."[19]

---

17 See below.

18 Article 6, clause 2.

19 *Annals of Congress*, 8 Cong., 1 Sess. (1803–1804), 44–45.

A still different interpretation was presented by John Taylor of Virginia in answer to the objections made to the treaty; first, that the United States could not constitutionally acquire territory; and second, that the treaty stipulated for the admission of a new state into the Union, a stipulation with which the treaty-making power could not comply. Taylor argued that before the formation of the Confederation, each state, being sovereign, possessed the right to acquire territory: this right it either still held, or had surrendered to the General Government. This power was not possessed by the states separately because the states were prohibited by the Constitution from engaging in war or entering into compacts with another state or with foreign powers. No other means of acquiring territory existed. By taking from each state the means of exercising the right of acquiring territory, the Constitution had taken from each state the right itself. On the other hand, neither the means nor the right of acquiring territory were forbidden to the United States; and the fourth article of the Constitution even empowered Congress "to dispose of and regulate the territory belonging to the United States." The right of the United States to hold territory was thus recognized. The means of acquiring territory consisted of war and compact. Both being expressly surrendered to Congress and prohibited to the several states, it followed, according to Taylor, that these attributes of sovereignty once held by each state were thus transferred to the United States, annexed to the treaty-making power, and the power of making war; or literally granted by the Constitution to the General Government.[20]

Nicholas held it to be rather extraordinary that arguments to show the unconstitutionality of the treaty should be made in the Senate, to prevent its execution, after the treaty had already

20 *Ibid.*, 50.

been ratified by that body. This action having been taken it was not necessary to answer arguments denying the power of the Government to make such a treaty. The only question at stake was whether the bill ought to pass at that time. The principle had been decided when the British Treaty was under discussion that the treaty-making power of the Government was so limited that the consent and coöperation of Congress was necessary before engagements to pay money could be carried into effect. In the Constitution the treaty-making powers were not specified nor were any reservations made; but from this it was not to be inferred that the treaty-making power was unlimited. If special grants of power to Congress were to be considered as limitations of the treaty-making power, the power of making treaties did not substantially exist in the Government, for a commercial treaty could not be formed without interfering with the Congressional power to regulate commerce, lay and collect duties, imposts, etc., and every other treaty would require the payment of money or some other stipulation calling for the exercise of some power vested in Congress.

To make ours a practical Government, [declared Nicholas] it must be understood that the treaty-making power may negotiate respecting many of the subjects upon which Congress may legislate, but that Congress are not bound to carry into execution such compacts (where an act of theirs is necessary to give them effect) unless they approve of them. And this must be fully understood by all nations with whom such compacts may be formed. Upon every other subject proper for a national compact, not inconsistent with our Constitution, and under the limitations by me stated, a treaty may be negotiated and absolutely concluded by the treaty-making power, so as to bind the nation. . . . By the British Treaty a great number of persons had a right to become American citizens immediately; not only without a law, but contrary to an existing law. And by that treaty many of the powers specially given to Congress were exercised by the treaty-making power.

. . . .

If the third article of the treaty is an engagement to incorporate the Territory of Louisiana into the Union of the United States, and to make it a State, it cannot be considered as an unconstitutional exercise of the treaty-making power; for it will not be asserted by any rational man that the territory is incorporated as a State by the treaty itself; when it is expressly declared that 'the inhabitants shall be incorporated in the Union of the United States, and admitted as soon as possible, according to the principles of the Federal Constitution.' Evidently referring the question of incorporation, in whatever character it was to have taken place, to the competent authority; and leaving it to that authority to do it, at such time, and in such manner, as they may think proper.

This would be done by Congress or by an amendment to the Constitution for in no other way could a State be admitted into the Union.[21]

Cocke of Tennessee pointed out that the objections being made to the treaty were not consistent with the opinions formally delivered by those who, a short time before, advocated the taking of New Orleans and the Floridas by military force.[22] He pertinently demanded whether the Constitution had formed a barrier then. Presenting an extremely broad interpretation of the Constitution, Cocke contended that the treaty-making powers were "competent to the full and free exercise of their best judgment in making treaties, without limitation of power; for, on every subject in which that power is called to act, it must act on its own responsibility." According to Cocke's interpretation, the treaty-making power passes out of the hands of the people by their consent, and for a time limited by them, is vested in the President and Senate. There it remains until the time set by the people for the resumption of their elective rights.[23]

So sweeping a power for the treaty-making branch of the Government was not held by many of Cocke's contemporaries but it met with growing favor in the years following the Spanish-American War of 1898.

---

[21] *Ibid.*, 68–71. It is very doubtful if a saner interpretation of the constitutional provision for the treaty-making powers has been made than this by Nicholas.

[22] See above.

[23] *Annals of Congress*, 8 Cong., 1 Sess. (1803–1804), 71–73.

The vote on the passage of the bill to create eleven million two hundred and fifty thousand dollars of stock to pay for Louisiana was carried in the Senate by a vote of twenty-six to five, those opposing it being Hillhouse and Tracy of Connecticut, Pickering of Massachusetts, and White and Wells of Delaware.[24]

Senator Plumer had voted against ratifying the treaty but voted in favor of the bill for creating the stock to pay for the territory. His justification of his action in the latter case was that the President and Senate, the only tribunal established to make treaties, had declared the instrument to be a treaty; and this question having been settled, the faith of the nation was pledged to make the necessary appropriations. The treaty, by action of the President and Senate, having become a law, Plumer did not consider himself at liberty to withhold his vote on the ground either that the treaty was unconstitutional, or that it was a bad bargain. Those questions as they related to the Senate, were, for him, definitely settled.

Plumer declined to say that the ratification made the treaty a constitutional one, if its articles violated the Constitution. Its ratification, however, bound the Government to carry it into effect so far as the Government had authority to do so. "Perish the eleven millions of stock," declared Plumer, "but preserve the *faith* of the nation." He then pointed out that cases might arise respecting the rights of individuals under the treaty in the courts of law in which the constitutionality of the treaty might be questioned. He could even conceive of cases in which it might become the duty of the judges, if such were their opinion, and if the nature of the case required it, to declare the treaty to be repugnant to the Constitution.[25]

---

[24] *Annals of Congress,* 8 Cong., 1 Sess. (1803–1804), 73.

[25] Plumer, ''Memorandum, 1803–1804,'' under date of Thursday, November 3, 1803 (p. 72). A briefer reference to his vote will be found in his letter to Daniel Plumer, November 15, 1803, in his *MSS* letters, and in Plumer, *Life of William Plumer,* 265.

Coming as it did only a few months after the decision of the Supreme Court in the case of *Marbury vs. Madison* (February, 1803), Plumer's last statement is very striking. In *Marbury vs. Madison* the Supreme Court of the United States, for the first time, had declared a law to be unconstitutional. Plumer's assertion that the judges had the power ''to declare a treaty repugnant to the Constitution'' is in harmony with that decision. Plumer does not say whether he had been influenced by the opinion of the Supreme Court or whether he had reached his conclusion independently. In either case, his statement is an interesting illustration of the development of constitutional interpretation.

The extent of the treaty-making power was, like practically all the other constitutional issues to which the Louisiana Purchase gave rise, one of interpretation. To a great degree it has remained so, yet precedent has added much to interpretation. Just as the decision at the time of the Jay Treaty was made use of in the debates on the Louisiana Treaty, so the latter has been cited each time the same question has recurred. That sectional interests have entered into these interpretations is of none the less interest and importance; for it goes to show how men sought, under the Constitution, a justification of their acts and votes.

CHAPTER V

THE DEBATE ON THE TREATY

(1) *The Right to Acquire Territory*

The right of the Government under the Constitution to acquire new territory did not, in itself, cause much debate in Congress when the Louisiana treaty was under discussion. This right, although generally complicated with some of the other points at issue, nevertheless, in some of its phases at least, stands apart. The doctrine that a republic ought not to cover too extensive an area was early introduced, as it had been during the days when the ratification of the Constitution itself was before the country.[1] This doctrine John Breckinridge of Kentucky, in the Senate, pronounced old and hackneyed. He, too, asked whether the principle would have been violated by including the island of Orleans and the Floridas. Since all parties seemed to think their acquisition essential, why not acquire on the west bank of the Mississippi as well as the east side? Instead of believing in the theory that a republic ought to be confined within narrow limits, he believed that the more extensive its dominion the more durable it would be.[2]

---

[1] *Federalist* (Ford, ed.), nos. 9, 10, 14. After the triumph of democracy in 1801, Jefferson wrote to Nathaniel Niles: ''It furnishes a new proof of the falsehood of Montesquieu's doctrine, that a republic can be preserved only in a small territory. The reverse is the truth. Had our territory been even a third only of what it is, we were gone. But when frenzy & delusion, like an epidemic, gained certain parts, the residue remained sound & untouched, and held on till their brethren could recover from the temporary delusion; and that circumstance has given me great comfort.'' Jefferson, *Writings* (Ford, ed.), VIII, 24. Quoted by Ford in his edition of the *Federalist*, 50, footnote.

[2] *Annals of Congress*, 8 Cong., 1 Sess. (1803–1804), 60.
The same idea crept into the printed pamphlets of the time, where supporters of the administration defended the extension of the Federal limits. See for example, David A. Leonard, *An Oration ... on the late acquisition of Louisiana. ... 1804*, 20; David Ramsay, *An Oration on the*

Upon the question of the right to acquire territory, Randolph of Virginia stood, in the House, as the champion of broad construction of the Constitution. He held that if, by the Constitution, the United States was restricted to the limits which existed at the time of its adoption, those limits must have been accurately defined and generally known at the time. The boundaries had been neither particularly described nor settled beyond dispute. They were unsettled on the northwestern, southern, and northeastern frontiers when the Constitution was adopted.

> It will not be denied, [said Randolph] that, among the powers which the Government possesses under the Constitution, there exists that of settling disputes concerning our limits with the neighboring nations.... The existence of this power will not be denied: it has been exercised in ascertaining our northeastern and southern frontier, and it involves in it the power of extending the limits of the Confederacy.... That the Constitution should tie us down to particular limits, without expressing those limits; that we should be restrained to the then boundaries of the United States, when it is in proof ... that no such bounds existed, or do now exist, was altogether uncomprehensible and inadmissible.[3]

Elliott of Vermont declared that the treaty-making power had been constituted by the American people with an eye to the law of nations; and that by virtue of this law, the Government and the people of the United States possessed the power and right of acquiring territory by conquest, cession, or purchase.[4]

Nicholson of Maryland traced historically the right of the United States to acquire territory. When, in 1776, allegiance was absolved from Great Britain, each state became a separate and independent sovereignty. Included among the rights of

---

Cession of Louisiana to the United States ... 1804, 19; Allan B. Magruder, *Political, Commercial and Moral Reflections, on the late cession of Louisiana to the United States*, 73; John B. Colvin, *Republican Policy, etc., 1802;* Sylvestris (pseud.), *Reflections on the Cession of Louisiana to the United States.*

[3] *Annals of Congress*, 8 Cong., 1 Sess. (1803–1804), 434–435.

[4] *Ibid.*, 447–448.

each state was that of extending its limits, either by conquest or by purchase. In 1781, under the Articles of Confederation each state surrendered a portion of its sovereignty for the common benefit of the whole. Among the rights surrendered was that of acquiring new territory, with the powers of peace and war. Again in 1788, the states resumed their original independence. The present Constitution was adopted, giving the right to declare war to Congress and the right to make treaties to the President and Senate. These were the means of acquiring territory.[5]

Nicholson's argument is interesting as an early application of the doctrine that the states did possess, at one time or other, complete sovereign powers, some of which were given up to the General Government.

The widest sweep of authority was claimed for the Government by Rodney of Delaware, who held that unless special restriction of the Constitution forbade it, there was no reason why the power of acquiring territory could not come under the clause providing for the general welfare and common defense. The territory of the United States might also be extended through war, and by the treaty-making power. Furthermore, added Rodney, since Congress had the right to purchase territory from a state for a capital, forts, arsenals, public buildings, etc., it must possess the power to purchase territory from a foreign state.[6] The claims to power made here were too broad even for the supporters of the treaty.

Mitchill of New York did not believe the framers of the Constitution intended to prevent the United States from acquiring territory. Such a restriction would have been contrary to the powers inherent in independent nations. Moreover, lands had been frequently obtained by treaty and purchase from the

---

[5] *Ibid.*, 468.
[6] *Ibid.*, 472–473.

Indians who were as much aliens as other foreign nations, and the question of the constitutionality of such acquisitions had never been raised. He declared his understanding revolted at a doctrine which held that there was no constitutional power to purchase and possess waste lands across the Mississippi to which the American people could spread when the eastern side had become overpopulated.[7]

Thus it will be seen that the great difference of opinion was not over the right to acquire territory, but over the means by which this could be done.

(2) *Status of the Acquired Territory*

The third article of the treaty with France for the cession of Louisiana to the United States provided that:

> The inhabitants of the ceded territory shall be incorporated in the Union of the United States, and admitted as soon as possible, according to the principles of the Federal Constitution, to the enjoyment of the rights, advantages and immunities of citizens of the United States; and in the meantime they shall be maintained and protected in the free enjoyment of their liberty, property, and the religion which they profess.

This article caused the principal struggle over constitutional interpretation aroused by the treaty. Whether the treaty-making power could guarantee such rights as were here laid down has already been discussed.[8] The right under the Constitution to incorporate into the Union the new territory, or any new territory, was questioned by opponents of the treaty. The wording of the article itself called for interpretation. Just what was meant by the term "incorporated in the Union of the United States"? What obligation was involved in the stipulation "as soon as possible"? What rights did the inhabitants

---

[7] *Ibid.*, 477–479.
[8] See above.

have in the interval between acquisition and statehood, allowing that ultimate statehood was to be the goal for Louisiana—which some vehemently denied?

The policy of the Government was of the greatest significance because of the precedents laid down, precedents cited in connection with every new acquisition of territory by the United States; and here again special attention must be called to the recent Insular Cases, where the arguments used in connection with the Louisiana purchase were gone over in detail.[9]

Some light is thrown on the intentions of the Jefferson Administration regarding the rights of the inhabitants of the acquired territory by an examination of the outline of the treaty drawn up by Madison for the guidance of Livingston and Monroe, dated March 2, 1803. Although this plan of a treaty was made with an eye to the purchase of the territory on the east side of the Mississippi only, yet the attitude towards the inhabitants was the same as if the purchase of Louisiana had been included. Article seven of the outlined treaty reads as follows:

> To incorporate the inhabitants of the hereby ceded territory with the citizens of the United States on an equal footing, being a provision which cannot now be made, it is to be expected, from the character and policy of the United States, that such incorporation will take place without unnecessary delay. In the meantime they shall be secure in their persons and property, and in the free enjoyment of their religion.[10]

Madison wrote in his instructions, March 2, 1803:

> This article is suggested by the respect due to the rights of the people inhabiting the ceded territory, and by the delay which may be found in constituting them a regular and integral portion of the union. A full respect for their rights might require their consent to the act of cession; and if the French Government should be disposed to concur in any proper

---

[9] See *Insular Cases*, passim. Also Charles E. Magoon, *Report on the Legal Status of the Territory and Inhabitants of the Islands acquired by the United States during the War with Spain*, Washington, 1900.

[10] *Annals of Congress*, 7 Cong., 2 sess. (1802–1803), Appendix, 1101; *American State Papers, Foreign Relations*, II, 542.

mode of obtaining it, the provision would be honorable to both nations. There is no doubt that the inhabitants would readily agree to the proposed transfer of their allegiance.[11]

An undated manuscript abstract of the terms of the treaty with France contained, as article three, the following provision:

All the rights which it is usual to reserve to the inhabitants of a ceded territory or country, are reserved in a manner the most ample possible to those of Louisiana, as well in the exercise of their religion as to retire wheresoever they please, to sell their lands and other property or transport their effects and persons without impediment of any [sort?] under any pretext whatever, except for debts or criminal offenses. The [term?] fixed for the said sale and removal or retreat shall be that of two years to commence from the day of the exch[an]ge of the ratification of the present treaty.[12]

Article three of the treaty as finally ratified contains an express stipulation that "The inhabitants of the ceded territory shall be incorporated in the Union, and admitted as soon as possible, according to the principles of the Federal Constitution, to the enjoyment of all the rights, advantages and immunities of citizens of the United States." How much of an obligation did this imply? There were various answers to this question. One was that of John Taylor, who, speaking in the Senate, denied that the third article of the treaty stipulated that Louisiana must be erected into a state:

It is conceded that the treaty-making power cannot, by treaty, erect a new State, however they may stipulate for it. . . . It has been proved that the United States may acquire territory. Territory, so acquired, becomes from the acquisition itself a portion of the territories of the United States, or may be united with their territories without being erected into a State. An union of territory is one thing; of States, another. . . . The United States possesses territory, comprised in the union of territory, and not in the union of States. Congress is empowered to regulate or dispose of State

---

[11] *Monroe Papers,* "Writings to Monroe," IX, November 9, 1800–September, 1803; *American State Papers, Foreign Relations,* II, 543.

[12] *Monroe Papers,* "Writings of Monroe," II, December 17, 1803–December 16, 1804.

sections of the Union. The citizens of these territorial sections are citizens of the United States, and they have all the rights of citizens of the United States; but such rights do not include those political rights arising from State compacts or governments, which are dissimilar in different States. Supposing the General Government or treaty-making power have no right to add or unite States and State citizens to the Union, yet they have a power of adding or uniting to it territory and territorial citizens of the United States. . . .

The third article declares that 'the inhabitants of the ceded territory shall be incorporated in the Union of the United States.' And these words are said to require the territory to be erected into a State. This they do not express, and the words are literally satisfied by incorporating them into the Union as a territory, and not as a State. The Constitution recognizes and the practice warrants an incorporation of a Territory and its inhabitants into the Union as a territory, without admitting either as a State. . . . For if the words 'the inhabitants of the ceded territory shall be incorporated in the Union of the United States' intended that Louisiana and its inhabitants should become a State in the Union of States, there exists no reason for proceeding to stipulate that these same inhabitants should be made 'citizens as soon as possible, according to the principles of the Federal Constitution.' Their admission into the Union of the States would have made them citizens of the United States. . . . If my construction is correct, all objections to the treaty and to this bill for fulfilling it, on the ground of unconstitutionality, are unfounded. The three distinct members of the third article will be each separately and distinctly complied with; first, by an incorporation of the territory and its inhabitants in the Union, as a Territory. Secondly, by admitting them to all the rights of citizens of the United States—under some uniform rule of naturalization; and thirdly, by protecting their liberty, property, and religion, by 'rules and regulations,' to be, 'in the meantime,' enacted by Congress, under a Constitutional power extending to Territories, but not to States.[13]

Taylor's interpretation was not acceptable to the opponents of the treaty of whom Tracy of Connecticut was a typical representative. Tracy held the meaning of the third article of the treaty to be that the inhabitants of Louisiana were incorporated by it into the Union on an equality with the territorial govern-

---

[13] *Annals of Congress*, 8 Cong., 1 Sess. (1803–1804), 50–52. Taylor's distinction between state and federal citizenship is a forerunner of the lengthy discussion of this point in the Dred Scott case, and more recently in the Insular Cases.

ments already existing, and similarly, this territory when the population had increased sufficiently, could be admitted as a state, with the same rights as the other states. He questioned the power of the President and Senate to guarantee this. Although it was true that the Constitution provided for the admission of new states by Congress, Tracy declared that the President and Senate alone could not admit Louisiana. Furthermore, even Congress could not admit new ''foreign'' states into the Union without the consent of the old partners.

The compact theory, so often the weapon of the party of opposition in the United States, was now pushed to the front and along with it came the reasons for much of the New England opposition to the treaty. The article of the Constitution alluded to, Tracy argued, referred only to ''domestic'' states. It was ''unreasonable to suppose that Congress should, by a majority only, admit new foreign States, and swallow up by it, the old partners, when two-thirds of all the members are made requisite for the least alteration in the constitution.'' The principles of the Government, the rights of the partners to the compact, forbade a measure which would introduce a large foreign element into the Union. This could only be done by the consent of all the partners. The reason for such an interpretation comes out in Tracy's frank statement that ''the relative strength which this admission gives to a Southern and Western interest, is contradictory to the principles of our original Union.''[14]

Breckinridge denied the charges of unconstitutionality against the third article of the treaty. Opponents of the treaty, he pointed out, had gone so far as to advocate the seizure of a part of the country under question. Where was the constitutional distinction between acquisition by conquest and purchase

---

[14] *Ibid.*, 54–56.

through a treaty? An amendment could be made to the Constitution to avoid all difficulty. Answering Tracy, Breckinridge said:

[The] gentleman from Connecticut admits that Congress may acquire territory and hold it as a territory, but cannot incorporate it into the Union. By this construction he admits the power to acquire territory, a modification infinitely more dangerous than the unconditional admission of a new State; for by his construction, territories and citizens are considered and held as the property of the United States, and may consequently be used as dangerous engines in the hand of the Government against the States and people.... As to the admission of new States the same gentleman observes that Congress may admit new States, the President and Senate who are but a component part, cannot. Apply this doctrine to the case before us. How can Congress by any mode of legislation admit this country into the Union until it is acquired? And how can this acquisition be made except through the treaty-making power? Could the gentleman rise in his place and move for leave to bring in a bill for the purchase of Louisiana and its admission into the Union. I take it that no transaction of this or any kind with a foreign Power can take place except through the Executive Department, and that in the form of a treaty, agreement, or convention. When the acquisition is made, Congress can then make such disposition of it as may be expedient.[15]

New England scruples were not yet overcome and Thacher of Massachusetts denied, as Tracy had done, the right to admit a new member into the partnership of states without the consent of all the partners: most assuredly, the President and Senate had no such power.[16]

Smilie of Pennsylvania considered the right of annexing territory to be incidental to all Governments. In the United States this right must reside in the General Government, because the states were expressly forbidden to form treaties or make war. Taking up the matter of the third article, Smilie said that if the principles of the Constitution forbade the admission of the

---

[15] *Annals of Congress*, 8 Cong., 1 Sess. (1803–1804), 60–63. Just how Breckinridge would have stood on the action taken by Congress in relation to Texas is an interesting topic for conjecture.

[16] *Ibid.*, 454–455.

inhabitants of Louisiana into the Union, there was no obligation to admit them. In this case the remedy would be an amendment of the Constitution authorizing the admission. If the people of the United States did not choose to pass such an amendment, the inhabitants of the territory could remain in a colonial state.[17]

Roger Griswold interpreted the third article to mean either that the inhabitants of the ceded territory were to be incorporated into the Union, by the treaty itself, or that the faith of the nation was pledged that this would be done within a reasonable time. He denied the right of the President and Senate to add new members to the Union by treaty, and, like other opponents, he declared that the consent of all the parties to the compact was necessary for the admission of a new partner.

> The Government of this country is formed by a union of States, and the people have declared, that the Constitution was established 'to form a more perfect union of the United States.' The United States here cannot be mistaken. They were the States then in existence, and such other new States as should be formed, within the limits of the Union, conformably to the provisions of the Constitution.[18]

The bringing in of a foreign nation, continued Griswold, would destroy the ''perfect union of the States'': a treaty so stipulating was void.

Taking up another line of attack, Griswold argued that a promise to incorporate was the same in principle as incorporation. If no incorporation of new territory could take place without an amendment to the Constitution, he denied the right of the treaty-making power to stipulate for such an amendment. Stipulations which created an obligation were void. Admitting that new territory and new subjects could undoubtedly be obtained by conquest and by purchase, Griswold maintained that

---

17 *Ibid.*, 457–458.

18 Compare the argument in the Dred Scott Decision and in the Insular Cases.

they must remain in the condition of colonies, and be governed as such. ''The. objection to the third article is not that the province of Louisiana could not have been purchased, but neither this nor any other foreign nation, can be incorporated into the Union by treaty or by law.''[19]

Griswold's interpretation, if followed, would have altered greatly the history of the United States. The policy adopted by the Government with regard to the steps by which the people of the territories have been prepared for statehood was laid down by Mitchill of New York in so clear a fashion that it seems justifiable to follow him at some length.

According to Mitchill, the inhabitants of the ceded territory were to have the choice of staying or leaving. If they chose to remain they were to be maintained and protected in the enjoyment of liberty, property and religion. They were to be trained in a knowledge of American laws and institutions. And so:

They are thus to serve an apprenticeship to liberty; they are thus to be taught the lessons of freedom; and by degrees they are to be raised to the enjoyment and practice of independence. All this is to be done as soon as possible; that is, as soon as the nature of the case will permit; and according to the principles of the Federal Constitution.... Secondly, after they shall have a sufficient length of time in this probationary condition, they shall, as soon as the principles of the Constitution permit, and conformably thereto, be declared citizens of the United States. Congress will judge the time, manner, and expediency of this. The act we are now about to perform will not confer on them this elevated character.... By degrees, however, they will pass on from the childhood of republicanism through the improving period of youth, and arrive at the mature experience of manhood. And then, they may be admitted to the full privileges which their merit and station will entitle them to. At that time a general law of naturalization may be passed. *For I do not venture to affirm that, by the mere act of cession, the inhabitants of a ceded country, become, of course, citizens of the country to which they are annexed. It would seem not to be the case, unless specially provided for.*[20]

---

[19] *Annals of Congress,* 8 Cong., 1 Sess. (1803–1804), 460–463.
[20] Italics mine.

Mitchill cited the treaty of 1794 with Great Britain as a precedent that, without an act of Congress, aliens could be converted into citizens by the provisions of a treaty duly ratified by the President and Senate. By the second article of that treaty it was stipulated that all British subjects continuing within the evacuated posts and precincts longer than a year, should be considered to have abandoned allegiance to the British Crown, and to have elected to become American citizens. By taking the oath of allegiance, they became at once, by act of treaty, citizens of the United States. In the Louisiana treaty the power of making citizens had not been exercised by the President and Senate but was left to Congress at some future day.[21]

John Randolph argued that a stipulation to incorporate the ceded territory did not imply that the inhabitants must ever be admitted to the unqualified enjoyment of the privileges of citizenship. It did not mean that they must be brought into the Union on an equal footing with the people of the original states, or with those created under the Constitution. It merely extended to them the rights and immunities of citizens,

being those rights and immunities of jury-trial, liberty of conscience, etc., which every citizen may challenge, whether he be a citizen of an individual State, or of a territory subordinate to and dependent on those States in their corporate capacity. In the meantime they are to be protected in the enjoyment of their existing rights. There is no stipulation, however, that they shall ever be formed into one or more States.[22]

The validity of Randolph's argument has divided political thinkers of the United States to the present day. One group, of whom Randolph is an early exponent, holds that although the Constitution grants to Congress the power of legislating for the territories, yet legislation by Congress is not necessary for the extension to the inhabitants of the territories of certain civil

---

[21] *Annals of Congress*, 8 Cong., 1 Sess. (1803–1804), 480–481.
[22] *Ibid.*, 487.

rights, such as those enumerated by Randolph. Such rights, it is claimed, are extended to the territories by the Constitution, *ex proprio vigore.*

The opposing school maintains that Congressional legislation is necessary in all cases, no exceptions whatever being made.

Just what action was taken with regard to the inhabitants of Louisiana will be narrated later.

(3) *Commercial Privileges Under the Treaty*

Another question which aroused the keenest controversy at the time and which left its legacy of constitutional difficulties for many years afterwards was that of an alleged preference given by article seven of the treaty to ports of the newly acquired territory over the other ports of the United States. Article seven provided "that the French ships coming directly from France or any of her colonies, loaded with the produce and manufactures of France or her said colonies," and the ships of Spain in similar fashion,

should be admitted during the space of twelve years in the port of New Orleans, and in all other legal ports of entry within the ceded territory, in the same manner as the ships of the United States coming directly from France or Spain, or any of their colonies, without being subject to any other or greater duty on merchandize, or other or greater tonnage than that paid by the citizens of the United States.

During this perid no other nation was to have the same privileges in the ports mentioned. This provision pertained to importations into Louisiana and was not to affect regulations of the United States concerning the exportation of the produce and merchandise of the United States. Article eight was really a supplement of the above, stipulating that, "In future and forever after the expiration of the twelve years, the ships of France shall be treated upon the footing of the most favored nations in the ports above mentioned."

Aside from the grant of commercial privileges to France and Spain, which New England ship owners opposed, did article seven of the treaty violate the provision in the Constitution that, "No preference shall be given by any Regulation of Commerce or Revenue to the Port of one State over those of another"?[23] Opponents of the treaty held that it did, while those who favored the treaty declared that this provision of the Constitution was for states only and that Congress might legislate as it chose for the territories. Senator Tracy of Connecticut said that a commercial preference to the ports of the ceded territory over the other ports of the United States was hereby granted because a duty of forty-four cents on tonnage was paid by all foreign ships or vessels in all the ports of the United States. He conceded, however, that if Louisiana were not admitted into the Union and if no promise to admit her existed, then his argument did not apply.[24]

The difference between state and territory is here recognized, a distinction which formed the basis of the controversy.

John Quincy Adams claimed that the seventh article contained engagements which he thought would necessitate an amendment or an addition to the Constitution.[25]

In the House of Representatives the seventh article of the treaty caused much more contention than it had in the Senate. Gaylord Griswold of New York maintained that a violation of the ninth section of article one of the Constitution would result if the newly ceded territory should ever become incorporated with the United States, because there would then be ports of entry in the United States into which French and Spanish ships might enter on terms different from those on which they could enter other ports of the United States.[26] The same view was

---

23 Article I, section 9, clause 6.
24 *Annals of Congress*, 8 Cong., 1 Sess. (1803–1804), 57.
25 *Ibid.*, 67.
26 *Ibid.*, 434.

held by Joseph Lewis of Virginia.[27]   Randolph introduced a novel interpretation in his denial of the unconstitutionality of the seventh article on the ground that the privilege given French and Spanish vessels was a part of the price of the territory.[28] Just how this satisfied the constitutional requirements of the case did not appear clear to many and Randolph's arguments were questioned.   Thacher of Massachusetts, for instance, asked how the preference could be considered a part of the purchase price when it applied to Spain as well as France.[29]

To the alleged unconstitutionality of the article in question on the ground that it violated the ninth section of the first article of the Constitution, Griffin of Virginia added another objection.   He deemed the seventh article of the treaty a commercial regulation.   Therefore, since to Congress had been given, by the eighth section of article one of the Constitution, power to regulate commerce with foreign nations, the treaty stipulation made by the President and Senate was a contravention of this constitutional investiture of Congress.   The President and Senate, in their executive capacity, had legislated, and by so doing, had infringed upon the rights of the House.[30]

Elliott of Vermont in defending the seventh article reiterated the statement of others that the provision of the Constitution applied only to states and not to the territorial acquisitions. Under the treaty, a complete discretion was left to the United States as to the time and manner of admission of the inhabitants of the ceded territory into the Union; and he had no idea that it would be necessary to admit them within the twelve years during which the commercial privileges were enjoyed by France and Spain.   There could, therefore, be no possible violation of the Constitution.[31]

---

[27] *Annals of Congress,* 8 Cong., 1 Sess. (1803–1804), 440–441.

[28] *Ibid.,* 437.

[29] *Ibid.,* 455.

[30] *Ibid.,* 442.

[31] *Ibid.,* 450.

Exactly what Elliott did not anticipate came to pass, for the lower part of the territory entered the Union as the state of Louisiana before the twelve-year period had elapsed.[32]

Crowninshield of Massachusetts combined the arguments of the defenders of the treaty by stating that it was not unconstitutional to receive the ships of France and Spain in the ports of the new territory upon any terms whatever because the stipulation was a mere condition of the purchase, a commercial regulation to be agreed to or disagreed to by the House. Since the privilege was extended only to ports in the ceded territory no injury was done to the rights of ports in the Atlantic states.[33]

Crowninshield's last statement did not pass unchallenged. Just as it was fear of losing political power which drove certain of the New Englanders to oppose the third article of the treaty, so it was sectional and economic interests which dictated their stand on the seventh. Roger Griswold presented the case clearly and frankly. To admit the ships of France and Spain into the port of New Orleans, on the same terms with American ships, would result in the development of French and Spanish shipping and the ruin of the trade of the Atlantic ports. "How gentlemen," he concluded, "under these circumstances can consider the interests of the Eastern States uninjured, is to me inexplicable."[34]

Once more was the distinction between state and territory, and the powers of the Government over the latter, set forth by Nicholson, when he said that Louisiana

is a territory purchased by the United States in their confederate capacity, and may be disposed of by them at pleasure. *It is in the nature of a colony whose commerce may be regulated without any reference to the Constitution.* Had it been the Island of Cuba which was ceded to us, under a

---

[32] Difficulties arising as a result of its admission are discussed in the latter part of this chapter.

[33] *Annals of Congress*, 8 Cong., 1 Sess. (1803–1804), 459.

[34] *Ibid.*, 464–465.

similar condition of admitting French and Spanish vessels for a limited time into the Havannah, could it possibly have been contended that this would be giving a preference to the ports of one State over those of another, or that the uniformity of duties, imports and excises throughout the United States would have been destroyed?[35] And because Louisiana lies adjacent to our territory, is it to be viewed in a different light?[36]

Territories, then, according to Nicholson, were beyond the pale of the Constitution. Not satisfied with this sweeping interpretation, defenders of the treaty found still other grounds of justification of the contested provisions. Rodney of Delaware even contended that if the territory of the United States benefited because of particular territorial regulations, the territory being the common property of the United States, every state in the Union reaped the benefit.[37]

It is very doubtful if Rodney's arguments carried any weight with the New England group, who felt not only their political power but also their shipping interests to be endangered. A common benefit to be derived by the states under the treaty was beyond their ken.

Mitchill, like Nicholson, considered the treaty-making power "unfettered by constitutional impediments and like that great charter of freedom itself, originates from its own source, supreme laws of the land." A treaty, therefore, according to Mitchill, could hardly be conceived as unconstitutional unless it outraged all common principles, rights and feelings. Thus interpreted, no charges of unconstitutionality could be brought against the seventh article of the treaty.[38]

---

[35] Nicholson was here approaching one of the questions involved in the Insular Cases. His speech is there quoted, in part, in *Insular Cases*, 316.

[36] *Annals of Congress*, 8 Cong., 1 Sess. (1803–1804), 471. Italics mine.

[37] *Ibid.*, 475. Cf. the argument in *Insular Cases*, 203: "All legislation for Territories being enacted by the Congress chosen by the States, and the Territory being the property of the United States, all the States are equally advantaged by whatever is done toward the regulation of such Territories."

[38] *Ibid.*, 481–482.

So radical a view found few supporters. It was a difficult matter to convince even the most ardent defenders of the treaty that the treaty-making power was on a plane with the very instrument which had brought it into existence.

John Randolph called attention to the fact that by the third article of the Treaty of London,[39] the United States was pledged not to impose on imports in British vessels from British territories in America, adjacent to the United States, any higher duties than would be paid upon such imports, if brought into the Atlantic ports of the United States in American vessels. Here was no distinction between territory and state, the ports being those of New York. Randolph said he did not defend the constitutionality of this provision; as a matter of fact, he had not voted to carry the treaty into effect. He desired to know how such men as Griswold of Connecticut. who had advocated the treaty, got over the constitutional difficulty which was urged against the Louisiana treaty. How could a preference be given to particular ports of certain states which could not constitutionally be given to the ports of New Orleans, not within a state?[40]

Years afterwards, James Madison described the nature of the provision concerning commercial privileges made by the Louisiana Treaty. Writing to Robert Walsh, November 27, 1819, he said:

In the case of Louisiana, there is a circumstance which may deserve notice. In the Treaty ceding it, a privilege was retained by the ceding party, which distinguishes between its ports & others of the U. S. for a special purpose & a short period. *This privilege, however, was the result, not of an ordinary legislative power in Congress; nor was it the result of an arrangement between Congress & the people of Louisiana. It rests on the ground that the same power, even in the nation, over that territory, as over the original territory of the U. S., never existed; the privilege*

---

[39] Jay's Treaty.
[40] *Annals of Congress*, 8 Cong., 1 Sess. (1803–1804), 483–484.

alluded to being in the deed of cession carved by the foreign owner out of the title conveyed to the purchaser. A sort of necessity, therefore, was thought to belong to so peculiar and extraordinary a case. Notwithstanding this plea, it is presumable that if the privilege had materially affected the rights of other ports, or had been of a permanent or durable character, the occurrence would not have been so little regarded. Congress would not be allowed to effect, through the medium of a Treaty, obnoxious discrimination between new and old States more than among the latter.[41]

Because of Madison's knowledge of the meaning of the Constitution, it is interesting to hear from him that the commercial privileges granted by the treaty were "in the deed of cession, carved by the foreign owner out of the title conveyed to the purchaser," and that the United States never possessed entire power over that territory as over the original territory of the United States.

As already shown, defenders of the constitutionality of the seventh article of the treaty based their arguments on the distinction between territory and state. During the debate on the seventh article, Elliott had declared that he had no idea that it would be necessary to admit the inhabitants of Louisiana to statehood within the twelve years during which the commercial privileges were to be enjoyed by France and Spain. The question is at once suggested: if Louisiana should be admitted before this twelve-year period had elapsed could the provisions of the treaty be carried out in the face of the apparent violation of the constitutional prohibition against granting preferences to ports of one state over those of another? A topic of conjecture became a definite fact, for Louisiana was admitted into the Union as a state, April 30, 1812, four years before the twelve-year period during which preferences were to be granted to the ships of France and Spain. Curiously enough, the New Englanders did not raise the point during the debates on the passage

---

[41] Madison, *Letters and Other Writings* (Congressional ed.), III, 153–154; *Writings* (Hunt, ed.), IX, 7–8. Italics mine.

of the bill admitting Louisiana into the Union.[42]   Attention was
called to it through the complaints made by the French minister,
Hyde de Neuville, to John Quincy Adams, Monroe's secretary
of state.[43]

Soon after the war of 1812, the United States adopted a plan
of reciprocity. Discriminating tonnage duties on foreign vessels
were to be repealed in favor of any nation whenever the President
should be satisfied that similar discriminating duties of
such foreign nation, so far as they should be operative against
the United States, had been abolished.[44]   England took advantage
of this offer,[45] and was followed by the Netherlands, Sweden,
Prussia and certain of the Hanseatic cities.[46]   France, however,
declined, and soon began to complain of discrimination against
her vessels. A formal complaint was lodged with Secretary of
State John Quincy Adams in 1817 by Baron de Neuville. This,
of course, was several years after the admission of Louisiana as
a state, and also after the expiration of the period during which
France and Spain were to enjoy commercial privileges in the
ports of Louisiana. De Neuville protested against the grant of
privileges to Great Britain in the ports of the United States,
and demanded similar privileges for France in the ports of
Louisiana, in accordance with article eight of the treaty of 1803
which stipulated that ''in future and forever after the expiration
of the twelve years, the ships of France shall be treated upon
the equal footing of the most favored nations in the ports above
mentioned.''[47]

---

[42] Adams to de Neuville, June 15, 1821, in *American State Papers,
Foreign Relations*, V, 182.

[43] See Max Farrand, ''The Commercial Privileges of the Treaty of
1803,'' in *American Historical Review*, VII, 494–499. This article was
closely followed. All of the documents bearing on the matter have been
consulted, however, and citations have been made directly to them.

[44] *U. S. Statutes at Large*, March 3, 1815, ch. 77.

[45] *American State Papers, Foreign Relations*, IV, 7–8.

[46] *Ibid.*, 738.

[47] De Neuville to Adams, December 15, 1817, *ibid.*, V, 152.

Adams replied that French vessels were so treated; that English vessels were granted privileges because of similar ones made to the United States; and that France could obtain the privileges held by vessels of Great Britain if she would make the same provisions for American ships in return. This would hold true for all the ports of the United States as well as those of Louisiana. Adams said it would be a violation of the Constitution to admit French vessels into the ports of Louisiana upon payment of the same duties as vessels of the United States, because the Constitution provides "that no preference shall be given to the ports of one State over those of another."[48]   De Neuville pointed out that France had enjoyed such privileges in 1815, despite the apparent constitutional difficulties and asked why they could not be enjoyed again.[49]

No answer was made at the time but nearly three years later de Neuville pressed for one[50] and Adams made his reply. He declared it to be a question for the Senate to decide whether the commercial privileges of the Louisiana treaty were compatible with the Constitution of the United States or not. There was no question, however, about the claim put forward by France; it was directly contrary to the provision of the Constitution that no preference could be given to the ports of one state over those of another. What had happened in the case of Louisiana did not alter the interpretation of the Constitution. Had any of the other states so desired, the act of admission of Louisiana might have been delayed until the twelve-year period had elapsed. Waiving this right and allowing the admission "can be considered in no other light than a friendly grant in advance of that which in the lapse of three short years might have been

---

[48] Adams to de Neuville, December 23, 1817, *ibid.*, 152–153.

[49] De Neuville to Adams, June 16, 1818, *ibid.*, 154–155.

[50] De Neuville to Adams, February 23, 1821, *ibid.*, 162–163.

claimed as an undeniable right.''[51] France had received no wrong, and therefore had no cause for complaint.[52] Soon after this the question was dropped, despite the efforts of de Neuville to continue negotiations.[53]

---

[51] Adams to de Neuville, March 29, 1821, *ibid.*, 163–165.

[52] Adams to de Neuville, June 15, 1821, *ibid.*, 180–184.

[53] De Neuville to Adams, June 30, 1821, *ibid.*, 186–192; de Neuville to Adams, August 15, 1821, *ibid.*, 193–194; de Neuville to Adams, October 15, 1821, *ibid.*, 194–195.

CHAPTER VI

THE GOVERNMENT OF THE ACQUIRED TERRITORY

Louisiana having been acquired by the United States, it was necessary that measures be taken for the occupation and government of that country. The attention of Congress was called to this fact by President Jefferson in the special message of October 21, 1803.[1] Congress took immediate action. On October 25, the following resolutions were delivered at the table of the clerk of the House, and read:

1. *Resolved,* That provision ought to be made for carrying into effect the treaty and conventions concluded at Paris on the thirtieth of April, 1803, between the United States of America and the French Republic.

2. *Resolved,* That so much of the Message of the President, of the twenty-first instant, as relates to the establishment of a Provisional Government over the Territory acquired by the United States, in virtue of the treaty and conventions lately negotiated with the French Republic be referred to a select committee; and that they report by bill, or otherwise.

3. *Resolved,* That so much of the aforesaid conventions as relates to the payment, by the United States, of sixty millions of francs to the French Republic, and to the payment, by the United States, of debts due by France to citizens of the United States, be referred to the Committee of Ways and Means.[2]

The first resolution was agreed upon in the House by a vote of ninety yeas to twenty-five nays.[3] The second was again read and amended, adding "occupation and" before "establishment," and was referred to a committee consisting of John Randolph of Virginia, Gaylord Griswold of New York, John Rhea of Tennessee, William Hoge of Pennsylvania, and George Bedinger of Kentucky. The third resolution was reported from the Committee of the Whole, read and agreed to.[4]

---

[1] Richardson, *Messages and Papers of the Presidents,* I, 362–363.

[2] *Annals of Congress,* 8 Cong., 1 Sess. (1803–1804), 488.

[3] *Ibid.*

[4] *Ibid.,* 489.

Two days later the House resolved itself into a Committee of the Whole on a bill from the Senate enabling the President to take possession of the ceded territory and empowering him to use the army and navy if necessary, and also so much of the sum appropriated by the acts as might be necessary.[5] Section two of the Senate bill provided:

> That, until Congress shall have made provision for the temporary government of the said Territories, all the military, civil, and judicial powers, exercised by the officers of the existing government of the same, shall be vested in such person and persons, and shall be exercised in such manner, as the President of the United States shall direct.[6]

It was certain that this section of the bill would not be allowed to pass without opposition on constitutional grounds. Party lines were not now held so strictly as when the provisions of the treaty were being discussed. For instance, the real objection to the passage of the section was voiced by John Randolph. While recognizing the necessity of vesting power in the Executive which would enable him to take possession of Louisiana, Randolph declared himself opposed to so extensive a grant as that contained in the bill. In order to have a check on the Executive, he moved an amendment substituting in place of the words, ''Congress shall have made provision for the temporary government of the said territories,'' the words, ''the expiration of the present session of Congress, unless provision for the temporary government of the said territories be sooner made by Congress.'' Thus the power of the President would cease at any time during the session provided Congress took action; at most, his power would continue only until the expiration of the session. Congress would be forced to take early measures leading to the reduction of the great power granted to the Executive.[7]

---

[5] *Ibid.*, 497.

[6] *Ibid.*, 498.

[7] *Ibid.*

Randolph was willing to support his party to a certain extent but he still kept a watchful eye on what to him was a source of grave danger—too extensive a power in the Executive.

Other members of the House were even more strongly opposed to the section of the bill than Randolph. Among these was Roger Griswold of Connecticut, who moved to strike out the whole of the section on the ground that ignorance of what the powers exercised by officials of the territory were might lead to trouble if their continuance was authorized. It was even probable, he contended, that some of them were inconsistent with the Constitution of the United States.[8] Furthermore, the transfer to the President of all the civil, military and judicial powers being exercised in the territory would be making him legislator, judge and executive, something which could not constitutionally be done.[9]

Griswold's motion was seconded by Elliott, who held that the grant of such extensive powers to the President, even over a territory, was unconstitutional. Should it be necessary to enact such a provision as that planned for in the section it was Congress who must take up the task of legislation.[10]

Nicholson defended the constitutionality of the bill. The President, according to his interpretation, was merely invested with the appointment of persons to exercise the civil, military and judicial powers of the existing government, and was not invested with the exercise of them himself. To Nicholson, this was not different from the powers exercised by the President in the appointment of officers under the Ordinance of 1787.[11]

Griswold answered that since the powers were to be exercised as the President should direct they were virtually exercised by him; and if Congress could not transfer to him legislative and

---

8 *Annals of Congress*, 8 Cong., 1 Sess. (1803–1804), 498–499.

9 *Ibid.*, 500–501.

10 *Ibid.*, 499.

11 *Ibid.*, 501.

judicial power in any other territory, they could not in Louisiana. Furthermore, the section of the bill was unconstitutional because it gave to the President full power to appoint *all* officers in the province, without the sanction of the Senate.[12]

Mitchill interpreted the Constitution differently. Congress, having the right to dispose of the territory and property of the United States, could empower the President to put others in a position to act. Instead of a claim of prerogative on the part of the Executive it was a constitutional deposit of powers in him by Congress.[13] On the other hand, Dana of Connecticut regarded the power granted to the President in the bill as creating "a complete despotism."[14]

In the light of future interpretation, the speech of Varnum of Massachusetts is fraught with significance:

We are told that we are about to exercise a power over the ceded territory not authorized by the Constitution. *He would ask if the Constitution were to take effect as soon as the United States take possession of the territory?* The treaty provides that 'the inhabitants of the ceded territory shall be incorporated in the union of the United States, and admitted as soon as possible.' How incorporated? By a legislative act? No, 'according to the principles of the Federal Constitution, to the enjoyment of all the rights, advantages, and immunities of citizens of the United States; and in the meantime they shall be maintained and protected in the full enjoyment of their liberty, property, and the religion which they profess.' In what meantime?

There is a time when the country is acquired, and a time when it will be admitted into the Union. Between these periods, in the meantime, the people are to enjoy their liberty, and the religion which they profess. I can devise no way of their enjoying these rights, until admitted into the Union, but by their continuing under the government of the law of Spain. The Senate have made provision for carrying into effect this part of the treaty, and it cannot be carried into effect in any other way.[15]

---

12 *Ibid.*, 510. Italics mine.
13 *Ibid.*, 502–504.
14 *Ibid.*, 504–506.
15 *Ibid.*, 505–506. Italics mine.

Another member from Massachusetts, Eustis, also supported the bill. The Government, according to him, had a constitutional right to acquire territory, and to take possession of it when acquired, the latter being not only a right, but a duty of the Government. Declaring this to be a new case, Eustis based the extent of power vested in the Executive on necessity. He was willing to give the President authority even to institute such powers as might be necessary for the well-being of the country until Congress should make the requisite laws. He failed to see any constitutional obstacles to the carrying out of the provisions of the bill.[16]

Elliott of Vermont[17] and Jackson of Virginia[18] aligned themselves with those who were against the second section of the bill because of its alleged infringement of the Constitution. Rodney of Delaware did not consider that the bill "infringed the Constitution in the remotest degree." The Constitution, by the third section of article four, as he understood it, vested Congress with full and complete power to exercise a sound discretion on the subject of the government of territories. "Congress," he said, "have a power in the Territories, which they cannot exercise in States, and the limitations of power, found in the Constitution, are applicable to States and not to Territories."[19]

The question on striking out the second section was lost, only thirty votes being cast in the affirmative. Randolph's motion to amend the section by the addition of the words, "for the maintaining and protecting the inhabitants of Louisiana in the full enjoyment of their liberty, property, and religion," was agreed to without a division.[20]

---

[16] *Annals of Congress*, 8 Cong., 1 Sess. (1803–1804), 506.

[17] *Ibid.*, 508.

[18] *Ibid.*, 511.

[19] *Ibid.*, 512–514.

[20] *Ibid.*, 514.

The bill enabling the President to take possession of the territories ceded by France and for the temporary government thereof was passed by the House, October 28, 1803, by a vote of eighty-nine to twenty-three,[21] and was approved by the President October 31.[22] The bill did not escape criticism. Senator Plumer took exception to the grant to the President of the appointment of *all* officers, *superior* and *inferior*, whereas the Constitution provided that Congress might vest the appointment of *inferior* officers in other places.[23]

Plumer's particular criticism in this instance can in itself be attacked because the very clause of the Constitution to which he referred allows Congress to vest the appointment of inferior officers in the President alone. Speaking broadly, that is what was done. There is more ground for Plumer's statement that, "Had such a bill been passed by federalists, the Democrats would have denounced it as *monarchial* but when enacted by the *exclusive friends* of the people, it is pure *republicanism.*"[24]

Somewhat similar is the complaint of Manasseh Cutler:

Look at the power given to the President by the provisional government of Louisiana. By one sweeping clause, he is made as despotic as the Grand Turk. Every officer is appointed by him, holds his commission during his pleasure, and is amenable only to him. He is the Executive, the Legislature, and the Judicature. What clamor a few years ago, lest the President should be vested with too much power, the department the most dangerous of all to be trusted.[25]

Supplementing what had already been done, an act was passed giving effect to the laws of the United States within the territories ceded by the treaty.[26]

---

[21] *Ibid.*, 546.

[22] *Laws of U. States*, III, 562.

[23] Plumer, "Memorandum, 1803–1804," 64–65, October 26, 1803.

[24] *Ibid.*

[25] Cutler and Cutler, *Life, Journals and Correspondence of Rev. Manasseh Cutler*, II, 148.

[26] Act approved February 24, 1804, *Annals of Congress*, 8 Cong., 1 Sess. (1803–1804), 1253–1258.

Jefferson had taken it for granted that the treaty would be ratified and provision made for the transfer of the territory to the United States. As early as July 18, 1803, only four days after the arrival of the treaty from France, he wrote to Governor Claiborne of Mississippi Territory that the government, public property and archives of Louisiana were to be delivered up immediately after the exchange of ratifications, which would take place between the seventeenth and thirtieth of October. Claiborne was to go there for the United States "to transact it, and to hold the place some little time, until Congress shall direct what is to be done more particularly."[27]   Claiborne replied from Natchez, August 12, that he would hold himself in readiness to embark for New Orleans immediately on receiving orders. He considered it a very high honor to be appointed to receive the ceded territory.[28]

Jefferson already had a good man in mind to be governor of Louisiana, so he informed Madison July 31. "Sumpter" he regarded "as perfect in all points as we can expect, sound judgment, standing in society, knowledge of the world, wealth, liberality, familiarity with the French language, & having a French wife." Jefferson professed that he did not know a more proper character for the place.[29]

Nor did Jefferson's friends await the transfer of the territory before making suggestions for the government of Louisiana. Among them was Thomas Paine who supposed that a provisional government formed by Congress for three, five, or seven years would be the best mode of beginning. In the meantime the

---

27 *Jefferson Papers,* "Letters from Jefferson, 1st Series," IX, (113).

28 *Jefferson Papers,* "Letters received at Washington, 2nd Series," XVII, (42).

29 *Madison Papers,* XXV, "Writings to Madison," Dec. 7, 1802–Nov. 2, 1803. This ideal governor was in all probability Thomas Sumter, Revolutionary War hero, and at the date of Jefferson's letter, United States senator from South Carolina. For some reason or other the appointment was not made.

people might be initiated into the practice of electing their municipal government, and thus prepare for the election of a state government. Characteristic of Paine is the additional note that it would be a good plan to let the people elect their church ministers, thus freeing them from papal control.[30]

Before going to New Orleans Claiborne made inquiries concerning the character of the inhabitants of Louisiana, the results of which he conveyed by letter to Jefferson. On September 29 he wrote that a previous statement of his that a majority of the citizens of Louisiana could read and write was based on incorrect information; on the contrary, they were "involved in great ignorance." The form of government which might be prescribed for Louisiana, Claiborne reported, was exciting great anxiety. The existing government of that territory he described as a despotism, partly civil, partly military, and in some degree ecclesiastical. To regenerate a system based on principles so abhorrent to those of the United States would be a difficult task. Although he felt that the Louisianians could be trusted very far, it was Claiborne's opinion, "that until a knowledge of the American Constitutions, Laws, Language and customs is more generally diffused, a State Government in Louisiana would not be managed with discretion."[31]

Claiborne's opinion of the political fitness of the Louisianians for self-government was to change many times during the next few years, as will be shown.

Jefferson had been busily engaged gathering material from many sources in order that Congress might be supplied with all information that might be of assistance in the framing of a form of government for Louisiana. The result was a state paper which he submitted to that body, November 14, 1803, covering a wide

---

[30] *Jefferson Papers*, "Letters received at Paris and Philadelphia," 2d Series, LXV, (193).

[31] *Jefferson Papers*, "Letters received at Washington," 2d Series, XVII, (38).

range of topics, such as boundaries, population, resources, existing system of government, exports and imports, and many others.[32]

General James Wilkinson was associated with Governor Claiborne as commissioner for the purpose of receiving Louisiana from the French officials. The two commissioners proceeded to New Orleans where the transfer took place December 20, 1803, Laussat representing the French Government.[33] Claiborne, who was to act as governor of the territory, made an address in which the people were assured of fair treatment and protection under the terms of the treaty of the cession.[34]

Steps were taken by the new governor to supply the needs of government, especially in New Orleans where the cabildo had been abolished by the French prefect. The doing away with this body Claiborne considered an act beneficial to the United States because the cabildo ''was created on principles altogether incongruous with those of our Government.''[35]

---

[32] *American State Papers, Miscellaneous,* I, 344–356.

[33] Claiborne to Madison, December 20, 1803, in *Claiborne Papers,* ''Claiborne's Correspondence relative to Louisiana, 1803–1804,'' I. For a description by an eye witness, see Robin, *Voyages dans l'interieur de la Louisiane,* II, 137–140. More recent accounts are given by Grace King, *New Orleans,* 160–163, and Gayarré, *History of Louisiana,* IV, 619–622. A copy of the instrument of cession, signed by Claiborne, Wilkinson, and Laussat is in the *Annals of Congress,* 8 Cong., 2 Sess. (1804–1805), Appendix, 1229–1231.

[34] *Annals of Congress,* 8 Cong., 2 Sess. (1804–1805), Appendix, 1232–1233.

[35] Claiborne to Madison, December 27, 1803, in *Claiborne Papers,* ''Claiborne's Correspondence relative to Louisiana,'' I; Robertson, *Louisiana under the Rule of Spain, France, and the United States,* II, 227. The cabildo had been established in accordance with the proclamation of November 21, 1769, issued by Don Alexander O'Reilly, who had been commissioned governor and captain-general of the province of Louisiana in April of the same year. The proclamation stipulated that the cabildo, which was substituted for the superior council, should be ''composed of six perpetual regidors, two ordinary alcaldes, an attorney-general-syndic, and a clerk; over which the governor would preside in person.'' The cabildo sat every Friday but might be convened by the governor at any time. In the absence of the governor one of the ordinary alcaldes presided. Martin, *History of Louisiana,* 209–210.

Claiborne was vested, temporarily, with all the powers previously held by the Governor-General and the Intendant of Louisiana. The inhabitants of the territory had expected a much more liberal form of government and were greatly disappointed because they were granted no voice in it. Moreover, the new governor was unacquainted with their language, and mutual misunderstandings and suspicions were, as a result, certain to arise.

Then, too, there were a number of American residents in New Orleans and the neighboring country who sought to gain political influence through exploiting the grievances of the Louisianians. Their knowledge of American theories of government and of American institutions gave them an opportunity of criticizing the territorial government and, on the whole, making the governor's position an exceedingly unhappy one.

Claiborne's opinion of the people fluctuated back and forth, now favorable, now unfavorable. Difficulties of government caused him much embarrassment and he urged the early establishment of some permanent government for the territory. The constitution to be given ought to be as republican as the people could safely be intrusted with. Training and tradition had rendered the people unprepared to take a very active part in government, however. Trial by jury would at first be an embarrassment to the administration of justice.[36] The better acquainted he became with the inhabitants the more convinced he was of their unfitness for a representative government. He considered it advisable that they remain for some years under the immediate guardianship of Congress. For the present a local and temporary government for Louisiana, upon principles somewhat similar to the present territorial government of the first grade ought to be established. In the same letter Claiborne reported that the merchants of the city desired a law to be passed

[36] Claiborne to Madison, January 2, 1804, in Robertson, *Louisiana under the Rule of Spain, France, and the United States*, II, 232–234.

for the regulation of commerce. They were complaining of great injury for want of registers for their vessels, and of being yet subject to export duties and other commercial inconveniences.[37]

A somewhat similar opinion was expressed to Jefferson a few days later, to which Claiborne added that he did not share the opinion of some that a military government could alone, for the present, insure good order and harmony. Louisiana could be governed without force. He "could wish Louisiana a State tomorrow but that would be impolitic."[38]

One of the questions which early presented itself to Claiborne was that of the importation of slaves. In a letter to Madison, January 31, 1804, he reported the arrival a few days before of a ship with fifty African negroes for sale. He was opposed to the traffic, but, doubting his authority to prevent it, appealed to Mr. Leonard, late Spanish contador at New Orleans, for information as to the status of the slave trade under Spain. Upon learning that the importation of African slaves had been permitted, Claiborne did not interfere.[39]

It might here be noted that the prohibition by law of the importation of slaves into the territory of Louisiana was urged upon Congress in a memorial of the "American Convention for promoting the abolition of slavery, and improving the condition of the African race" to the House, January 23, 1804. The memorial was referred to the committee on the government of Louisiana.[40]

---

[37] Claiborne to Madison, January 10, 1804, in *Claiborne Papers*, "Claiborne's Correspondence relative to Louisiana," I.

[38] Claiborne to Jefferson, January 16, 1804, in *Jefferson Papers*, "Letters received at Washington, 2d Series," XIX, (19).

[39] *Claiborne Papers*, "Claiborne's Correspondence relative to Louisiana," I; Robertson, *Louisiana under the Rule of Spain, France and the United States*, II, 240; *American State Papers, Miscellaneous*, I, 390.

[40] *Annals of Congress*, 8 Cong., 1 Sess. (1803–1804), 940. The memorial itself is in the *American State Papers, Miscellaneous*, I, 386, no. 171. In this connection see Mary S. Locke, *Anti-Slavery in America*, 147–148, 162–163.

On February 6, 1804, Claiborne reported the inhabitants of New Orleans as manifesting great solicitude for a form of government, and the merchant class, in particular, desiring commercial regulations. A spirit of restlessness pervaded the territory. Claiborne felt that a majority of the inhabitants were well disposed towards the United States but the attachment to France was still strong.[41] A few days later he repeated his statement that the people were anxious for some form of permanent government. The rapid increase in population, bringing into the territory all sorts of adventurers, further complicated the situation.[42]

One of Claiborne's first measures as governor had been to establish a Court of Pleas. This had been done by ordinance, issued December 30, 1803. The ordinance provided for a court to be composed of not less than seven justices appointed by the governor, any three of whom might hold court. In civil matters their jurisdiction was limited to cases not exceeding in value three thousand dollars, from which there was an appeal to the governor when the amount in litigation was over five hundred dollars. Their criminal jurisdiction was to extend over all criminal cases involving punishment not to exceed two hundred dollars fine and sixty days imprisonment. Each of the justices was to have jurisdiction over all debts under one hundred dollars, with right of appeal to the Court of Pleas, the seven justices sitting together in court.[43]

This Court of Pleas was not used by the people to any extent. The people preferred the governor to the court so Claiborne decided to set apart one day in every week for the hearing and

---

[41] Claiborne to Madison, February 6, 1804, in Robertson, *Louisiana under the Rule of Spain, France, and the United States*, II, 248–249.

[42] Claiborne to Madison, February 13, 1804, in *ibid.*, II, 250–251.

[43] Gayarré, *History of Louisiana*, IV, 3; Martin, *History of Louisiana*, 319.

deciding of causes until Congress should provide some fixed government to relieve him of what he considered a painful duty.[44]

Among other matters Claiborne was somewhat puzzled as to the status of the people under his charge with respect to their relation to the United States. Citizens of Louisiana passing by water to the United States or to Europe requested passports or letters of protection. Having had no instructions on this subject, Claiborne acted with some reluctance. Considering the request reasonable, however, he issued to such applicant an instrument in writing, providing proof were given that he had been before, and on December 20, 1803, the date of the transfer of Louisiana to the United States, an inhabitant of Louisiana.[45]

There was a desire on the part of the people for a delegate in Congress and Claiborne suggested that in the formation of a government for Louisiana, Congress might make provision for one, placing him on an equal footing as regards privileges with the delegates from other territories.[46]

Claiborne admitted being compelled to exercise more authority than he had contemplated, and feared his decrees and ordinances would present a novel appearance in Washington. This species of legislation he entered into only when necessary.[47]

Such were some of the difficulties of the governor of Louisiana at the outset of his administration. How he fared later will

---

[44] Claiborne to Madison, February 13, 1804, in *Claiborne Papers*, ''Claiborne's Correspondence relative to Louisiana,'' I; Robertson, *Louisiana under the Rule of Spain, France, and the United States*, II, 250.

[45] Claiborne to Madison, February 20, 1804, in *Claiborne Papers*, ''Claiborne's Correspondence relative to Louisiana,'' I. For the history of the passport in the United States, see Gaillard Hunt, *The American Passport*. Claiborne's issuance of passports is not mentioned by Hunt.

[46] Claiborne to Madison, March 1, 1804, in Robertson, *Louisiana under the Rule of Spain, France, and the United States*, II, 254. Before the date of this letter the Senate had already debated on and declined to grant a delegate to Louisiana. See the report of the debate in the Senate, Chapter VII, below.

[47] Claiborne to Madison, March 2, 1804, in *Claiborne Papers*, ''Claiborne's Correspondence relative to Louisiana,'' I.

be discussed in due time. We must turn now to the activities of the federal authorities at Washington.

Jefferson had, in the meantime, been making plans for the government of the territory. An outline of what he considered proper was submitted to Gallatin in a letter of November 9, 1803, in which he says:

The following articles belong to the legislature.

The administration of justice to be prompt. Perhaps the judges should be obliged to hold their courts weekly, at least for some time to come. The ships of resident owners to be naturalized, and in general the laws of the U. S. respecting navigation, importation, exportation, &c; to be extended to the ports of the ceded territory.

The hospital to be provided for.

Slaves not to be imported, except from such of the U. S. as prohibit importation.

Without looking at the old territorial ordinance, I had imagined it best to found a government for the territory or territories of *lower* Louisiana on that basis. But on examining it, I find it will not do at all; that it would turn all their laws topsy-turvy. Still I believe it best to appoint a governor & three judges, with legislative powers; only providing that the judges shall form the laws, & the governor have a negative only, subject further to the negative of a national legislature. The existing laws of the country being now in force, the new legislature will introduce the trial by jury in *criminal* cases, first; the habeas corpus, the freedom of the press, freedom of religion, etc., as soon as can be, and in general draw their laws and organization to the mould of ours by degrees as they find practicable without exciting too much discontent. In proportion as we find the people there riper for receiving these first principles of freedom, congress may from session to session confirm their enjoyment of them.[48]

This letter is of importance for the light it throws on Jefferson's idea of a government for the new territory. Jefferson, who had drawn up the Declaration of Independence, is here found planning a form of government in which the people to be governed were to have no voice whatever. All rights, even those of jury trial, habeas corpus, freedom of the press and of religion, had to be legislated into the territory. Congress had

---

[48] Jefferson, *Writings* (Ford, ed.), VIII, 275–276, footnote.

complete power to regulate these rights and privileges as they saw fit. It was a practical scheme of government, but it was far removed from the abstract principles of government which Jefferson had been accustomed to quote in putting forth the claims of the American colonists against the British Government.

With regard to Upper Louisiana, Jefferson, in a postscript in the letter quoted, wrote that it was his idea that this region should be continued under its present form of government, only making it subordinate to the national government and independent of the lower part of Louisiana.[49] The division of the territory into two parts was here early decided upon.

Writing to Dewitt Clinton, December 2, 1803, Jefferson said that much difference of opinion manifested itself as to the manner of governing Louisiana. He added that, "Altho' it is as yet incapable of self-government as children, yet some cannot bring themselves to suspend its principles for a single moment."[50]

Whether the settlement of Upper Louisiana should be prohibited gave rise to three groups holding different opinions thereon. One wished to prohibit it until the Constitution could be amended to provide for it, claiming that if the legislature were allowed to open a land office there, this would have a great influence on elections and end in a "yazoo scheme," to quote Jefferson. The second group would have the legislature prohibit settlement, fearing that an amendment of the Constitution could not be obtained. The last group was in favor of permitting immediate settlement.[51]

It had been Jefferson's idea that the upper portion of the territory should be closed to settlers. This he had stated to George D. Erving as early as July 10, 1803.[52] John Breckin-

---

[49] Jefferson, *Writings* (Ford, ed.), VIII, 275–276, footnote.

[50] *Ibid.*, VII, 283.

[51] *Ibid.*

[52] *Jefferson Papers*, "Letters from Jefferson, 1st Series," IX, (99).

ridge of Kentucky, however, informed Jefferson that it would be impossible to prevent the Americans from crossing the Mississippi, "as they can do so with equal ease in every part of it for an extent of upwards of 1000 miles. When they have once crossed it, it will be the Rubicon to them. They have taken this resolution & will hazzard all the consequences."[53] Jefferson, despite his letter to Erving, seems to have reached the same conclusion as Breckinridge, for in a letter already quoted he had declared that after the filling up of the eastern side of the Mississippi range after range of states would be laid off on the western side.[54]

The progress made in planning the government for the territory can be traced in Jefferson's correspondence. On January 17, 1804, he wrote to Thomas McKean:

We are now at work on a territorial division & government for Louisiana. It will probably be a small improvement of our former territorial governments, or first grade of government. The act proposes to give them an assembly of Notables, selected by the Governor from the principal characters of the territory. This will, I think, be a better legislature than the former territorial one & will not be a greater departure from sound principle.[55]

To Doctor Joseph Priestley, Jefferson expressed himself well pleased with the "duplication of area for extending a government so free and economical as ours." Whether the country remained united or formed into Atlantic or Mississippi confederacies he did not consider vital to the happiness of the people. He was willing to do all he could for either part.[56]

---

[53] John Breckinridge to Jefferson, September 10, 1803, in *Jefferson Papers*, "Letters received at Washington, 2nd Series," IX, (8).

[54] See his letter to Breckinridge, above. Compare also the arguments on this question in the Senate debate of January–February, 1804, on the Breckinridge Bill, in Chapter VII, below.

[55] Jefferson, *Writings* (Ford, ed.), VIII, 293.

[56] Jefferson to Priestley, January 29, 1804, *ibid.*, 295.

In a letter of January 31, 1804, to Robert R. Livingston, Madison stated that a form of government was under discussion but its precise form was not yet known. It was certain, however, that:

The provisions generally contemplated will leave the people of the District for awhile without the organization of power dictated by Republican theory; but it is evident that a sudden transition to à condition so much in contrast with that in which their ideas and habits have been formed, would be as inacceptable and as little beneficial to them as it would be difficult for the Government of the United States. It may fairly be expected that every blessing of liberty will be extended to them as fast as they shall be prepared and disposed to receive it.[57]

The extent to which Congress at that time considered the Louisianians prepared to receive the ''blessings of liberty'' will now be related.

---

[57] Madison, *Writings* (Hunt, ed.), VIII, 115.

CHAPTER VII

THE DEBATE IN THE SENATE ON THE LOUISIANA GOVERNMENT BILL[1]

The law of October 31, 1803, which had placed the administration of the Louisiana territory, until further action by Congress, in the hands of the President, was recognized as a temporary measure and steps were soon taken to provide a different government. With this object in view, it was moved in the Senate on November 28 that a committee be appointed to form such a government.[2] This motion was taken into consideration December 5, and being agreed to, Senators Breckinridge of Kentucky, Wright of Maryland, Jackson and Baldwin of Georgia and Adams of Massachusetts were selected.[3] The committee, through Breckinridge, reported on December 30[4] the bill which bears Breckinridge's name. According to the provisions of the bill, as finally passed, the purchased territory was divided into

---

[1] The material used in the writing of this chapter is taken principally from Senator William Plumer's "Memorandum of the proceedings of Congress, Particularly of the Senate, from October 17, 1803, to March 27, 1804," cited as Plumer's "Memorandum." The part of the "Memorandum" which reports the Senate debate of January-February, 1804, on the Louisiana Government Bill was contributed by the present writer to the *American Historical Review*, XXII, 340–364.

Plumer's "Memorandum" seems to have escaped the attention of previous writers of American history. William Plumer, Jr., beyond quoting a few paragraphs from it, did not make use of it in his *Life of William Plumer*. The statement that this debate in the Senate was not reported has been made by Henry Adams, *History of the United Statse*, II, 122–123; F. A. Ogg, *The Opening of the Mississippi*, 571; and Curtis M. Geer, *The Louisiana Purchase and the Westward Movement*, 242.

Chapter VII, therefore, is an entirely new contribution to United States history.

[2] *Annals of Congress*, 8 Cong., 1 Sess. (1803–1804), 106.

[3] *Ibid.*, 211.

[4] *Ibid.*, 223. As might be inferred from the personnel of the committee, the framing of this bill was not accomplished without considerable difficulty. Senator John Smith of Ohio wrote to Jefferson that the committee "have met two or three times but cannot agree on the principles of the bill." December, 1803. [Letter received December 12.] *Jefferson Papers*, "Letters received at Washington, 2d Series," LXXVI.

two parts, that north of the thirty-third parallel to be called the "District of Louisiana," and connected, for purposes of government, with the territory of Indiana. The name "Territory of Orleans," was applied to the southern area.[5] For this region the bill provided for a governor, appointed by the President for a term of three years; a secretary, similarly appointed, for four years; and a legislative council of thirteen members, appointed annually by the President. The governor was given power to convene and prorogue the council at will. The judicial officers were to be appointed by the President for a term of four years. The right of trial by jury was granted in capital cases in criminal prosecutions; and in all cases, criminal and civil, in the superior court, if either party required it. The slave trade in the territory was restricted to slaves brought from states of the Union by American citizens going there to settle, and who at the time were bona fide owners of such slaves. The importation of slaves from abroad into Orleans Territory was prohibited, and slaves imported since May 1, 1798, were to be excluded from the territory.[6]

The provisions of the Breckinridge Bill and of amendments thereto formed part of the programme in the Senate from January 10, when Adams moved the three resolutions already noted,[7] until February 18, 1804, when the bill passed the Senate.

[5] For a discussion of the terms *territory* and *district*, see Max Farrand, "Territory and District," in *Am. Hist. Rev.*, V, 676–681.

[6] For the full text of the bill, approved by Jefferson, March 26, 1804, see the *Annals of Congress*, 8 Cong., 1 Sess. (1803–1804), Appendix, 1293–1300; *Statutes at Large*, II, 283.

The act of April 7, 1798, which authorized the establishment of a government in the Mississippi territory, contained a section forbidding the introduction into that territory of slaves from without the United States. On this point see Du Bois, *The Suppression of the African Slave-Trade*, 88–89, and Appendix B, 239. The act of 1798, together with the fact that it antedated the reopening of the foreign slave trade by South Carolina, explains the reason for the insertion of the date 1798 in the Louisiana bill.

[7] See above; also *Annals of Congress*, 8 Cong., 1 Sess. (1803–1804), 228–229; Adams, *Writings* (Ford, ed.), III, 25–30; Adams, *Memoirs*, I, 286–287.

Senators Dayton, Nicholas and Jackson considered Adams's resolutions as being alarming and dangerous in principle; however, they did not point out any particular evil that would result from their adoption. Plumer held them to be "mere abstract propositions, not connected with any business immediately before the Senate," and declared that a vote in favor of them would settle nothing.[8]

On January 16, Worthington of Ohio moved to amend the fourth section, which made provision for the appointment and powers of the legislative council, so as to authorize that body to elect a delegate to Congress with the right to debate but not vote.[9] This motion gave rise to an interesting debate concerning the status of the inhabitants of the ceded territory. Breckinridge of Kentucky favored the motion as a means of conveying useful knowledge to Congress. Samuel Smith of Maryland held a somewhat similar view. So, too, did John Smith of Ohio, who considered the amendment both necessary and important. Dayton of New Jersey, on the other hand, thought the legislative council of the territory could better inform Congress of conditions in the territory by memorials. Pickering of Massachusetts took the stand that since Louisiana was not incorporated into the Union, it would be absurd to admit a delegate from there to debate in Congress. Louisiana was a purchased province and must be governed as such. Opposition came also from White of Delaware, who argued that since the legislative council was to be created by the President and vested with the power of choosing a delegate to Congress, this delegate would be in reality the representative of the President, an arrangement which he denounced as wrong. Bradley of Vermont held the same point of view. Jackson of Georgia was of the opinion that it was

---

[8] Plumer, "Memorandum," Tuesday [January] 10, 1804.

[9] *Annals of Congress*, 8 Cong., 1 Sess. (1803–1804), 233.

too soon to allow the Louisianians representation in Congress. Worthington came to the support of his motion with the assurance that no danger could arise from the measure. Dayton, again participating in the debate, declared the motion unconstitutional. He said:

'The Constitution has provided only for the representation of States, and no man will pretend that Louisiana is a State. It is true by the confederation[10] provision was made for delegates from territories and our Constitution has provided that all *contracts and engagements entered into before its adoption shall be valid* (Art 6th) but no man will have the hardihood to say that Louisiana was included in that engagement.

John Quincy Adams also sided with the opposition, owing to constitutional scruples. Cocke of Tennessee saw no comparison between the government of Louisiana and other territorial governments. He realized that the Senate was face to face with a new problem, an original system, founded on new principles, which must be worked out on its own merits. He denied that the bill violated the Constitution, and, answering the argument that the people were ignorant, he claimed that they, knowing the necessity of it, would always elect worthy representatives. He expressed his veneration for these people because they lived in the west. Breckinridge added his voice to those who denied there was any infringement of the Constitution, and Samuel Smith brought the debate to a close with the argument that since the Constitution did not prevent the Senate from admitting delegates from old territories he could see no power restraining that body from allowing Louisiana to send a delegate to the other House.[11] The motion failed by a vote of eighteen nays to twelve yeas.[12]

---

[10] By the Ordinance of 1787, sec. 12.

[11] Plumer, ''Memorandum,'' Monday, January 16. Compare the statement in John Quincy Adams, *Memoirs*, I, 290, under the same date: ''The Louisiana Government bill was further discussed; but no decision had.''

[12] *Annals of Congress*, 8 Cong., 1 Sess. (1803–1804), 233–234. The liberal tendencies of the West are seen in the vote on this measure. With

Mere abstract theory of government played little part in this debate. The principal grounds of argument were those of constitutional restrictions and of expediency.

The doctrine that territories must pass through varying stages of progress before definite privileges were granted to them is here applied to newly acquired foreign territory as well as to that originally held. This was true not only of the one question already discussed; it can be traced throughout the entire debate. On the very next day following the refusal to grant a delegate in Congress to Louisiana, a motion to extend to that country the trial by jury in all criminal cases was defeated.[13]

The Breckinridge Bill was debated on January 18[14] and on January 23. On the latter day a difference of opinion was manifest as to how much of the operative part of our political institutions could be carried into direct effect in the new country, and as to the mode by which the spirit and principles of these institutions could be most effectually introduced. The immediate cause of debate was a motion to strike out a part of what related to the legislative council. It was urged, on the one side, that the legislative council ought to be chosen by the governor from certain qualified settlers of the different parts of the country, men who should be able to give information con-

---

the exception of John Brown of Kentucky the western states voted solidly in favor of allowing the Louisianians a delegate in Congress. Those voting aye were Anderson and Cocke of Tennessee, Breckinridge of Kentucky, John Smith and Worthington of Ohio, Ellery and Potter of Rhode Island, Logan of Pennsylvania, Israel Smith of Vermont, Samuel Smith of Maryland, and Nicholas and Venable of Virginia. The nays were Adams and Pickering of Massachusetts, Armstrong of New York, Baldwin and Jackson of Georgia, Bradley of Vermont, Brown of Kentucky, Condit and Dayton of New Jersey, Franklin and Stone of North Carolina, Hillhouse and Tracy of Connecticut, Maclay of Pennsylvania, Olcott and Plumer of New Hampshire, and Wells and White of Delaware.

13 *Annals of Congress*, 8 Cong., 1 Sess. (1803–1804), 235. Plumer does not report the debate on this motion, nor does John Quincy Adams (*Memoirs*, I, 290). The bill limited trial by jury in criminal cases to those which were capital.

14 *Annals of Congress*, 8 Cong., 1 Sess. (1803–1804), 236.

cerning their respective sections. The governor, having power to dissolve this council at discretion, could check factious dispositions; while, since the members were to be chosen annually by the governor, who was responsible for their choice, no injury could arise. Information could be acquired on the state of things and the representative element of our government be introduced gradually and progressively. This mode of procedure was considered necessary and expedient, on the one hand, because of lack of information on the part of Congress of the local conditions, and on the other, from the attitude of mind of the inhabitants due to long subjection to a form of government very different from our own. If elections were held, there was a danger that persons would be elected who did not know our language and who, from want of necessary information in our principles of government, would be incapable of proceeding with legislation.

Those favoring the extension of legislative rights to the Louisianians contended that capable men could be found in every district. Furthermore, admitting the people of Louisiana to be "next to a state of nature," it was inconsistent with the third article of the treaty to allow them to remain so. Having guaranteed to them in due time equal rights and laws with ourselves, the first step in effecting that extension of civil and political liberty to them was to grant the election of a legislative council. Not to grant this would be perpetuating ignorance, that "great source of human enslavement." It would be better to allow them to experiment while their numbers were few rather than wait until more numerous settlers would render errors arising from ignorance extensive and dangerous. The theory of free government appeared in the statement:

That we best understood what is fit and what will be good or acceptable in the eyes of others by placing ourselves in their situation and that if we were in their situation now we should hardly complain or object to the conduct of those who should proffer to us the same means of happiness, freedom and prosperity which had rendered our benefactors the admiration of mankind.[15]

On January 24, an amendment was offered authorizing the governor to divide the territory into twenty-four districts, in each of which the resident householders were to elect annually two properly qualified persons, from whom the governor was to select twenty-four, one from each district, to form a legislative council.[16] Jackson declared that the inhabitants of Louisiana were not citizens of the United States; they were in a state of probation and were as yet too ignorant to elect a legislature. This view received the support of Samuel Smith, Nicholas and Pickering, who considered the people absolutely incapable of governing themselves, of electing their rulers, or of appointing jurors. They would be in favor of granting a free government as soon as the people were ready for it. Maclay of Pennsylvania favored the amendment, as did Cocke, who opposed the original bill as tyrannical. Anderson was surprised that the third article of the treaty had been lost sight of. To him the original bill had not "a single feature of our government in it—it is a system of tyranny, destructive of elective rights. We are bound by treaty, and must give that people, a free elective government."

The proposal of an amendment to extend to the new territory the act of February 28, 1803, forbidding importation of slaves into states which prohibited their importation,[17] brought forth the remark from Jackson that "slaves must be admitted into

---

[15] *Aurora,* January 27, 1804. The correspondent's communication is dated Washington, January 23. Curiously enough, this was the only lengthy newspaper report on any part of the debate which the writer was able to find. The *Aurora* correspondent contented himself the next day, January 24, with a brief statement to the effect that the debate in the Senate was continued along much the same lines as the day before. See the *Aurora* for January 28.

[16] *Annals of Congress,* 8 Cong., 1 Sess. (1803–1804), 238–239.

[17] *Ibid.,* 7 Cong., 2 Sess. (1802–1803), Appendix, 1564–1565.

that territory; it cannot be cultivated without them.'' This assertion opened the way for a heated discussion of slavery and the slave-trade which became the central theme of the debate until the final passage of the bill. Nearly all the arguments for and against the institution of slavery which were to become so familiar in the years to follow, were advanced. The light thrown by Plumer on the position of the Senate on this question is one of the most important of his contributions to our knowledge of current congressional action.

The statement of a Georgia man, Jackson, was immediately attacked by other Southerners, Franklin of North Carolina and Breckinridge of Kentucky, both of whom declared themselves opposed to slavery. Breckinridge expressed the hope that the time was ''not far distant when not a slave will exist in the Union.'' He feared a slave uprising similar to that which had occurred in San Domingo.[18]

Slavery had not yet divided the country along geographical lines, although such a division was hinted at during this debate.[19] Dayton, senator from New Jersey and a native of that state, took upon himself the defense of slavery on the ground that the newly acquired territory would never be inhabited unless slavery should be permitted there. White men could not bear the burning sun and damp dews of that country. Dayton based his statement on first-hand evidence, having traveled over a large part of Louisiana. He was opposed, also, to limiting the trade in slaves to the states of the Union, for this would lead the slave dealers of the United States to collect and ship into the new territory the worst type of slaves.

Dayton, however, was not the only senator who possessed first-hand knowledge of Louisiana. John Smith of Ohio had

----

[18] Frequent reference to this slave revolt shows how deep an impression was made by it on the minds of the people of the South. See Du Bois, *The Suppression of the African Slave-Trade,* 70–93.

[19] See the speech of Hillhouse, p. 112.

spent considerable time there. He did not agree with Dayton and maintained that white men could cultivate that land. Slaves introduced from foreign countries would soon become so numerous as to endanger the government and ruin the new country. He, however, favored the admission of slaves from the states. This would be the means of scattering the negroes more equally through states and territories and thus check their power. He professed his admiration of the policy of New England in excluding slavery, and thanked God there were no slaves in Ohio.[20]

Franklin asserted gravely that, ''Slavery is in every respect an evil to the States in the south and in the west; it will, I fear, soon become a dreadful one.'' The great danger, however, arose from negro insurrections. In support of his contention he pointed to the laws of Virginia and North Carolina, made for the purpose of guarding against and suppressing these rebellions.[21]

The debate on the slave trade was resumed the next day. Bradley of Vermont was in favor of permitting slavery in Louisiana because this right was claimed by the inhabitants and was made binding on the United States by the treaty. He preferred, however, to omit entirely the slave question from the bill.[22] Hillhouse pointed to the great increase in the number of negroes in the United States—nearly two hundred thousand for the ten years ending with the last census. He regarded slavery as a serious evil and desired to check it wherever possible. An increase in the number of slaves in Louisiana would necessitate

---

[20] The words *slavery* and *slave trade* are used rather loosely by Plumer and sometimes lead to obscurity of meaning although, as a rule, it is not difficult to ascertain from the context which is meant.

[21] Plumer, ''Memorandum,'' Tuesday, January 24. Cf. John Quincy Adams, *Memoirs*, I, 292, under the same date: ''The amendments to the Louisiana Government bill were taken up, and some progress made in them. Mr. Venable's amendment, to give them the beginning of a popular representation, failed for want of one vote. Yeas fourteen, nays fourteen. On the section prohibiting the slave trade, no question was taken.

[22] See Adams's comments on Bradley's action, p. 110.

the maintenance of a standing army to protect the people against insurrections. In conclusion, he said that if the new country could not be cultivated without slaves it would prove a curse to the United States, particularly to some of the states nearest it.

Bradley favored the establishment of a general, not a particular form of government. He cited the government of the District of Columbia as proof of the fact that Congress was incompetent to deal with particulars.

Adams held slavery in a moral sense to be an evil, but as connected with commerce it had important uses. Considering that the regulations offered to prevent slavery were insufficient, he announced his intention of voting against them. Dayton repeated his argument of the previous day that negro slave labor was necessary for the cultivation of the soil of Louisiana. Reverting to other sections of the bill, he declared that an elective government and trial by jury would be a curse to the people, but that slavery was essential to their existence.

Hillhouse and John Smith both took exception to Dayton's remarks. The former claimed that the Constitution permitted a republican government and no other. "We must," he said, "apply the Constitution to that people in all cases or in none. We must consider that country as being within the Union or without it—there is no alternative. I think myself they are not a part or parcel of the United States."[23] Smith's opposition was simply a reiteration of his earlier statement that negroes were not necessary for the tillage of the soil; white men could cultivate it. He, too, emphasized the dangers and horrors of negro rebellions, and again referred to the one in San Domingo.

---

[23] The division of opinion on this point has continued to the present day. One needs only to examine the magazines and newspapers of the period immediately following the acquisition of our insular possessions to see how live an issue this still is among students of political science and constitutional history. The Insular Decisions of the Supreme Court throw further light on the controversy. It has played a prominent part in the discussions following each new acquisition of territory. The importance of Louisiana as a precedent is once more emphasized.

Jackson, arguing from experience as a Georgia rice-planter, held that slavery was necessary. To exclude slaves would depreciate the value of lands in Louisiana fifty per cent. The third article of the treaty, according to his interpretation, forbade the exclusion. Full of serious portent for the future, tinged with what might be well called the "higher law," was his statement: "You cannot prevent slavery—neither laws moral or human can do it. Men will be governed by their interest, not the law."

Opposition to the extension of slavery in the west was voiced by Anderson of Tennessee. In his opinion its spread into Louisiana would prove a curse to the west.

The bitterness aroused by the debate, a bitterness which was to grow until the ties of union were broken by southern secession, did not escape men at the time and called forth the grave remark from White of Delaware: "I think it unfortunate that whenever this question is stirred, feelings are excited that are calculated to lead us astray." It was his hope that Congress would use every means within its power to prevent "this disgraceful traffick in human flesh." Nothing in the treaty guaranteed to the people of Louisiana the power, much less right, of holding slaves. He inquired whether the statement that Louisiana could not be cultivated by white men did not rise from the fact of their having slaves. He believed white men could accustom themselves to the fatigue of labor in that climate. In conclusion he put forth an argument for free white labor which was to be used many times afterwards, and one which the southern planters were unwilling to admit:

Examine the state of this Union. In the Eastern States where slavery is not suffered, their lands are highly cultivated, their buildings neat, useful and elegant, and the people are strong, powerful and wealthy. But as you travel south, the instant you arrive to where slavery is, you find the lands uncultivated, the buildings decaying and falling into ruins and the people, poor, weak, and feeble. This is not the effect of the climate, for our southern climates are more favorable than the eastern and northern.

Bradley had a hard time making his attitude clearly understood. Opposed to slavery in the "eastern states," he declared his intention of voting against the measure under consideration because it admitted of the principle of slavery. Hillhouse pointed out that this stand, if adhered to, would throw open the new territory to slaves imported directly from Africa, whereas support of the bill would limit the traffic to the United States.

Samuel Smith of Maryland claimed a constitutional right to prohibit slavery in Louisiana but doubted the wisdom of exercising it. Israel Smith of Vermont considered the provision proposed to be insufficient; it would increase rather than prevent slavery. Although opposed to the slave trade, he did not think Congress could prohibit it effectually until 1808. Many slaves existed in Louisiana and the change proposed would be too sudden. It would encourage South Carolina to import slaves. He was against present action in the matter.[24]

No vote was taken and the debate was continued on the next day. Hillhouse, in introducing a new amendment to the provision concerning slavery, denied the accusation that he was unfriendly to the new territory, and that he was bringing in measures merely to embarrass the Administration, and asserted his sincere desire to promote the interests of the Union. He then uttered a remark fraught with significant meaning:

It has been said on this floor that I am an *Eastern man.* I am so, but *while* I am the representative of a State which is *yet* a member of the

[24] Plumer, "Memorandum," Wednesday, January 25. Cf. John Quincy Adams, *Memoirs*, I, 292: "In Senate the debate continued all day upon the question of the admission of slaves into Louisiana. Mr. Hillhouse is to prepare a section to the same effect, but differently modified." Mention of the debate is made in the *Aurora*, January 30, and in the *Federal Gazette & Baltimore Daily Advertiser*, February 1, dated from Washington, January 25.

South Carolina had, by successive amendments, from 1787 to 1803, forbidden the importation of slaves, but the trade had been reopened by the repeal of these laws, December 17, 1803. For statistics on the number of slaves imported into Charleston after December, 1803, see DuBois, *The Suppression of the African Slave Trade*, 90–91.

Union, I hope I shall have as much influence as if I was a *Southern man.* I did not expect *so soon* to hear on this floor the distinction of *eastern and northern, and southern, men.* Has it indeed come to this—are we to be designated by a geographical line!

Hillhouse's amendment declared it unlawful for anyone to import, or assist in importing, any slaves into Louisiana from without the United States. Persons convicted of this offense were to be fined, and the slaves freed.[25]

The attack on the amendment was begun by Jackson, who still insisted that unless slavery were established in that country the territory must be abandoned. Personal interest inclined him to favor the prohibition of slavery in Louisiana because this would prevent its settlement and thereby raise the value of estates in Georgia. Duty, he said, outweighed personal or state interest. Like many other Southerners of his day, Jackson believed it would be for the interest of the United States to end slavery altogether, but this could not be done. Reverting to familiar arguments, he said that although he disliked the traffic in human flesh, the decision must be made not on the morality but the policy of the case. Furthermore, it was an improper time to prohibit the importation of slaves into Louisiana, our government not yet being established there. Anticipating the later "popular sovereignty" doctrine, Jackson said: "Let those people judge for themselves—the treaty is obligatory upon us."

The treaty obligation was emphasized by Dayton, who maintained that the faith of the nation was pledged, by treaty, that the rights of the Louisianians should be secured to them: one of their rights was slavery.

Both the doctrine of "popular sovereignty" and the rights under the treaty were to rise again and again to plague the Government until their settlement became issues of the Civil War.

---

[25] *Annals of Congress,* 8 Cong., 1 Sess. (1803-1804), 240.

Not all of the senators agreed with Jackson and Dayton as to the treaty obligations. The right, under the treaty, to hold slaves was denied by Breckinridge, himself a Southerner. Much less, according to him, did the treaty pledge the faith of the Union to support the slave traffic. Alarmed at the increase of slaves in the southern states, he, considering slavery an evil, desired to confine it within as small a compass as possible.

Some of the senators felt uncomfortable because of the stand they felt forced to take on the question before the Senate. Bradley opposed the amendment as insufficient. Desirous of abolishing slavery completely, he did not think the proper time had come. He wished nothing at all to be done on the subject. Samuel Smith found himself in similar difficulties. He stated his intention of voting against the amendment, although he wished it understood that he was opposed to slavery. On the other hand there were those in the Senate who were willing to vote for what could be obtained. Franklin was of this group. His wish was to exclude all slaves from the territory except those carried by actual settlers from the United States, but despairing of a vote in the Senate which would accomplish this exclusion, he was willing to vote for such a prohibition as he could get. With regard to all foreign importation of slaves, Franklin expressed his willingness to send a frigate to Charleston to prevent the landing of slaves from Africa, and *"frittering those nefarious traders to pieces."*

Jackson again asserted that human power and invention could not prevent the importation of slaves; that it was vain to make laws on the subject. Slaves directly from Africa were preferable to those who had been long in this country, or born here. He was sorry the constitution of Georgia probihited the slave trade.[26] Jackson's idea of the futility of laws on the

---

[26] Constitution of Georgia, 1798, Art. IV, sect. 11, Thorpe, *Federal and State Constitutions,* II, 801.

subject was shared by a New Englander, Israel Smith of Vermont. Although opposed to slavery, Smith considered as useless all laws made to prevent it. Such legislation would be as futile as an attempt to prevent by law the use of cider in New England. No effective law against the slave trade, he argued, could be carried into effect until 1808. South Carolina was within her rights in importing slaves from Africa. Any laws passed at the present time would give encouragement to the states in 1808 to resist laws which might then constitutionally be made to abolish the slave trade. He hoped nothing would now be done on the matter.

Jackson attempted to prevent a vote on the provision by moving an adjournment, which was refused. He considered it to be unfair for a majority to press the subject. The question was taken on the amendment and passed in the affirmative, twenty-one to six.[27]

<hr />

[27] Plumer, ''Memorandum,'' Thursday, January 26. For the text of the amendment under discussion, and the vote thereon, see *Annals of Congress*, 8 Cong., 1 Sess. (1803–1804), 240–41. John Quincy Adams in his *Memoirs*, I, 292–293, under date of January 26, says:
''The section for prohibiting the admission of slaves from abroad into Louisiana was again debated all day. It was at last taken by yeas and nays—seventeen to six. [An error. Compare the vote in the *Annals*.— E. S. B.] The discussion of this question has developed characters. Jackson has opposed the section *totis viribus*, in all its shapes, and was very angry when the question was taken—called twice for an adjournment, in which they would not indulge him, and complained of unfairness. Dayton has opposed the section throughout with equal vehemence, but happened to be absent when the question was taken. Smith, of Maryland, who has been all along extremely averse to the section, but afraid to avow it, complained bitterly that the yeas and nays were taken in quasi committee, instead of waiting to take them on the ultimate question in the Senate. But, finding his party on this point stiff to him as if he was in the minority, he left his seat, to avoid voting at all, in the yeas and nays. Bradley, of Vermont, after trying various expedients to give the slip to the real question, finally moved an amendment to prohibit the admission of slaves altogether, as well from the United States as from abroad. The object was to defeat the thing by its own excess, and made his abhorrence of all slavery the ground of his argument to oppose the partial prohibition. He therefore took the yeas and nays upon his own proposed amendment before they were taken on Mr. Hillhouse's section. The workings of this question upon the minds and hearts of these men opened them to observation as much as if they had had the window in the breast.''

The slavery issue with respect to Louisiana was by no means settled. On Monday, January 30, Senator Hillhouse moved an amendment to the Louisiana Bill, providing that no person brought into the territory from any state or territory of the Union or from any territory in America belonging to any foreign Prince or State after a day to be decided could be held by law to serve for more than one year after reaching the age of twenty-one years for males and eighteen for females, unless bound by their own voluntary act after reaching that age, or bound by law for the payment of debts, damages, fines or costs. It was also provided that this act should not affect fugitives from other states or territories, who must be delivered up in the manner prescribed by law.[28]

Practically no discussion of this amendment is reported, brief remarks in favor of it by Hillhouse and Bradley alone being noted. The measure was rejected.[29]

Hillhouse promptly offered another amendment, the first part of which made it unlawful for any person to import into the territory, from any place within the limits of the United States, or to assist in importing, any slaves brought since [blank] date into any part of the limits of the United States, from any place outside those limits. If convicted of such an offense in any competent court of the territory, the offender was liable to fine.[30]

Dayton pointed to the fact that South Carolina had a constitutional right, which she was exercising, to import slaves from Africa, and the proposed amendment would impair that right. Hillhouse admitted this, adding that it would do so justly. Jackson touched on one of the real difficulties in any settlement of the slavery question when he said it was unfortunate that

---

[28] *Annals of Congress,* 8 Cong., 1 Sess. (1803–1804), 241–242.

[29] Plumer, ''Memorandum,'' Monday, January 30. For the vote see *Annals of Congress,* 8 Cong., 1 Sess. (1803–1804), 242.

[30] *Annals of Congress,* 8 Cong., 1 Sess. (1803–1804), 242.

slaves were owned, but having them it was unsafe to free them. He said that a very few negroes would revolutionize Louisiana. Georgia had prohibited the manumission of slaves.[31] He expressed his willingness to join in *exporting* all the slaves.

The difficulty of finding a solution to the slave problem was apparent to all. The danger of a sudden, general manumission could not be overlooked; nor was it, even by the very man who by his many amendments showed his desire to check the growth of slavery. Hillhouse held to his opinion that slavery was a real evil, but he was not in favor of freeing all the slaves at once; slavery must be extinguished by degrees. Adams stated his opposition to slavery but added that he had voted against the provisions to prohibit and lessen it. His reasons for so doing were those advanced in his amendments proposed January 10; namely, that he was opposed to legislating at all for Louisiana; and that the Senate was proceeding with too much haste on such an important question.[32]

The first division of the amendment was adopted, but the second part was postponed until the next day.[33] By this second division it was provided that no slaves should be introduced into

---

[31] A Georgia act of 1801 made manumission illegal unless accompanied by act of the legislature.

[32] Plumer, "Memorandum," Monday, January 30. Cf. John Quincy Adams, *Memoirs*, I, 293, for same date, where merely a brief note of the continuance of the discussion is mentioned. The *National Intelligencer and Washington Advertiser*, the Administration paper, under date of January 30, has the following to say: "The Senate have, for some days past, been engaged on the bill for the government of Louisiana. After a debate of considerable length, it has been decided—yeas 22—nays 7—to prohibit the importation into Louisiana of slaves from all foreign countries. We flatter ourselves that this important principle will be confirmed by the ultimate vote of the two Houses, and that Congress will thereby evince an unabating spirit to exert every legitimate power, with which they are invested, to rescue the national character from its greatest degradation, and save the people they represent from the deepest evils which futurity might otherwise have in store for them." The same statement appears in the *Federal Gazette & Baltimore Daily Advertiser*, Wednesday, February 1, 1804.

[33] *Annals of Congress*, 8 Cong., 1 Sess. (1803–1804), 242.

the territory except by persons removing thence for actual settlement, and being, at the time of removal, *bona fide* owners of such
slaves. The penalty for violation of this regulation was freedom
for the slaves.[34] An attempt to strike out this section and insert
another proposed by Breckinridge was defeated,[35] but not until
the matter had been debated ''warmly,'' to use the phrase of
Adams.[36] Something of the warmth of the discussion is to be
seen in Plumer's report of it. Much was repetition of what had
already been said, and yet there were sufficient new phases of
the question laid open and old phases emphasized in new ways
to make an examination of the debate exceedingly profitable.
The depth of the problem was voiced by Samuel Smith:

> When the prohibition of slavery was first introduced into the bill I was
> much alarmed. I foresaw it would take up time—that it would create
> alarm and even endanger the peace and security of these States holding
> slaves—especially when the subject is debated in the other House—and
> those debates published in the newspapers.[37] God knows that I am not
> friendly to slavery, although I own slaves and live in a state where slavery
> is established by law. I am unwilling to think much less to speak on this
> subject.

Smith here voiced an attitude toward the slave question
which became all too common at a later date. The absolute
impossibility of avoiding the topic in this manner was recognized
by another Southerner, Franklin of North Carolina, in the following words: ''We cannot wink this subject out of sight—if we
leave it, it will follow us.'' Legislation on this question he
considered imperative. The evil of slavery was felt in North
Carolina; yet while Franklin was in favor of restraining foreign importation, he did not wish to go further. Breckinridge

---

[34] *Annals of Congress*, 8 Cong., 1 Sess. (1803–1804), 243.

[35] *Ibid.*, 243–244.

[36] John Quincy Adams, *Memoirs*, I, 293.

[37] Although the Senate was no longer closed to the public except when
special matters were under discussion, the debates in the House were given
much wider publicity, a fact to which Smith here bears witness.

believed firmly in the power of the Government to make laws concerning slavery, and to carry those laws into effect. If this could not be done then our power was too feeble to govern the Union. Breckinridge emphasized the importance of the problem —the legislation for a large section of the country. In considering this matter, said he, immediate effects of legislation must be overlooked. The fundamental issue was: ''Can it be right to extend and foist slavery into that country?'' Yet in answering his own question, Breckinridge could not forget the interests of his own and neighboring states. He argued, as had been done before, that it would be good policy to permit slaves to be sent into Louisiana from the United States because this would disperse the negroes over a wider area and thus free the southern states from a part of their black population. Unless slaves could be carried into the territory from the states, wealthy southern men would be prohibited from going to Louisiana to settle.

Answering a charge made by Bradley that liberty and slavery could not exist together, Breckinridge declared that such a condition did exist in the slave states. He enlivened the discussion by asserting that the Constitution not only recognized slavery but expressly protected it. This was denied by Adams who said: ''The Constitution does not recognize *slavery*—it contains no such word—a great circumlocution of words is used merely to avoid the term *slaves*.'' He in turn was answered by Venable who admitted that while the Constitution did not contain the actual word *slave*, nevertheless it admitted the *thing* and protected it, and Congress had uniformly acted accordingly.

The whole situation from the point of practical statesmanship was summed up by Nicholas as follows:

One State only, South Carolina, can now import slaves—and that is a right derived not from Congress, but from the Constitution—it is a mere temporary right. The people of Louisiana cannot therefore complain of the partiality in Congress because we deny them the liberty of importing foreign slaves—It is no more than what we long since denied to the Mississippi and Ohio territories. We are now making a form of government for Louisiana, not establishing a common and ordinary law—I am for prohibiting the people of that country from importing slaves from foreign countries, and leave it optional with the government of Louisiana, when they have one, to prohibit it from the United States also, if they should think best.[38]

The vote on Hillhouse's proposition was not then taken[39] but the measure was passed the following day in an amended form, limiting to "a citizen of the United States" instead of "a person or persons," in describing the right to take slaves into Louisiana. The proposed change in wording and the slave problem in general precipitated another debate on the subject, which, added to what had already been carried on, led to statements which showed how bitter the feeling had become. Hardly had the matter been raised again before Wright of Maryland stated what was later to be one of the last defenses of the slave-holder: "It is wrong to reproach us with the *immorality* of *slavery*—that is a crime we must answer at the bar of God—We ought not therefore to answer it here—for it would be unjust that we should be punished twice for the same offence."

Jackson opposed the amendment because it did not authorize foreigners who might go there to settle to carry their slaves with them. The settlement of that country should be the first object aimed at; and interest dictated the admission of Englishmen there as soon as possible.[40] The amendment, however, was passed.[41]

---

[38] Plumer, "Memorandum," Tuesday, January 31. Plumer adds a note to the effect that the real reason why the senators from the Southern States desired the prohibition of the foreign importation of slaves into Louisiana, was that such action would raise the price of their own slaves in the market, and give them a chance to get rid of dangerous slaves.

[39] John Quincy Adams, *Memoirs*, I, 293 (January 31).

[40] Plumer, "Memorandum," Wednesday, February 1. Cf. John Quincy Adams, *Memoirs*, I, 293–294, for February 1.

[41] *Annals of Congress*, 8 Cong., 1 Sess. (1803–1804), 244; Plumer, "Memorandum," Wednesday, February 1; John Quincy Adams, *Memoirs*, I, 293–294.

The slavery question having been settled for the time being, the Senate turned its attention to other provisions of the Louisiana Government Bill. Anderson moved to strike out the eighth section which concerned the government of the upper district, known specifically as the District of Louisiana.[42]

Jackson argued against the establishment of a regular government and the opening of Upper Louisiana to settlement because it would destroy the western states. It was too soon to settle Upper Louisiana. The placing of large uncultivated tracts on sale would open the way for bribery as it had done in Georgia, where he had been offered half a million acres to keep still, an offer he had refused.[43] Not only would the value of the lands be greatly lowered by the settlement of Louisiana but a separation of the Union would result. Worthington of Ohio answered that the western states would not separate unless the eastern states by their conduct rendered it absolutely necessary.[44]

The debate on striking out the eighth section of the bill continued. The principal provisions of this section, as now amended, pertained to the transfer of the form of government of Upper Louisiana which existed previous to the cession to one under the direction of the United States Government. This district was to retain its name and government except that the executive and judicial powers of the former government should be exercised by a governor, appointed by the President. The

---

[42] Adams, *Memoirs*, I, 294, under date of February 1. No mention of Anderson's motion is made in the *Annals of Congress*, nor does Plumer state the exact question which came up but his report of a debate following the passage of the amendment on the slave trade corroborates Mr. Adams's statement.

[43] In 1796 Jackson had been the leader of the ''Anti-Yazoo Party'' in the Georgia house of representatives. Jackson's reference to his own honesty brought forth the rather sarcastic rejoinder from Cocke: ''I am glad Georgia has one uncorrupt man, and I rejoice that he is a senator. I trust we may have many such in the nation.''

[44] Plumer, ''Memorandum,'' Wednesday, February 1; John Quincy Adams, *Memoirs*, I, 294, February 2 [Louisiana Government Bill] ''Debate until four o'clock, and the question not taken.''

powers of the former commandants of posts or districts were to be vested in civil officers, to be appointed by the President in the recess of the Senate, but at the next meeting thereof to be nominated for their advice and consent. Salaries for these officers were provided for in the bill.[45]

The question now before the Senate allowed free expression of theories as to the government of acquired territory. Abstract theories in general, expediency, treaty rights and obligations, and constitutional restrictions were all enunciated. The establishment of an arbitrary government in order to prevent the settlement of Louisiana was opposed by Hillhouse. He contended that under the treaty this could not be done, for much of the land had been granted to Spaniards, and they must be given such a government as they could live under; otherwise they would not be protected in the enjoyment of their rights as stipulated in the treaty. A practical government was necessary, not one like that of the United States, with which the people of the territory were unacquainted. Nor would a military form do, for that would be too arbitrary. Trial by jury ought not to be extended to the inhabitants until they were able to express their desire for it by their own legislature, and to make laws regulating that form of trial.

John Smith considered a military government at variance not only with the third article of the treaty but also with the letter and spirit of the Constitution. Furthermore, now that the country was ours it would be impossible, by any law that could be passed, to prevent people from emigrating and settling there. Cocke believed the people of the territory would be more satisfied with their old government than with a new one, even though the latter might, theoretically, be better. He was in favor of allowing them their old laws and customs with the addition, however, of trial by jury. Boldness and resolution were neces-

---

45 *Annals of Congress*, 8 Cong., 1 Sess. (1803–1804), 245.

sary in the government of the inhabitants. "Tell that people you shall have justice, but you shall obey the laws," represents Cocke's stand in the matter. The people, he said, were not so ignorant as senators considered them to be. Jackson, as before, opposed western settlement because of the resulting depreciation of public lands already held. He never wished to see our people go beyond the Mississippi. Anderson bluntly described the eighth section as a military despotism; unconstitutional; opposed to the spirit and genius of our country. The only power to legislate for the new country was derived from the Constitution and that required the grant of a republican form of government and no other. Even though this injured his own state, Tennessee, and all the western states, yet a constitutional government must be established. According to Anderson, there were about eight thousand inhabitants in Upper Louisiana, more than two-thirds of whom were Americans, most of them emigrants from Virginia, who understood and would demand their rights. Dayton wanted to know in what part of the Constitution Mr. Anderson found any authority to legislate for Upper Louisiana. He denied that any such authority was granted by the Constitution. Going beyond the Constitution he said, "We derive our power and right from the nature of government. That Country is a purchased territory and we may govern it as a conquered one." To Dayton the only safe government to establish in Upper Louisiana was a military one. He hoped the settlement of that country might be prevented forever. If settled it would separate from the Union, form a new empire and become the enemy of the United States. Dayton then alluded to a favorite proposal of the time when he said he believed the Indians on the eastern side of the Mississippi could be induced to move to the other side.[46] He favored the retention of the eighth section of the bill.

[46] See Miss Abel, "History of Events resulting in Indian Consolidation West of the Mississippi," in American Historical Association, *Annual Report, 1906*, I, 249. Miss Abel did not use Plumer's "Memorandum."

The distinction, under the Constitution, between states and territories was brought out by Wright, another advocate of the eighth section. Alluding to the opposition of the section on constitutional grounds, Wright claimed that while the Constitution required that the governments of the states should be republican, this was not true of territories. He added that to extend jury trial to that country would, in reality, be a denial of justice because the people lived too remote from each other to derive any benefit from the jury system.

A rather new and novel interpretation of republican government was laid down by Samuel Smith who considered the eighth section of the bill republican in principle, Congress being the people's legislators and the commandants only the agents of Congress. This view certainly would have found little favor in colonial times, substituting Parliament for Congress and the American colonists for the inhabitants of Upper Louisiana. It had been essentially the British point of view and one bitterly opposed by the colonists. Theory and practice could thus vary greatly in the space of a few short years, according as the parties to the action shifted.

Pickering considered it an error to apply the Constitution to Upper ·Louisiana: it did not extend there. The Senate was bound, however, by the treaty to extend protection to the people of that country and secure to them their rights and privileges. He held that they must be considered and governed as a colony. Once more Pickering advanced the futility of attempts to prevent settlement of the new country by legislation: if the people found it to their interest to settle it, prohibition would be unavailing.

Pickering's statements are interesting to us as we look back over the rapid expansion of the United States. Not yet is it settled in the minds of scholars whether, theoretically, the Constitution extends to the territories or not, although there is little doubt that they are governed as colonies. The utter futility of attempting to prevent settlement by legislation has been seen time and again. Interest has predominated and the resistless tide of American expansion has moved westward, despite treaties with Indians to the contrary, and despite Spanish and Mexican attempts to stem it. "When one bird flies and goes ahead, commonly more will follow," was the picturesque statement of one of the Indian chiefs in the early days of the Republic in his complaint to the United States Government against American encroachment on the lands of his tribe, in violation of treaty agreements. The tide might be temporarily halted but it found its way around, if not through, the immediate barrier, and moved onward.

After a few more brief remarks for and against the eighth section, the question was taken and the section struck out.[47]

The section providing for the government of Upper Louisiana having been struck out, the way was open for further legislation and discussion on that point; and accordingly the Senate took the matter up on February 3. Jackson opposed the establishment of a civil government in that country because of the proposed plan of the Government to induce the Indians to move across the Mississippi, exchanging their present lands for lands in Upper Louisiana. He maintained that the Indians would already have moved there if the Spaniards had not prevented them. The establishment of a civil government would lead to settlement by whites and, as a result, to expensive and dangerous Indian wars.

Nicholas expressed the hope that Upper Louisiana would not for many years be admitted as a state or states: New Orleans,

---

[47] Plumer, "Memorandum," Thursday, February 2. Cf. John Quincy Adams, *Memoirs*, I, 294, February 2: "The debate on Mr. Anderson's motion was continued this day in Senate until four o'clock. The eighth section was struck out; yeas sixteen, nays nine." For the vote, see *Annals of Congress*, 8 Cong., 1 Sess. (1803–1804), 245.

perhaps, must soon be admitted as such. Jackson then brought
the question to an issue by moving to annex Upper Louisiana to
the Indiana Territory. Breckinridge immediately agreed. Hillhouse, however, pointèd to difficulties in effecting an immediate
change; namely, the difference in governments, laws, customs,
manners, and habits of the countries. Samuel Smith approved
the measure as a means of lessening the number of officers
required and, consequently, the expense; and also because it
would stop slavery there.[48]   Wright agreed to unite the two
territories governmentally but not territorially.   Hillhouse
desired to know how the separate rights of each territory could
be guaranteed.   Who was to legislate for them?   Were they to
be governed by different laws?   Such a union, he thought, would
make one of the territories a mere colony of the other.   Wright
answered part of the query by saying that the territories must
be governed by different laws.   While expressing a willingness
to accord with the majority, John Smith preferred to have a
part of Upper Louisiana annexed to the Mississippi Territory.
While approving, Venable saw a difficulty in the fact that it
was not yet settled that Louisiana was a part of the United
States.   He would not therefore join the two territories together
but would extend the authority of the government of the Indiana
Territory to the territory of Upper Louisiana.[49]

On February 7, the debate on the Louisiana Government Bill
was over the disqualification and exclusion of people of color
from serving on juries.   It was decided to exclude them.[50]

---

[48] By provision of the Ordinance of 1787.

[49] Plumer, ''Memorandum,'' Friday, February 3.   Cf. John Quincy
Adams, *Memoirs*, I, 294, February 3:   ''The debate on Mr. Anderson's
motion was renewed, and General Jackson proposed, by way of substitute,
that the government of Upper Louisiana should be annexed to the Indiana
Territory.   The question was not finally taken, but will doubtless finally
prevail.''

[50] Plumer, ''Memorandum,'' Tuesday, February 7.   Plumer adds,
''Democrats in general voted in favor of exclusion.''   See *Annals of
Congress*, 8 Cong., 1 Sess. (1803–1804), 247–248; John Quincy Adams,
Memoirs, I, 294, February 7.

The same bill was before the Senate the next day and the amendment to annex Upper Louisiana to Indiana was withdrawn. Nicholas then offered an amendment authorizing the officers of the Indiana Territory to govern the Upper District of Louisiana and establishing the existing laws of Louisiana in that district. This was adopted and the act as amended was ordered to be printed. The principles of the bill had been settled by the Democratic senators in caucus on the preceding night, according to Plumer, and they agreed to it in the Senate without debate.[51]

The Senate discussion of the Breckinridge Bill was rapidly drawing to a close. An amendment was offered, February 10, by Anderson, providing for the election of representatives when a certain number (left blank) of free white male inhabitants had been reached. The number of representatives was to increase in proportion to the increase of population; but a limit was to be set. The manner of electing the legislative council by the representatives and the President was also stipulated. Qualifications and terms of office for each body were laid down.[52] The amendment failed, receiving only five votes in its favor.[53]

Three days later, February 13, another attempt at amendment was made. It was proposed to change the fourth section, so as to provide for the laying off of the territory by the governor into twenty-four districts, from each of which the free male householders were annually to elect one person to compose the legislative council. This amendment failed by the narrow margin of one vote, the final count being thirteen yeas to thirteen nays. The bill then passed to the third reading.[54]

---

[51] Plumer, ''Memorandum,'' Wednesday, February 8. Cf. *Annals of Congress*, 8 Cong., 1 Sess. (1803–1804), 248. John Quincy Adams, *Memoirs* of this date have no information on the subject.

[52] *Annals of Congress*, 8 Cong., 1 Sess. (1803–1804), 250–251.

[53] *Ibid.*, 251.

[54] *Ibid.*, 251–252; John Quincy Adams, *Memoirs*, I, 294–295.

While the Senate was busy on the third reading the question of salaries for the officers of the territorial government arose. There was quite a divergence of opinion over the amount to be paid. On the salary of the governor of Orleans Territory, Jackson, Dayton, Samuel Smith and Logan spoke for $8000 per annum, but only seven voted for it. Breckinridge and John Smith favored $6000. Twelve senators voted for this sum. Olcott, Franklin and Cocke argued for $5000, and eighteen votes being cast in favor of it, the motion was carried. The salary of secretary was set at $2000; that of the three judges at $2000 each; district judge, $2000; attorney, $600, and marshall, $200. The members of the legislative council were each to have four dollars per diem while attending the council.[55]

One final attempt to amend the bill with regard to the slave trade was made in a motion to strike out of the tenth section, the words: ''And no slave or slaves shall directly or indirectly, be introduced into said Territory except by a citizen of the United States removing into said Territory for actual settlement, and being at the time of such removal *bona fide* owner of such slave or slaves.'' The amendment failed.[56] Two other proposed amendments to the same section suffered the same fate. The last proposed favored the extension of the prohibition of the importation of slaves into Louisiana ''from any State authorizing the importation of slaves from any foreign port or place.''[57]

This attempted amendment was the cause of a further enunciation of opinion on the slavery question. Stone of North

---

[55] Plumer, ''Memorandum,'' Thursday, February 16. During the course of this debate, Plumer says that Jackson and Samuel Smith observed ''That the people must be governed more by pomp, parade, and shew than by reason—that splendid retinue and armed men are more convincing than arguments.'' Cf. Adams, *Memoirs*, I, 295, February 16, ''In Senate they were engaged in the Louisiana bill.''

[56] *Annals of Congress*, 8 Cong., 1 Sess. (1803–1804), 255.

[57] *Ibid.*

Carolina summed up the position of the slaveholder and his rights in language which might have been quoted verbatim in the majority decision in the Dred Scott case. "Slaves," he held, "are property. The rights of property are by the Constitution guaranteed and why should the holders of this kind of property be prohibited from sending and selling their slaves in Louisiana?" Maclay said that the country was purchased as an *outlet* for the United States, and to admit slaves there would defeat that object. Jackson hinted at disastrous results if South Carolina were prohibited from sending slaves into Louisiana because she imported them from Africa. To put it plainly, South Carolina, if offended, would reject the Twelfth Amendment of the Constitution, then under consideration, and her rejection would prevent its ratification. Jackson also defended the plan of the Administration to exchange lands in Louisiana with the Indians for their lands on the eastern side of the Mississippi. He had been assured by the President that this was a favorite measure of his; furthermore, sixteen of the Cherokee chiefs had already consented to make the exchange.[58]

The Louisiana Government Bill was finally passed on February 18, 1804, with only five votes—those of Adams, Hillhouse, Olcott, Plumer, and Stone, all New Englanders except Stone—against it.[59] The last speech in opposition to the bill was that of John Quincy Adams, who, true to his principles throughout, based his opposition on the ground that a government was being formed for a people without their consent; a principle contrary to republican government in which all power is derived from the people.

The people of that country [Louisiana] have given no power or authority to us to legislate for them. The people of the United States could

---

58 Plumer, "Memorandum," Friday, February 17.

59 *Annals of Congress*, 8 Cong., 1 Sess. (1803–1804), 256. The passage of the bill was reported in the *National Intelligencer, and Washington Advertiser*, February 22, 1804.

give us none, because they had none themselves. The treaty has given us none, because they were not parties to it—it was made without their knowledge. To pass this bill is an encroachment on their rights—it's a commencement of assured power—it's establishing a precedent for after Congresses destructive of the essential principles of genuine liberty.... This bill contains arbitrary principles—principles repugnant to our Constitution. The Legislative Council are to be appointed by the Governor, who is a creature of the President's—not elected by the people.

The judges are to legislate—make laws and expound them—this is the essence of tyranny.

In the other territorial governments, even in the departure from liberty, there is a reverence for it—for it provides that when its inhabitants are increased to a certain number they shall elect a representative.

This bill provides that the officers shall be appointed by the President *alone* in the recess of the Senate—Why this departure from the Constitution.

The Judicial officers are to be appointed for a term of years only, and yet the bill is not limited. The constitutional tenure for judicial officers is *during good behavior.*[60]

The proper procedure in such a case is next laid down by Adams:

The first thing Congress ought to have done in relation to that country, should have been to propose an amendment to the Constitution, to the several States to authorize Congress to receive that Country into the Union. We ought to have applied to the inhabitants of Louisiana to recognize our right to govern them. This we ought to have done, and there is no doubt that the United States and that territory would have given the authority before the next session.

Adams advanced objections to legislating for the territory because of ignorance of conditions there. The bill itself contained certain incongruous articles. The governor's appointing and proroguing the council he branded as tyranny. The people were not ready for trial by jury. The importance of precedent

---

[60] This was not, however, the interpretation adopted later by the Supreme Court. In *American Insurance Co. vs. Canter* (I Peters, 546), it was held that courts in the territory of Florida were legislative courts created by Congress and did not come under the restrictions of the third article of the Constitution. It was not required, therefore, that the judges presiding over those courts should hold office during good behavior.

was not overlooked. "This," he argued, "is a Colonial system
of government. It is the first the United States have established.
It is a bad precedent—the U. S. in time will have many colonies
—precedents are therefore important."[61]

Adams's plea for the republican theory of government was
unavailing as against the doctrine of practical expediency. For
good or ill, the latter policy was adopted, to serve as the precedent, as Adams said it would, on later occasions. So far as
Louisiana was concerned it only remained to see what action the
House of Representatives would take.

---

[61] Plumer, "Memorandum," Saturday, February 18. On this important
speech John Quincy Adams in his *Memoirs*, I, 295, merely states: "I spoke
against it, alone, and was very shortly answered by Mr. Wright, alone.
On the question, the yeas were twenty, the nays five. Messrs. Dayton, Pickering, Tracy, Wells, and White absent. Mr. Stone alone of the major party
voted against the bill, and thus terminates the introductory system for the
government of Louisiana. I have thought it placed upon wrong foundations. It is for time to show the result."

CHAPTER VIII

THE LOUISIANA GOVERNMENT BILL IN THE HOUSE

Closely connected with the problem of a frame of government for Louisiana, bills were introduced in the House for the regulation of affairs in the newly-acquired territory. During the debate on them many novel interpretations of the Constitution were advanced. It was proposed by one of these bills to allow all citizens of the United States and all inhabitants of Louisiana who had been resident there on the thirtieth of April, 1803, on taking an oath of allegiance to the United States, to obtain registry for their vessels. Varnum of Massachusetts, George W. Campbell of Tennessee, Bedinger of Kentucky, Dennis of Maryland, Sloan of New Jersey, and Holland of North Carolina supported this measure, while Nicholson of Maryland, Dana of Connecticut, and Hastings of Massachusetts opposed it. Those favoring the bill cited the rights and privileges guaranteed to the inhabitants of the territory under the third article of the treaty, which included the "enjoyment of their liberty, property and religion." Vessels being property, it was argued, all rights attached to them were guaranteed to all those who were inhabitants at the time of cession, without discrimination. To allow residents of five years standing to register their vessels, while those who had resided in the territory a shorter period were prohibited—a distinction which had been suggested—would be an invasion of rights of the latter. The treaty was the supreme law of the land, and Congress could not violate it. To do so would not only cause· dissatisfaction in the territory but might afford a pretext on the part of the ceding power to obstruct the execution of the treaty.[1]

---

[1] *Annals of Congress*, 8 Cong., 1 Sess. (1803–1804), 977–978.

The opponents of the measure stated that Congress was authorized by the Constitution to fix one uniform rule of naturalization, and that Congress had passed a law requiring five years' residence previous to the naturalization of an alien;[2] furthermore, by the revenue laws of the United States only citizens were permitted to register their vessels.[3] The extension of this privilege to all the inhabitants of Louisiana would be to grant them an unconstitutional preference over the inhabitants of the United States who were not citizens. When the inhabitants of the ceded territory should be admitted into the Union, they would be entitled to all the rights of citizens of the United States; until that time "they must be viewed in the light of colonists, subject to the discretionary government of the United States." It would be unjust to extend privileges to the inhabitants of Louisiana which were denied by law to some of the citizens of the United States. A citizen could not "naturalize" a foreign bottom, yet this measure would permit the people of Louisiana to "naturalize" their ships, which must be considered foreign bottoms. The claim that the right must be granted because of a treaty stipulation, was a reason for the rejection of the motion because, if agreed to, it would establish the principle that the President and Senate in the exercise of the treaty-making power, could make citizens of as many foreigners as they pleased.[4]

To this last statement it was replied that,

the treaty-making power was unquestionably under the constitutional control of Congress, who might, or might not, carry a treaty into effect; but that, after having carried it generally into effect, as had been the case with the Louisiana Convention, it became the supreme law of the land, and a discretion ceased to exist in the Government to fulfil it.

The motion was agreed to by the House by a vote of fifty-five to forty-eight.[5]

---

2 Act approved April 2, 1802; *Laws of U. States*, III, 475–478.

3 Act of December 31, 1792; *Laws of U. States*, II, 313; Act of February 18, 1793, *ibid.*, 332.

4 *Annals of Congress*, 8 Cong., 1 Sess. (1803–1804), 978.

5 *Ibid.*, 979.

On February 20, 1804, a message from the Senate informed the House that the Senate had passed a bill entitled, "An act erecting Louisiana into two Territories, and providing for the temporary government thereof"; to which the concurrence of the House was desired.[6]

On the same day a memorial from the merchants of New Orleans was read begging for relief from the existing state of affairs. They asked for the extension to them of the laws of the United States and for proper documents which would enable them to use their ships. This memorial was referred to the Committee of the Whole.[7] Two days later the House took up the discussion of a bill from the Senate providing for the recording, registering, and enrolling of ships, or vessels in the District of Orleans. By the bill, all who had been inhabitants of Louisiana on the thirtieth of April, 1803, and all citizens of the United States residing therein, were authorized to register their vessels. A motion to strike out the part of the provision extending the right of registry to citizens of the United States was made by Roger Griswold, and caused considerable debate. Those advocating the amendment did not consider it just to extend such a right to citizens of the United States in the ceded territory while the same right was refused to citizens in the Atlantic states. Citizens of Louisiana would be enabled to "naturalize" foreign bottoms which they had purchased and to trade with them in the ports of the United States as well as in those of Louisiana, thus affecting the rights of shipowners who had obtained registers under the existing navigation system. The opponents of the amendment declared that citizens of the United States in general ought to be placed on an equal footing with the inhabitants of Louisiana; otherwise great dissatisfaction would result.[8]

---

[6] *Annals of Congress*, 8 Cong., 1 Sess. (1803–1804), 1038.

[7] *Ibid.*

[8] *Ibid.*, 1044–1046.

The amendment was lost, and the Senate bill was passed on February 23.[9]

The House next proceeded to take up the bill from the Senate making plans for the erection of Louisiana into two territories and providing for their government.[10] The fourth section, which provided for the legislative powers, aroused immediate opposition. Under this section, the legislative powers were to be vested in the governor and thirteen persons of the territory, to be called the legislative council, who were to be appointed annually by the President. Certain qualifications as to residence and the holding of real estate were to be required. The governor, with the advice and consent of the council, was given power to alter, modify or repeal the laws in force at the commencement of this act. The legislative powers were to extend also to all rightful powers of legislation, with the usual restrictions requiring consistency with the Constitution and laws of the United States, and guaranteeing religious freedom. The governor must have the laws published throughout the territory and report them to the President, to be laid before Congress for approval or disapproval. The governor and legislative council were to have no power over the primary disposal of the soil; nor could they tax the lands of the United States, nor interfere with claims to land within the territory. The governor could convene or prorogue the legislative council whenever he should deem it expedient. It was also his duty to keep the President informed of matters pertaining to the inhabitants of the territory.[11]

Leib and Gregg, both from Pennsylvania, were opposed to the power granted to the governor.[12] Varnum of Massachusetts believed that provision ought to be made for the election of a

---

9 *Ibid.,* 1048–1049.

10 For the Senate debate see the preceding chapter.

11 *Annals of Congress,* 8 Cong., 1 Sess. (1803–1804), 1054.

12 *Ibid.,* 1055.

legislative body by the people. Elliott of Vermont thought that the section under consideration was not consistent with the spirit of the Constitution but that a small amendment might make it so.[13] Eustis of Massachusetts declared it to be very difficult to form a system of government for the territory in question, conformable with the ideas of civil liberty under the Constitution. Quoting the third article of the treaty he said that the real difficulty lay in determining whether this article had or had not admitted the people of Louisiana into the Union with all the rights of citizens of the United States. He thought that the people of the territory were unprepared for exercising electoral power, and the first object of the Government would be to protect them in their rights. It was necessary that the Government of the United States should assert its authority until the admission of the territory into the Union admitted the people to the enjoyment of state rights. The government laid down in the bill Eustis considered as a new thing in the United States, but so were the people of the country different from the citizens of the United States. He continued with the statement:

> I am one of those who believe that the principles of civil liberty cannot suddenly be engrafted on a people accustomed to a regimen of a directly opposite hue. The approach of such a people to liberty must be gradual. I believe them at present totally unqualified to exercise it.... I consider them as standing in nearly the same relation to us as if they were a conquered country. By the treaty they are entitled to the enjoyment of all the rights advantages and immunities of citizens of the United States, and to be incorporated into the Union as soon as possible according to the principles of the Federal Constitution—but can they be admitted now? Are they at this minute so admitted? If not, they are not entitled to these rights; but if they were, I should doubt the propriety of extending them to them.[14]

Lucas of Pennsylvania agreed with Eustis,[15] while Lyon of Kentucky thought the people should have at least a certain

---

[13] *Annals of Congress*, 8 Cong., 1 Sess. (1803–1804), 1056.
[14] *Ibid.*, 1057–1059.
[15] *Ibid.*, 1061.

amount of participation in government.[16] Speaker Macon of North Carolina moved that the fourth section be struck out. He was opposed to the establishment of a species of government unknown to the laws of the United States. Macon recognized three descriptions of government in the United States: that of the Union, that of the states, and territorial governments. In his estimation, the territorial government established by the Ordinance of 1787 was the best adapted to the circumstances of the people of Louisiana, and he believed that it could be modified so as best to promote their convenience.[17]

George W. Campbell of Tennessee, bitterly denounced the form of government contemplated. He declared that:

It really establishes a complete despotism, that it does not evince a single trait of liberty; that it does not confer one single right to which they are entitled under the treaty; that it does not extend to them the benefits of the Federal Constitution or declare when, hereafter, they shall receive them. I believe it will, on investigation, be found difficult to separate liberty from the right of self-government, and hence arises the question, now to be decided, whether we shall countenance the principle of government by despotic systems of government, or support the principle that they are entitled to be governed by laws made by themselves, and to expect that they shall, in due time, receive all the benefits of citizens of the United States under the Constitution.

He was opposed to the establishment of a despotic form of government in Louisiana and favored a territorial government similar to that of Mississippi Territory.[18]

Another opponent of the measure was Jackson of Virginia. He held that since the guarantee of incorporation of the inhabitants of Louisiana into the Union could be made under the Constitution, Congress was bound to admit them to the rights guaranteed by the treaty. Both policy and moral obligation dictated the establishment of a system of government different from that contained in this section of the bill. Holland of North

---

[16] *Ibid.*, 1059–1060.

[17] *Ibid.*, 1062.

[18] *Ibid.*, 1063–1067.

Carolina, on the other hand, said the object of the bill was to extend the laws of the United States over Louisiana, not to enable the people of Louisiana to make laws. The people there were not prepared for self-government. Sloan of New Jersey was desirous of allowing the people of Louisiana the elective franchise, which he considered "not only as their inherent and inalienable right, but as a right we are bound to give them to fulfill the treaty of cession." Smilie of Pennsylvania favored giving the people of Louisiana more of a voice in their government, "of bestowing every blessing consistent with the provisions of the Federal Constitution." Boyle of Kentucky was against granting such great powers to the President, for he considered it to be a dangerous precedent. Reverting to history, he compared the American objection to the Declaratory Act of Great Britain with the present bill.[19]

In the face of so general an objection to this section of the bill it was clear that it could not pass. By a vote of eighty to fifteen it was struck out.[20] A substitute was offered by George W. Campbell. This provided that the governor and judges should adopt and publish in the territory such laws of the original states as were suitable to the needs of the territory. They could also make laws, which of course must be submitted to Congress. Such laws, subject to the approval of Congress, were to be in force until the organization of a territorial general assembly, which could alter or repeal them. The governor and judges were to divide the territory into counties in which the governor should appoint the necessary officers. After the organization of the general assembly, the powers and duties of the magistrates and other civil officers were to be regulated and defined by the assembly. During the continuance of the temporary government, all magistrates not otherwise provided for were to be appointed by the governor.

---

19 *Annals of Congress,* 8 Cong., 1 Sess. (1803–1804), 1069–1076.
20 *Ibid.,* 1078.

The general assembly, or legislature, was to consist of a legislative council and a house of representatives, the latter to consist of members chosen from the counties. Only free white males, owners of two hundred acres of land, were eligible to election as representatives, certain residence qualifications being also required. No property qualification was required of voters, nor were the words "white" and "male" used, although perhaps understood. Representatives were to serve for one year. The number of members of the legislative council was left blank. Their term was one year. The governor was to select them from a list submitted by the representatives. The general assembly was to be the law-making body. All laws had to receive the governor's signature. Restrictions of power over the primary disposal of the soil, taxing the lands of the United States, and interference with claims to land, were made.[21]

The fifth section of the Senate bill for the government of Louisiana was the next one to receive attention. This section stipulated that, "The judicial power shall be vested in a superior court, and in such inferior courts, and justices of the peace, as the Legislature of the Territory may, from time to time, establish." All judges and justices were to hold office for the term of four years. The superior court was to consist of three judges, any one of whom should constitute a court. They were to have jurisdiction in all criminal cases, and exclusive jurisdiction in capital ones; and original and appellate jurisdiction in all civil cases of the value of one hundred dollars. An important clause read: "In all criminal prosecutions which are capital, the trial shall be by jury of twelve good and lawful men of the vicinage; and in all cases criminal and civil, in the superior court, trial shall be by a jury, if either of the parties require it." Then follows another provision important in its bearing on territorial government and the power of Congress thereover. Once more

---

[21] *Ibid.*, 1078–1079. For further action on this section, see below.

assuming that all rights and privileges must be legislated into the territories and that no part of the Constitution, by the mere act of acquisition, took effect in the territory, the section provided that:

> The inhabitants of the said Territory shall be entitled to the benefits of the writ of *habeas corpus;* they shall be bailable, unless for capital offences, where the proof shall be evident or the presumption great; and no cruel and unusual punishments be inflicted.[22]

George W. Campbell moved to strike out the clause containing a restriction of the rights of jury trial to capital cases and to insert "the trial shall be by jury, and in all civil cases above the value of twenty dollars." He claimed that in legislating for Louisiana, Congress was bound by the Constitution and did not have the right to establish courts in that territory on any other terms than it could in any of the states. "Whenever courts were established in a Territory, they must be considered as courts of the United States."[23] After quoting the Constitution on the right of jury trial, Campbell concluded with the remark that the bill did not secure that right as contemplated by that instrument.[24]

The motion was lost. The report for the rest of the debate is not given because at this juncture the reporter left to attend the trial of impeachment of Judge Pickering in the Senate.[25] However, it is noted that Campbell offered a new section of the

---

[22] *Annals of Congress*, 8 Cong., 1 Sess. (1803–1804), 1128–1129.

[23] Compare Marshall's decision in *American Insurance Co. vs. Canter*, I Peters, 546, where territorial courts are considered not as constitutional but as legislative courts, created in virtue of the right of sovereignty existing in the Government, or in virtue of the power granted to Congress to make all needful rules and regulations respecting the territory of the United States. A distinction between state and territorial courts was here recognized.

[24] *Annals of Congress*, 8 Cong., 1 Sess. (1803–1804), 1129. Cf. *Callan vs. Wilson*, 127 U. S. 540; *Hawaii vs. Mankichi*, 190 U. S. 197; *Dorr vs. U. S.*, 195 U. S. 138; J. W. Garner, "The Right of Jury Trial in the Dependencies," in *American Law Review*, XL, 340–355.

[25] *Annals of Congress*, 8 Cong., 1 Sess. (1803–1804), 1129.

bill providing for the election of a legislature by the people of Louisiana instead of a council appointed by the President as provided for in the Senate bill. This amendment suffered the same fate as his previous one.[26]

The Senate bill which had reached the House on February 20, was discussed at intervals through the early weeks of March.[27] Various were the interpretations as to the extent of the power of Congress to legislate for the territories. For instance, Leib of Pennsylvania moved an amendment extending to the inhabitants of Louisiana the Naturalization Act of the United States.[28] Such extension was opposed by Roger Griswold, who deemed it inexpedient to vest the courts of Louisiana with the power of naturalization. Joseph Clay of Pennsylvania supported the amendment on the ground that it extended to the inhabitants of the territory the privileges promised them by the treaty. However, a residence of five years would be required, since the privileges promised were to be received under the Constitution. There was a wide difference, he declared, between naturalizing the inhabitants of Louisiana, and admitting them into the Union. The amendment failed to pass.[29]

On March 14, Sloan of New Jersey introduced an amendment to prohibit the admission of slaves into Louisiana, both from the United States and from foreign parts. No detailed report on this question is given, the record containing the bare state-

---

[26] *Ibid.*, 1130.

[27] These difficulties were expressed by Manasseh Cutler in a letter to the Rev. Dr. Dana, March 3, 1804. ''The Democrats of both Houses are much perplexed about establishing a system of government in Louisiana. A bill has long been before the Senate, and has at length come to the House. It has been repeatedly taken up and as often laid down, without making any progress.'' Governor Claiborne's letter stating the difficulties of forming a government on the principles of the Constitution is referred to. ''His sentiments and opinions have extremely embarrassed our worshipers of the idol of Democracy, and what is to be done in this case is difficult to conjecture.'' Cutler and Cutler, *Life, Journals and Correspondence of Rev. Manasseh Cutler*, II, 165–166.

[28] Act of April 14, 1802, *Laws of U. States*, III, 475–478.

[29] *Annals of Congress*, 8 Cong., 1 Sess. (1803–1804), 1185–1186.

ment that "Mr. S. concisely stated his reasons in favor of this provision, when the question was taken, and the amendment agreed to—ayes 40, noes 36."[30]

The fourth section of the bill was again taken up on March 14, when Early of Georgia moved a substitute for this section.[31] On the next day Early's substitute was agreed to. The House then voted to strike out the fourth section of the original bill and insert the new section. By it, the legislative power was to be vested in the governor and thirteen persons of the territory, to be called the legislative council. Members of the council were to be appointed by the President of the United States from holders of real estate, resident at least one year in the territory and holding no office of profit under the territory, or the United States. Their term of service was set at one year. The territory was to be divided into convenient counties by the legislative council. After the first year members of the legislative council were to be chosen annually by persons qualified to vote. Those entitled to vote were: (1) Free white male persons twenty-one years of age, resident in the territory on April 30, 1803, and resident therein one whole year next before election, provided they could produce satisfactory proof that they had taken an oath of allegiance to the United States, agreeably to the Naturalization Act of April 4, 1802; (2) citizens of the United States, who had become residents in the territory since April 30, or who should thereafter become residents, or who had resided there a year, six months of which previous to the election must be in the district or county voted in.

The legislative council was to make all necessary regulations concerning elections. If no one should be elected, the governor and council were to appoint a person to serve for the district. The governor, with the consent of the legislative council, could

---

[30] *Ibid.* The lack of information on this particular topic in the House renders all the more valuable Plumer's report of the Senate debate on the slave question.

[31] *Annals of Congress*, 8 Cong., 1 Sess. (1803–1804), 1188.

alter, modify or repeal the laws in force at the commencement of the act. Their legislative powers were to extend to all rightful objects of legislation, restricted only by conformity with the Constitution of the United States and the prohibition of interference with the religious freedom of the inhabitants. The governor was to publish the laws throughout the territory and also to report them to the President to be laid before Congress. Restrictions of legislation over the primary disposal of soil, taxing of lands of the United States, and interference of claims to land were made. The governor could convene or prorogue the legislative council whenever he deemed it expedient. It was also to be his duty to inform the President as to the customs, habits, and dispositions of the inhabitants of the territory.[32]

Certain minor changes in the bill led to conferences between managers appointed by the Senate and the House for this purpose[33] and the bill was finally passed. It was limited in duration to one year from October 1 following and thence to the end of the next session of Congress. The President was to appoint a governor, to hold office for four years, an annual legislative council, composed of inhabitants of Louisiana, and judges. The principle introduced by the Senate, of withholding for the present the right of suffrage from the people of Louisiana prevailed, subject to the time limitation introduced in the bill by the House of Representatives.[34]

Whether the differences of opinion in Congress over Louisiana could be sufficiently harmonized to allow the establishment of a more permanent form of government for that territory was a question in which Jefferson professed interest. He expressed his fear that because of these differences the present government would be continued another year, but hoped this would not be

---

32 *Ibid.*, 1191–1193.
33 *Ibid.*, 1206, 1208, 1229, 1230.
34 *Ibid.*, 1230.

the case; and that a government would be established in Louisiana capable of meeting its own emergencies.[35]

While the Breckinridge Bill was still under discussion in the House, Nahum Mitchell of Massachusetts wrote an interesting letter to Edward H. Robbins, in which he reviewed the whole Louisiana question, and, incidentally, looked into the future with more or less prophetic insight. Although possessing a great deal of printed information respecting Louisiana, Mitchell said he had little knowledge as to the disposition of the lands. He had heard that Spain, previous to putting Louisiana into the hands of France, had made grants of most of the valuable parts to individuals and companies. Whether this should prove to be the case or not, Mitchell believed the intention of the Adminitration was to take no measures for the immediate settlement of the country. On this matter, however, there was a difference of opinion. One group, whom Mitchell considered visionary, hoped to induce the Indians on the eastern side of the Mississippi to exchange their land for lands across the river; and to persuade the white inhabitants on the western side to cross to the eastern. Mitchell said this plan would fail because the whites would not move back.[36]

Another scheme, according to Mitchell, was to send all the negro slaves from the southern states into Louisiana, as soon as practicable. Again, Mitchell considered the plan visionary, for he was persuaded that the New England states would sooner become black than the southern states white; in other words, that slavery would rather increase and extend itself all over the Union, than be diminished and limited, much less extinguished. He expressed surprise at the zeal with which the right to hold slaves was guarded in the South. Slaves were increasing in numbers faster than the whites. Then, too, South Carolina was

---

[35] Jefferson to William Dunbar, March 13, 1804, in Jefferson, *Writings* (Memorial ed.), XI, 23.

[36] See the correspondence between Jefferson and Breckinridge, above.

importing slaves, and many more were imported surreptitiously against the law in other parts of the Union. Petitions from the western part of the country for the admission of slaves served, in Mitchell's opinion, to show the disposition of the people.

Land jobbers and speculators on the eastern side of the Mississippi were in favor of preventing the settlement and sale of lands in Louisiana for the present. Jackson, of Georgia, whom Mitchell considered as an index to the intentions of the party in power, said it would be ruinous to the southern states to open the sale of lands of that country and it must not be done.[37] Mitchell did not doubt that it would be postponed for the present. Many of the politicians of the South also opposed the settlement of Louisiana, fearing it would draw off inhabitants of their states. Many others, on the other hand, were anxious for an immediate settlement, because of the opportunity for speculation. Mitchell thought the purchase a foolish and unconstitutional bargain, which instead of a source of revenue would become a drain on the population and money of the Union; and would create no end of trouble.

Mitchell then turned to another ·phase of the question in which he showed much keener immediate insight than many of his friends. He stated it as his sincere belief that the purchase would have a beneficial influence on the "Eastern and Northern States." On this point he wrote:

The Western section of this Union have hitherto been altogether under the controul of Virginia and the Carolinas, because to them they looked for aid and protection, while they were the frontier of the U. States. Now while they are no longer a frontier people and all fears for their security, which is the first object, are at an end, they will no longer consider their neighbours as their natural protectors; and will be left in future to attend to their private interest and prosperity. In viewing them in this situation we shall see that their trade and intercourse will be altogether with the commercial states. They are dependent on their neighbours for no single article of life, and whatever they may receive of them will be through the hands of merchants and the navigation of the Mississippi, Ohio, and other

[37] Compare Jackson's speeches in the Senate on the Breckinridge Bill, Chapter VII.

rivers leading into it. This will render them more acquainted with the Eastern States. Besides they are the natural competitors and rivals of the Southern States in the market. While I am penning this sentence I overhear several members talking of a Northern and Western coalition. This language is already in vogue, and whether there will be any weight in my observations on this subject, you can judge better than I.[38]

The importance of a "Northern and Western coalition" cer-tainly came to be recognized and was to play a great political rôle in the years following the War of 1812 when New England and western interests were linked together on the platform of protection and internal improvements.

The form of government for Louisiana established by the law of March 26, 1804, did not escape the attacks of Jefferson's critics. The *New England Repertory* declared the source of that government novel in the political progress of the United States, because not one of the people to be governed would have a voice in the government. It was a despotism, with the President of the United States as the fountain of all power. "Louisiana is a part of the empire of the United States or it is not. If it is not, we have nothing to do with it. If it is, the establishment of a monarchy over a large country appertaining to the United States, is a gross violation of the spirit of the Constitution."[39]

The *New York Herald* stated that a perusal of the sketch of the debates in Congress would show that the "friends to the equal rights of man" were considerably hampered by the diffi-culties presented in the Breckinridge Bill. The proposal of the President "to erect a government about as despotic as that of Turkey in Asia," had the approval of his friends, but they were afraid of consequences; while the *Herald* said they might well be, "unless they can contrive to silence all the presses in the nation."[40]

---

[38] Nahum Mitchell to Edw. H. Robbins, Washington, March 12, 1804, in *Robbins Papers, 1800–1838,* VII.

[39] *New England Repertory,* Tuesday, March 6, 1804. Copied in *Thomas's Massachusetts Spy, or Worcester Gazette,* Wednesday, March 14.

[40] *New York Herald,* Wednesday, March 7, 1804.

CHAPTER IX

PROBLEMS OF TERRITORIAL GOVERNMENT

The inhabitants of Louisiana had expected a more liberal form of government and were greatly disappointed in the one provided. The report of the passage of a law by the Senate prohibiting the importation of foreign slaves into Louisiana caused great agitation, according to Governor Claiborne. The people considered it a serious blow at the commercial and agricultural interests of the province. Importation of slaves into South Carolina served to increase discontent. The people generally could not be made to understand the present power of the state authorities with regard to the importation of such persons. Many thought Congress connived at this.[1] A mass meeting was held to protest to Congress on the question of the slave trade, commercial restrictions, and government in general, and a committee was appointed to draw up a memorial.[2]

Prohibition of the importation of foreign slaves was a grievance which was raised continually, and will be referred to again.

Whether the governor's voice was final in judicial matters in the new territory was a question Jefferson was called upon to answer. Under the Spanish Government the Louisianians had been allowed an appeal from their governor to the governor general in Cuba. Such an appeal from a decision of Governor Claiborne came to the President. Jefferson did not believe that Congress when it authorized him to give any person all the power of the officers of the "then existing government," had intended to include the governor general of Cuba or the King of Spain. After asking the advice of Attorney General Levi

---

[1] Claiborne to Madison, March 10, 1804, in *Claiborne Papers*, "Claiborne's Correspondence relative to Louisiana," I.

[2] Claiborne to Madison, March 16, 1804, *ibid.*

Lincoln on this point,[3] Jefferson informed Claiborne that it was an error to presume that there was an appeal to the President. No authority had yet been created paramount to that of the governor. Such being the case, Jefferson remanded such matters to Claiborne for a second consideration, the remanding "to be considered as a measure of course, and not conveying in the slightest degree an opinion or even a suspicion that there is or is not error in the first proceedings."[4]

The course of territorial government did not run as smoothly as might have been desired by those in authority. The correspondence which passed between Governor Claiborne and the President and Secretary of State in Washington is filled with various opinions and recommendations. After the passage of the Breckinridge Bill, Jefferson asked Claiborne to communicate to him the names of the men best fitted to be appointed members of the legislative council. Jefferson thought a mere majority of them ought to be Americans and the rest French or Spanish.[5] Desirous of placating the native inhabitants though he might be, Jefferson nevertheless wanted to keep the control in American hands.

Claiborne kept the federal authorities well informed on conditions in the territory under his control, at least so far as frequent letters could do it. The extension of registry to vessels owned by Louisianians gave general satisfaction and removed one cause of discontent. The prohibition of the importation of foreign slaves was still viewed by the citizens as a great grievance,[6] yet quiet prevailed and Claiborne expressed the opinion

---

[3] Jefferson to the Atty. Genl., March 14, [18]04, in *Jefferson Papers,* "Letters from Jefferson, 1st Series, 1802–1803," IX, (39).

[4] Jefferson to Governor Claiborne, March 18, [18]04, in *ibid.,* (44). Quoted in part in J. F. H. Claiborne, *Mississippi as a Province, Territory and State,* I, 251–252.

[5] Jefferson to Governor Claiborne, April 17, 1804, in *Jefferson Papers,* "Letters from Jefferson, 1st Series," IX, (67).

[6] Claiborne to Jefferson, April 15, 1804, in *Jefferson Papers,* "Letters received at Washington, 2d Series," XIX, (3).

that unless the natives of the United States should excite discontent, the Louisianians would become well pleased with the temporary government.[7]

Only four days after the writing of this letter the Mayor of New Orleans, Étienne de Boré, resigned. The municipal body, composed of a mayor, a council of twelve, and a clerk, which had been established by Laussat in place of the abolished cabildo, had been carried over under the government of the United States. Boré, in an address to the council, May 16, 1804, asked that a formal protest be made against the form of government on the ground that it annihilated the rights of the Louisianians. He held it to be a departure from the principles of American government and an infringement of the natural rights of the people of the territory and of the third article of the treaty of cession. The council declining to make such a protest because it believed this to be the province of the people at large and not the municipal council, Boré resigned.[8]

Other evidences of discontent led Claiborne to write that as soon as the state of society would permit, he "would like to see the representative system in its fullest latitude extended to this territory." However, he thought Congress had been wise in not immediately conferring the privilege of self-government on the people, as this would probably have proved a misfortune to Louisiana. The natives of Louisiana he considered a pacific, amiable people. Adventurers from outside were the ones who caused trouble among a credulous people.[9] Who some of these "adventurers" were Claiborne also informed Madison. Among the most distinguished and active of those who disapproved of the measures of the Government in relation to Louisiana was

---

[7] Claiborne to Madison, May 12, 1804, in *Madison Papers*, XXVI, "Writings to Madison, Nov. 6, 1803–Aug. 21, 1804."

[8] Fortier, *History of Louisiana*, III, 14–15.

[9] Claiborne to Jefferson, May 29, 1804, in *Jefferson Papers*, "Letters received at Washington, 2d Series," XIX, (7).

Edward Livingston.[10]   Another of the discontents was Daniel
Clark, whom Claiborne considered disgruntled because he had
expected a greater reward for his services than he received.[11]

Livingston busied himself with a draft of a memorial to
Congress protesting against the government of Louisiana.   He
took the stand that, under the treaty, Louisiana was entitled to
immediate admission into the Union as a state.   Claiborne suspected Livingston of ulterior motives because it seemed to him
impossible ''that a man of reflection, can suppose the people of
Louisiana at this time, prepared for a complete Representative
System.''[12]   Claiborne did favor, however, the introduction of
representative government as soon as possible.   He expressed a
desire to see the legislative council elected by the people.[13]

The troublesome third article of the treaty on which the
Louisianians were to base their grounds for complaint in their
memorial to Congress, needed interpretation from other stand-
points.   One of these led to a further enunciation by Jefferson
of the meaning of the article.   Among other claims under it were
those of a monopoly of Indian commerce.[14]   Jefferson considered
the third article to have been worded with ''remarkable caution''

---

[10] Livingston had moved to New Orleans in 1804 and was destined to
play an important part in the history of the state of Louisiana.   Aside from
his connection with the famous Batture Case he was the author of a legal
code for Louisiana, acted as its representative in Congress in the Eighteenth,
Nineteenth and Twentieth Congresses, and served as United States senator
from Louisiana from December 7, 1829, until his resignation, May 24, 1831.
Livingston was secretary of state from May 24, 1831, to May 29, 1833,
under President Jackson, and Minister Plenipotentiary to France May 29
to April, 1835.   He died May 23, 1836.

[11] Claiborne to Madison, June 3, 1804 (Private), in *Madison Papers*,
''Writings to Madison,'' XXVI.   Clark was an old resident of Louisiana,
having been a subject of Spain there previous to the American occupation.
Jefferson had appealed to him for information concerning the territory.
Jefferson to Clark, July 17, 1803, in Jefferson, *Writings* (Memorial ed.), X,
406–407.   Clark was selected as delegate from the territory of Orleans to
the Ninth Congress.

[12] Claiborne to Madison, June 29, 1804 (Private and confidential), in
Madison Papers, ''Writings to Madison,'' XXVI.

[13] Claiborne to Jefferson, July 1, 1804, in *Jefferson Papers*, ''Letters
received at Washington, 2d Series,'' XIX, (10).

[14] The reclamations of Girod & Chote against the claims of Bastrop.

on the part of the American negotiators.   The people of Louis
iana according to him,

> shall continue under the protection of the treaty, until the principles of our
> constitution shall be extended to them, when the protection of the treaty
> is to cease, and that of our own principles to take its place. But as this
> could not be done at once, it has been provided to be as soon as our rules
> will admit. Accordingly Congress has begun by extending about 20 par-
> ticular laws by their titles, to Louisiana. Among these is the act concern-
> ing intercourse with the Indians, which establishes a system of commerce
> with them admitting no monopoly. That class of rights therefore are now
> taken from under the treaty & placed under the principles of our laws.[15]

That definite acts of legislation were necessary to bring about
a change in the laws of the territory acquired was emphasized
in another letter of Jefferson's at a later date, when he wrote:
"Louis XIV having established the Constumes de Paris as the
law of Louisiana, this was not changed by the mere act of transfer; on the contrary, the laws of France continued and continues
to be the law of the land, except where specially altered by some
subsequent edict of Spain or act of Congress."[16]

The doubt which existed in the minds of the government
officials over the real status of the Louisianians found vent in
hostile newspaper comment of which the following is typical:

> Mr. Jefferson gave us first to expect they were immediately to be in-
> ducted to the blessings of *self-government*, and were to be made citizens,
> as soon as convenient, implying a short time. Vice Roy Claiborne talked to
> them sometime as citizens, sometimes as aliens; but in his official letter,
> gave Government to understand that the people we had been buying must
> be *subjects*, (not citizens) for fifty years to come. But in a Baltimore
> paper we are again bewildered by the following toast—'the people of Louis-
> iana—no longer subjects but citizens.' "[17]

Claiborne's appointment as governor of Louisiana was a
temporary one. He, himself, thought that the office would be

---

[15] Jefferson to Secretary of State Madison, July 14, [18]04, in Jefferson,
Writings (Ford, ed.), VIII, 313.

[16] Jefferson to the Secretary of State, May 19, 1808, in Jefferson, *Writings* (Memorial ed.), XII, 58–59.

[17] The *Repertory* (Boston), Tuesday, May 29, 1804.

bestowed later on someone else. A report that Monroe would probably be the permanent governor of Orleans Territory reached Claiborne and he expressed his belief that this would be very pleasing to the Louisianians.[18] Monroe was offered the position but declined.[19]

In sending to Claiborne his commission as governor of Orleans Territory, Jefferson stated frankly that the office was "originally destined for a person (LaFayette) whose great services and established fame would have rendered him peculiarly acceptable to the nation at large. Circumstances however exist which do not now permit his nomination, & perhaps may not at any time hereafter."[20] Claiborne acknowledged receipt of his commission, October 3, 1804.[21] John Quincy Adams expected that some opposition would be made to the reappointment of Claiborne but when the vote was taken in the Senate only one voice answered in the negative.[22]

---

[18] Claiborne to Madison, June 9, 1804, in *Claiborne Papers*, "Claiborne's Correspondence relative to Louisiana," II.

[19] Jefferson, *Writings* (Ford, ed.), VIII, 288, 290; IX, 37. Monroe, *Writings* (Hamilton, ed.), IV, 153, 156, 477–478; V, 109–111.

Andrew Jackson hoped that he might be appointed to this position. His ambitions in this respect are revealed in a letter to his friend Representative G. W. Campbell, April 28, 1804. This letter is printed in full in James Parton, *Life of Andrew Jackson*, I, 237–238. It is mentioned in Parton, *Life of Thomas Jefferson*, 656.

[20] Jefferson to Claiborne, August, 30, 1804, in *Jefferson Papers*, "Letters from Jefferson, 1st Series," IX, (153). J. F. H. Claiborne, *Mississippi as a Province, Territory and State*, I, 251. In his "Memorandum of the Eighth Congress," under date of December 10, 1804, Plumer wrote: "The fact was I did not then know it—president originally intend the Marquis La Fayette for that office."

Although wishing to appoint Lafayette to the governorship, Jefferson, according to Parton, "demed it best not to gratify a sentiment by an act which might be construed as a reflection upon the seller [Napoleon]." James Parton, *Life of Thomas Jefferson*, 656.

[21] Claiborne to Madison, October 3, 1804, in *Claiborne Papers*, "Claiborne's Correspodence relative to Louisiana," II.

[22] John Quincy Adams, *Memoirs*, I, 321. December 12. 1804. John Randolph referred to Claiborne as a *"pompous nothing."* News of complaint from Louisiana called from Randolph the expression of a wish to send some thousands of troops into that territory "who can speak a language perfectly intelligible to the people of Louisiana, whatever that of their Governor may be." Henry Adams, *John Randolph*, 117–118.

Attacks on Governor Claiborne and the administration of his power became so bitter that he felt it necessary to send a lengthy refutation and explanation to Madison. One political pamphlet in particular,[23] seemed to demand an answer. Admitting that some of the statements made against him were true, Claiborne said others were not. For instance, it was untrue that Americans held all the lucrative positions under the temporary government; many were held by native Louisianians. After a defense of his government, he declared that the third article of the treaty rendered changes in the old system necessary to prepare the people for statehood. He said he was forced by conditions to assume great judicial powers against his own wishes.[24]

Meanwhile the memorial to Congress had been put in circulation. Claiborne, after seeing one sheet of the original, stated that it was in the handwriting of Edward Livingston. He did not doubt that all of it had been written by Livingston, with the aid of Daniel Clark and Evan Jones.[25]

If Claiborne's information was correct, there were not many people present at the meeting held for the drawing up of the memorial. It was afterwards carried through the territory and many signed without reading it, while others did so with no understanding of its contents. The names of others were affixed without their seeing it. Louisianians, continued Claiborne, had never before been called upon to sign a political paper. Some thought their grievances were real, others were made to think so.

---

[23] *Esquisse de la situation politique et civile de la Louisiane, depuis le 30 Novembre 1803 jusqu' au 1er Octobre 1804. Par un Louisianais à la Nouvelle-Orleans.* This pamphlet was translated into English.

[24] Claiborne to Madison, October 16, 1804, in *Claiborne Papers,* ''Claiborne's Correspondence relative to Louisiana,'' II; Robertson, *Louisiana under the Rule of Spain, France, and the United States,* II, 268–278.

[25] Claiborne to Madison, July 13, 1804 (Private), in *Madison Papers,* ''Writings to Madison,'' XXVI; also Claiborne to Madison, July 26, 1804, in *Claiborne Papers,* ''Claiborne's Correspondence relative to Louisiana,'' II, wherein Claiborne enclosed a paper containing a copy of the memorial, and added that Livingston acknowledged being the author.

Few were really interested in the fate of the memorial, except as it related to the African slave trade. He did not expect any disturbance if the petition were denied.[26]

Despite their anxiety over the question of the African slave trade, it cannot be said that the political situation of the inhabitants of Louisiana was altogether lost sight of. For instance, "Fellow Citizen" opposed the interpretation of the words "as soon as possible" to mean never or a time so indefinite that it might never arrive. He declared that the government was more oppressive than that which the United States had spurned in 1776, and asked the citizens to unite in a respectful demand upon the Government of the United States for those privileges to which they were entitled by nature and compact.[27]

A committee which met in New Orleans, August 9, 1804, adopted a report laying before the citizens of Louisiana the address which the United States in Congress assembled sent to Canada, October 26, 1774; and asking the citizens what relation there was between the present situation of the inhabitants of Louisiana and that of Canada at the time when Congress put the Canadians in mind of their rights and privileges, which the agents of England would not allow them. The report bore the signatures of Boré, president, and Robelot, secretary of the committee.[28]

Interspersed among general criticisms of the system of government were personal attacks on the governor. The latter led to a defense of Claiborne by James Workman who wrote under the nom de plume of "Laelius." In answering charges brought against Claiborne, "Laelius" admitted that it was to be re-

---

[26] Claiborne to Jefferson, October 27, 1804, in *Jefferson Papers,* "Letters received at Washington, 2d Series," XIX, (14). Also, Claiborne to Madison, November 5, 1804 (Private), in *Madison Papers,* "Writings to Madison," XXVI.

[27] *Louisiana Gazette,* August 7, 1804.

[28] *Ibid.,* August 14, 1804.

gretted that Congress had not immediately established some temporary legislative and judicial authorities, composed of the best informed men who could have been secured. Claiborne, however, had no power to bring this about, so could not be blamed.[29]

This called forth a lengthy reply in which all the complaints against the governor and the government were reiterated.[30]

The memorial to Congress having been duly circulated and signed, three agents were selected to bear it to Congress. They were Messrs. Pierre Derbigny, Jean Noel Destréhan and Pierre Sauvé, all natives of France. Derbigny, Claiborne described as "a man of good information, and I believe of strict integrity; pleased with the principles of our Government but much attached to his native country." Destréhan, he characterized as "a Frenchman in politics and affection," "one of the tools of M. Laussat and greatly mortified at the cession of Louisiana to the United States." He would endeavor to be the most prominent man in the mission. Sauvé was "an able good man, a wealthy planter universally esteemed by his neighbors and will be a good citizen under our Government; but I fear he will take little part in the agency." All were warm advocates of the slave trade.[31]

---

[29] *Ibid.*, November 9, 1804.

[30] *Ibid.*, January 11, 15, 22, 29, 1805. We are indebted to Isaac Briggs for information concerning the alignment of forces in this newspaper war. Claiborne's chief opponents were Livingston, I. B. Prevost, and Daniel Clark, who appeared under various signatures, principally, "An Inhabitant," and "Public Accuser." The friends of the governor were Lewis Kerr under the signature of "Curtius" and "Projector," and James Workman as "Laelius." Isaac Briggs to Jefferson, February 9, 1805, in *Jefferson Papers*, "Letters received at Washington, 2nd Series," IX, (18).

Briggs had been appointed surveyor of lands south of Tennessee by Jefferson, who characterized him as "a Quaker, a sound republican and of a pure and unspotted character," highly qualified for his new task. Jefferson to Claiborne, May 24, 1803, in Jefferson, *Writings* (Memorial ed.), X, 394–395.

[31] Claiborne to Madison, July 13, 1804 (Private), in *Madison Papers*, "Writings to Madison," XXVI.

An interesting picture of the memorialists in Washington is given by Senator Plumer, who with Pickering and others entertained them at dinner. He describes them as all Frenchmen, of whom Derbigny and Sauvé could speak English fluently, gentlemen of respectability, men of talents, literature and general information, men of business, and well acquainted with the world. They had little of "French frippery" about them and resembled New Englanders more than Virginians. Sauvé had one hundred and fifty acres of sugar cane, and Destréhan two hundred. The latter claimed that it would take sixty negroes to manage his crop. He stated that his ground generally produced on the average by the acre one hogshead of sugar weighing twelve hundred pounds and a hogshead of molasses.

The memorialists complained of the government which Congress had established over them at the last session. Plumer continues:

They say nothing will satisfy that people but an elective government. That under the Spanish government they paid only six per cent duty upon their imports & exports; & the whole charge of their religion & government was then supported by the Crown. That the duties they now paid are greater than what they then paid—& are themselves beside obliged to support their religion & internal government. So that they now pay more money for public uses than when they were subjects of a royal government, & enjoy less real liberty. That Claiborne, the present governor, is unable to speak a word of French, the language that is most generally used in that country. That the proceedings in the courts of law are in a language that most of the people do not understand—That they have in many instances been convicted of breaches of laws of the existence of which they were ignorant. That Claiborne is incompetent to discharge the duties of Government.

That the President had selected some very respectable men whom he has appointed members of the legislative Council. That out of these all except three have positively declined the appointments. That no man who wishes to enjoy the friendship & esteem of the people of that country can accept of an office under the existing system of government.

They say that they have visited Mr. Jefferson—that he has not made any enquiries of them relative either to their government, or the civil or natural history of their country—That he studiously avoided conversing with them upon every subject that had relation to their mission here.

They say that the city of New Orleans is situated on the banks of the Mississippi—that those banks are from one hundred to 120 feet deep—And that a considerable part of the city is in danger of being undermined by the stream—the land being sandy—That it will require immense expence to secure the town—that they must either sink rafts covered with the rocks on the bank next to the city, or cut down the bank on the opposite side of the river, That the country around the city & for a very considerable distance up the river is very good land for the width, on an average, of three quarters of a mile from the river—that beyond that distance from the river much of the land is a sunken swamp. That there is in the Country a considerable of good upland.[32]

The memorial was presented to the Senate, December 31, 1804, by Giles of Virginia. After an examination of the form of government laid down for the territory of Orleans, which showed that the people in the territory had no voice in their government, the memorial proceeded to state more specific grievances, using language which must have had a decidedly familiar sound for those who remembered the statement of grievances of the American colonists against the British Government. Objections were made to a governor whom the people had not chosen, and who might be ignorant of the language and institutions of the people. This government was vested with all executive and almost unlimited legislative authority, because of the power of the executive in the choice of members of the council and his authority to prorogue them freely. The memorial continued:

Taxation without representation, an obligation to obey laws without any voice in their formation, the undue influence of the executive upon legislative proceedings, and a dependent judiciary, formed, we believe, very important articles in the list of grievances complained of by the United States, at the commencement of their glorious contest for freedom; the opposition to them, even by force, was deemed meritorious and patriotic,

[32] Plumer, ''Memorandum,'' Saturday, December 15, 1804. Publication of Plumer's account at so great length seems justified because of the amount of information it contains, and because it has never before appeared in print. See my article on ''The Louisiana Memorialists to Congress, 1804,'' in the *Louisiana Historical Quarterly*, I, 99–102.

and the rights on which that opposition was founded were termed fundamental, indefeasible, self-evident, and eternal; they formed as your country
then unanimously asserted, the only rational basis on which Government
could rest; they were so plain, it was added, as to be understood by the
weakest understanding; not capable of alienation, they might always be
reclaimed; unsusceptible of change, they were the same at all times, in
all climates, and under all circumstances; and the fairest inheritance for
our posterity, they should never, it was firmly asserted ... be abandoned but
with life. ... Are truths, then, so well founded, so universally acknowledged,
inapplicable only to us? Do political axioms on the Atlantic become problems when transferred to the shores of the Mississippi?

Referring to the third article of the treaty, the memorialists
interpreted it to mean that there should be no longer delay in
the incorporation of the inhabitants into the Union than was
required to pass the necessary laws and ascertain the representation to which they were entitled. The government act under
fire did not satisfy the requirement of this provision of the
treaty. On this point the memorial ran:

A Territory governed in the manner it directs may be a province of the
United States, but can by no construction be said to be incorporated into
the Union. To be incorporated into the Union must mean to form a component part of it; but to every component part of the United States the
constitution has guaranteed a republican form of Government, and this
... has no one principle of republicanism in its composition; it is therefore
not a compliance with the letter of the treaty, and is totally inconsistent
with its spirit, which certainly intends some stipulations in our favor. For
if Congress may govern us as they please, how are we benefitted by its
introduction? If any doubt, however, could possibly arise on the first
member of the sentence, it must now vanish by a consideration of the
second, which provides for their admission to the rights, privileges, and
immunities of citizens of the United States. But this Government ... is
totally incompatible with those rights. Without any vote in the election
of our Legislature, without any check upon our executive, without any one
incident of self government, what valuable 'privilege' of citizenship is
allowed us, what 'right' do we enjoy, of what 'immunity' can we boast,
except, indeed, the degrading exemption from the cares of legislation, and
the burden of public affairs. ...[33]

[33] *American State Papers, Miscellaneous*, I, 396–398; *Annals of Congress*,
8 Cong., 2 Sess. (1804–1805), Appendix, 1597–1606.

In the next part of the memorial, that dealing with the prohibition of the slave trade, a clear demand was made for the very thing which at a later date was called "popular sovereignty." Reference was made to the fact that while the African trade was absolutely prohibited in the new territory, it was free to the Atlantic states and as far as related to procuring slaves from other states, it was permitted even in the Territory of Mississippi. "We only ask," ran the memorial, "the right of deciding it ourselves, and of being placed in this respect on an equal footing with other States." Slave labor was declared to be peculiarly necessary for the species of cultivation carried on and for the repair of the levees, the heat and moisture being intolerable to whites. The prohibition of the slave traffic would mean the cessation of cultivation.[34]

A similar remonstrance against the form of government established in the territory was communicated to the House of Representatives, January 4, 1805. One of the grievances cited was that of the division of Louisiana into two parts, because without the division there would be sufficient population to admit Louisiana into the Union as a state. This division, it was argued, was authorized neither by the Constitution, nor in the treaty with the French Republic. Endless divisions might postpone indefinitely the admission of a part of the territory into the Union.[35]

Both the Senate and House took action as a result of the memorial. The House referred the memorial received by it to a committee of which John Randolph of Virginia was chairman. Reporting for the committee, Randolph stated that the grievances set forth were those inseparable from sudden transitions of government. The committee recommended, however, "every

[34] *American State Papers, Miscellaneous*, I, 399; *Annals of Congress*, 8 Cong., 2 Sess. (1804–1805), Appendix, 1606.

[35] *Annals of Congress*, 8 Cong., 2 Sess. (1804–1805), Appendix, 1608-1620.

indulgence not incompatible with the interests of the union, to be extended to the inhabitants of Louisiana.'' Previous forms of government employed by the United States for remote territories were considered not to be worthy of imitation in the case of Louisiana. The object of the committee was to give Louisiana a government of its own choice, administered by officers of its own appointment. Certain restrictions would be made, among them ''a prohibition of the importation of foreign slaves . . ., restrictions against the establishment of any form of government, other than a representative Republic; against violations of the liberty of conscience, the freedom of the press, and the trial by jury; against the taxation of the lands of the United States,'' to which was added the usual restriction of requiring the approval of Congress to acts passed. A resolution was then submitted for providing by law for the extension to the inhabitants of Louisiana of the right of self-government.[36]

In the Senate the memorial was referred to a committee composed of Giles of Virginia, Franklin of North Carolina, Anderson of Tennessee, Tracy of Connecticut, and Baldwin of Georgia, who reported a bill providing for the government of the territory of Orleans. This bill authorized the President to establish a government similar to that of the Mississippi Territory. The inhabitants were to be entitled to and enjoy all the rights, privileges, and advantages, secured by the Ordinance of 1787, and enjoyed by the people of Mississippi.

There was to be a general assembly of twenty-five members elected by the voters of the territory. Annual meetings were provided for. Laws in force in the territory at the commencement of this act, and not inconsistent with it, were to continue in force until altered or repealed by the legislature. Whenever the population should have reached a number to be determined

---

[36] *Annals of Congress*, 8 Cong., 2 Sess. (1804–1805), 1014–1017; *American State Papers, Miscellaneous*, I, 417–418.

[sixty thousand], arrangements should be made for the establishment of a state government and admission into the Union upon the footing of the original states, conformably to the third article of the treaty of cession. The constitution to be established must be republican and not inconsistent with the Constitution of the United States, nor with the Ordinance of 1787 so far as it should be made applicable to the territorial government to be established. Congress was to be at liberty at any time prior to the admission of the inhabitants of the territory to the rights of separate statehood, to alter the boundaries; but no alteration could be made which would delay admission as a state. So much of the act for temporary government as was repugnant with this act was to be repealed (time left blank).[37]

This bill was rushed through in the closing hours of the session. It was passed by the Senate March 1, 1805,[38] by the House March 2,[39] and was approved by the President on the same day.[40]

Echoes of the compact theory were still to be heard, for at least one senator gave as his reason for voting against the bill, the provision that when the territory had sixty thousand inhabitants it was to be admitted into the Union, upon the footing of the original states. This, in Plumer's opinion, was unconstitutional. A new partner could not be admitted into the Union, from without the original limits of the United States, without the consent, first obtained, of each of the original partners to the federal compact.[41]

Upon their return home, Derbigny, Destréhan and Sauvé reported, May 2, 1805, on their experience in Washington. They

---

[37] *Annals of Congress*, 8 Cong., 2 Sess. (1804–1805), 45–46; *Laws of U. States*, III, 648–650.

[38] *Annals of Congress*, 8 Cong., 2 Sess. (1804–1805), 69.

[39] *Ibid.*, 1215.

[40] *Ibid.*, Appendix, 1674–1676.

[41] Plumer, *Life of William Plumer*, 328.

admitted failure to get all they had asked for, and objected to the arbitrary setting of the number required for statehood at sixty thousand. However, the right to initiate laws had been gained. The House of Representatives was willing to grant unlimited right of self-government but the Senate was opposed; nevertheless, the attitude of the House was encouraging. The term fixed for admission into the Union though arbitrary was not irrevocable.[42]

Claiborne hoped that the people would be contented with the new order of things. He was convinced that an early introduction of the entire representative system into Orleans Territory would be a hazardous experiment. He expressed serious doubts whether the second grade of territorial government would be conducted with discretion.[43]

Rufus Easton had a short time previously to this written to Gideon Granger that a representative form of government would be advisable for the Orleans Territory, as it would attach the people to the Federal Government. He suggested that one branch of the legislature be composed of representatives from districts, elected by the people. The rest of the government might remain for the present the same or similar to that of territories of the first grade; with the exception that the governor's veto would be operative only until the opinion of Congress through the representation of a territorial delegate should be known.

Easton took the opportunity to warn against prohibiting settlement on the western bank of the Mississippi, a policy which he declared had originated with the landed interests. If carried into effect, "it would be injurious to the United States—ruinous to the western country and infringe the rights of the people." Should trouble with the Indians occur, the navigation of the

---

[42] *Louisiana Gazette,* June 11, 1805. (Translated from the *Moniteur.*)

[43] Claiborne to Madison, May 4, 1805, in *Claiborne Papers,* ''Claiborne's Correspondence, Orleans Territory,'' III.

Mississippi would be shut off, causing great loss and discomfort to the people of the western country. He was willing to concede that it might be a good policy to draw a frontier line some distance beyond the Mississippi and halt settlers there.

Granger considered these suggestions of sufficient importance to forward them to Jefferson.[44]

As Claiborne had inferred, there was little outward sign of disappointment at the failure of Congress to grant to the people of Orleans Territory everything for which they had asked. After an excursion to Point Coupé, he reported that the citizens were happy and apparently well disposed to the American Government.[45] He was persuaded that the great body of the citizens could not be shaken in their allegiance, or be made to think that they were not greatly benefited by their annexation to the United States.[46]

On December 28, 1805, Jefferson wrote to the speaker and the house of representatives of the territory, felicitating them on their many blessings, among them that of being joined to the United States. He praised their choice of representatives, which augured well for their future political happiness.[47]

Yet Jefferson was not altogether satisfied with conditions as they existed in the new territory. On April 2, 1806, he expressed himself to Senator Plumer on a bill which provided that two million acres of land in the territory of Orleans be surveyed and divided into townships and lots, each alternate lot of one hundred and sixty acres to be given to every free able-bodied male not an inhabitant of the territory or of the Mississippi Territory on condition that he would live there and cultivate the same

---

[44] Gideon Granger to Jefferson, April 1, 1805, in *Jefferson Papers*, "Letters received at Washington, 2nd Series," XXXVI, (74 and 75). Granger was Postmaster General at this time.

[45] Claiborne to Madison, May 31, 1805, in *Claiborne Papers*, "Claiborne's Correspondence, Orleans Territory," III.

[46] Claiborne to Madison, June 6, *ibid.*

[47] *Jefferson Papers*, "Letters from Jefferson, 1st Series," XI, 1805–1806, (83).

............years and render............years of military service in the militia of the United States. Jefferson declared the bill to be the most important then pending in Congress. Louisiana was exposed and it was necessary that provision be made for its defense. Nearly half of its present inhabitants were such that they could not be depended on in case of an invasion. It would be impolitic and expensive to raise a standing army; and it was doubtful if the militia from the states would consent to go and stay there any great length of time. There was no means of compelling them to do it. If lands were given as bounties, able-bodied men would go there and settle and have an interest in defending the territory.

Plumer answered that he considered it as establishing a new principle in our Government, a sort of feudal system, based on military tenure. He required more time to satisfy himself how far it would affect the Constitution and legal system. He feared the danger of sudden innovations in government.[48]

The bill to which Jefferson referred was introduced March 6, by Senator Worthington of Ohio. The tract of land was to be located between the Achafalaya, the Red River and a meridian line passing by the fort at Natchitoches.[49] The bill was passed to the third reading only by the deciding vote of the president of the Senate.[50] On April 4, two days after Jefferson's conversation with Plumer, further consideration was postponed until the next session.[51] This seemingly put an end to the bill for although on February 6, 1806, Worthington gave notice that he would on the next day, ''bring in a bill to encourage a settlement in the western district of Orleans,'' presumably his former measure, no further mention of it was made.[52]

---

[48] ''Plumer's Register,'' 1, April 3, 1806. This is really the third volume of Plumer, ''Memorandum of the proceedings in Congress,'' but as it is marked as above on the cover, it is so cited here.

[49] *Annals of Congress*, 9 Cong., 1 Sess. (1805–1806), 164.

[50] *Ibid.*, 207.

[51] *Ibid.*, 228.

[52] *Ibid.*, 9 Cong., 2 Sess., 62.

Jefferson, however, did not give up his idea immediately, as is shown by a letter which he wrote to John Dickinson on January 13, 1807. He said that discontent in the territory of Orleans was due to the prohibition of the importation of foreign slaves; to the administration of justice in forms foreign to the people, and all the more abhorrent because of corruption of lawyers; and to the question of land titles.[53] Because of trouble with the French element Jefferson proposed the enlistment of thirty thousand native-born Americans, to be transported at the public expense, and settled on bounties of one hundred acres of land each, west of the Mississippi, on condition of two years military service should that country be attacked within a period of seven years. Besides providing on the spot for the defense of the country, the addition to the population would entitle the territory to become a state, with a majority of Americans, thus making it an American rather than a French state. "This," concluded Jefferson, "would not sweeten the pill to the French but in making that acquisition we had some view to our own good as well as theirs, and I believe the greatest good of both will be promoted by whatever will amalgamate us together."[54]

As a President confronted with practical problems to solve, Jefferson could deviate far from the theories of the framer of the Declaration of Independence, and salve his conscience with the doctrine that "the greatest good of both will be promoted by whatever will amalgamate us together."

This was not the only case in which Jefferson thought an explanation of his action necessary. In a letter to General William Smith, May 4, 1806, in stating his belief that his appointment of General Wilkinson as military governor of

---

[53] These are the chief causes of discontent enumerated in a letter of Claiborne's to Madison, May 16, 1806, in *Claiborne Papers*, "Claiborne's Correspondence, Orleans Territory," IV.

[54] *Jefferson*, Writings (Memorial ed.), XI, 135–137. For the policy of the United States Government on the holding of the western boundary of Louisiana against Spain, see Marshall, *A History of the Western Boundary of the Louisiana Purchase, 1819–1841*.

Upper Louisiana, was as good as could have been made, he nevertheless admitted a "qualm of principle" in the union of the civil and military authority. He had refused to appoint Wilkinson to the governorship of the Mississippi Territory for that very reason. In the appointment to Upper Louisiana he did not think himself departing from his principle because he considered it "not as a civil government, but merely a military station." That idea had been sanctioned by the legislative body by the establishment of the office of commandant, in which the civil and military powers were blended. "It seemed therefore that the governor should be in suit with them." At the very time of passing the stricture on the union of authorities, the House of Representatives had passed a bill making the governor of Michigan commander of the regular troops which should at any time be within his government.[55] By the action of the Legislature, rather than by strict adherence to theory, did Jefferson thus defend his action.

There arose, also, certain questions incidental to the transfer of jurisdiction over the territory from France to the United States. A Spaniard residing in the territory was arraigned on a murder charge. His counsel demanded a jury composed in part of Spaniards. While conceding that the prisoner was an inhabitant of Louisiana at the time of cession to the United States, and was still an inhabitant thereof, it was nevertheless contended that since he had not taken an oath of allegiance to the United States, he was an alien, and a subject of the King of Spain. Some of the American lawyers settled in New Orleans thought an oath of allegiance to the United States necessary before the people could be considered American citizens. Claiborne did not agree with them and, in this instance, was pleased with the decision of the Superior Court, which held that all persons who resided in the territory at the period of cession and had not withdrawn with the Spanish or French authorities could not

---

[55] Jefferson, *Writings* (Memorial ed.), XI, 112.

be considered otherwise than as citizens of the United States.[56]

Another of these questions grew out of the excitement incident to the Burr Conspiracy. It is not necessary here to trace the history of that conspiracy, which has been treated fully by various writers.[57] Apprehensive of danger, Claiborne, in a message to the territorial legislature, recommended that it suspend the writ of habeas corpus.[58] The answer of the house of representatives of the territory was a resolution of February 17, 1807, refusing to suspend the writ, on the ground that after an examination of the Constitution of the United States and the ordinance of Congress by which the territory was governed, they had reached the conclusion that to suspend the writ would be a violation of the Constitution.[59]

Although the judges and the district attorney agreed with the decision of the legislature, Claiborne held a contrary view. He argued that although the Ordinance of 1787 provided, ''That the people shall always be entitled to the privilege of the writ of Habeas Corpus and the trial by jury,''[60] and that therefore the power nowhere existed to suspend the writ in the Northwest Territory, yet this was changed when the Constitution became the supreme law of the land. In the clause of the Constitution declaring that ''the Habeas Corpus shall not be suspended except in times of rebellion, or danger of invasion,''[61] a power to suspend was recognized. This power not being exclusively delegated to Congress, or prohibited to the states, was reserved

---

[56] Claiborne to Madison, June 25, 1806, in *Claiborne Papers*, ''Claiborne's Correspondence, Orleans Territory,'' IV; Gayarré, *History of Louisiana*, IV, 148–149.

[57] See Walter F. McCaleb, *The Aaron Burr Conspiracy;* Henry Adams, *History of the United States*, III, 219–343, 441–471; James Parton, *Life and Times of Aaron Burr*.

[58] Gayarré, *History of Louisiana*, IV, 181.

[59] *Claiborne Papers*, ''Claiborne's Correspondence, Orleans Territory,'' V, resolution signed by John Watkins, Speaker of the House of Representatives; Gayarré, *History of Louisiana*, IV, 182.

[60] Art. II.

[61] Art. I, sec. 9, cl. 2.

by amendment ten of the Constitution to the states. Claiborne contended that if a state could suspend the writ of habeas corpus, so could a territorial legislature, because "their powers extend to all the rightful subjects of legislation, and those are rightful which the supreme law of the land in (the Constitution) recognizes."[62]

If the opinion of the territorial legislature were correct, Claiborne saw the necessity of amending the Ordinance of Government, vesting the right of suspension of the writ of habeas corpus in *all*, or some *one* of the branches of the territorial legislature. The experience of the Burr Conspiracy had shown the need of this in time of rebellion.[63]

The Federal authorities were also experiencing difficulty over the writ of habeas corpus. Following Jefferson's message of January 22, 1807, giving information to Congress concerning the Burr conspiracy,[64] the Senate, January 23, took up the question of suspending the privilege. By unanimous consent the rules were suspended, and a bill for the suspension of the privilege of the writ of habeas corpus was rushed through its three readings and passed, all in a single day.[65] The bill was then sent to the House in the form of a confidential message. The House was accordingly cleared, but when the bill had been read and its nature ascertained, that body voted, one hundred and twenty-three to three, to open the doors during the discussion.[66]

---

[62] Gayarré, *History of Louisiana*, IV, 183–184.

[63] Claiborne to Madison, February 20, 1807, in *Claiborne Papers*, "Claiborne's Correspondence; Orleans Territory," V.

[64] Richardson, *Messages and Papers of the Presidents*, I, 412–417, Jefferson did not ask for the action which the Senate proceeded to take. In 1788 when discussing with Madison the provisions of the Constitution, Jefferson had opposed the suspension of the privilege of the writ of habeas corpus on all occasions, even in cases of insurrections and rebellions. Jefferson, *Writings* (Ford, ed.), V, 46–47.

[65] *Annals of Congress*, 9 Cong., 2 Sess. (1806–1807), 44.

[66] *Ibid.*, 402–403.

The Senate bill was then taken up and received very little support. The principle of the bill was vigorously denounced. The action asked for was considered unnecessary. It was argued that the public safety did not require the suspension and only when that emergency arose could this great power be constitutionally exercised. Furthermore, a dangerous precedent would be established if the bill should pass. Such a precedent could be used by 'a corrupt and vicious administration in a manner destructive to the liberties of the people.[67] The bill was rejected by a vote of one hundred and thirteen to nineteen.[68]

It is worth noting that during the debate on the measure, Representative Eppes of Virginia made the statement, which went unchallenged, that the Constitution had vested the power of suspension of the privilege of the writ of habeas corpus in Congress.[69] The same opinion was expressed by Chief Justice Marshall in *Ex parte Bollman*,[70] a case which grew out of this same Burr conspiracy. This seems to have been the accepted view of the matter[71] until the Civil War when President Lincoln assumed the power himself. With the opposition which this action of the President aroused and the flood of literature which it precipitated we are not here concerned.[72]

---

[67] *Ibid.*, 403–424.

[68] *Ibid.*, 424–425.

[69] *Ibid.*, 409–410.

[70] 4 Cranch 75.

[71] As for instance by Story in his *Commentaries on the Constitution of the United States*, par. 1342.

[72] See for example, Horace Binney's pamphlets on *The Principles of the Writ of Habeas Corpus;* Joel Parker, ''Habeas Corpus and Martial Law,'' in *North American Review*, XCIII, 471–518 (October, 1861) ; George R. Curtis, *Constitutional History of the United States*, II, Appendix, 668--686; S. G. Fisher, ''The Suspension of Habaes Corpus during the War of the Rebellion,'' in *Political Science Quarterly*, III, 454–488. For further references consult the list of pamphlets published during the Civil War appended to Fisher's article.

CHAPTER X

DEMANDS FOR STATEHOOD AND THE QUESTION
OF WEST FLORIDA

The people of Orleans Territory had shown their loyalty to
the Federal Government during the period of the Burr intrigues;
and with a rapidly growing population and prosperity, looked
towards statehood. On May 19, 1809, Claiborne sent to Secretary of State Robert Smith a copy of the memorial to Congress
which had been adopted by the legislative council and the house
of representatives of the territory at their last session, asking
for early admission into the Union as a state. Claiborne expressed his belief that a territorial government was still a necessity, for although the people were peaceable and amiable they
were not prepared for statehood. He furnished, also, some interesting statistics on the condition of the territory. The census
of 1806, set the population at 52,998 people, of whom 23,574
were slaves, 3,355 free people of color, leaving 26,069 whites.
Of the latter at least 13,500 were natives of Louisiana, for the
most part descendants of the French; about 3,500 natives of the
United States, and the rest Europeans, including native French,
Spaniards, English, Germans and Irish. Since 1806, there had
been only about 3,000 or 4,000 free immigrants, two-thirds of
whom were native Americans. It was expected, however, that
many of the French people who had been banished from Cuba
would come to the territory.[1]

---

[1] The European War had caused many Frenchmen to leave Cuba and
seek refuge in Louisiana. Claiborne did not relish this influx of foreign
blood and tried to stem the tide of immigration. At the same time he was
kind to the refugees who did come. The fact that the French brought
their slaves with them caused him some anxiety because it was a violation
of the law. He thought best, however, not to be too severe on an unfortunate people and allowed the owners to keep their slaves provided a bond,

The memorial had met with great opposition in the territorial house of representatives, the final vote in its favor being eleven to seven, and Claiborne doubted that a majority of the people favored statehood. The rights of the citizens were little understood and a general apathy prevailed at territorial elections. In conclusion, Claiborne recommended changes in the government as related to the supreme judiciary, and also an increase in number of the members of the legislative council.[2] On March 12 of the next year Giles, in the Senate, presented another memorial of the legislature of the territory of Orleans, praying for the admission of the territory into the Union.[3] The memorial was referred to a select committee[4] which reported a bill acceding to the request of the memorialists.[5] An attempt was made by Hillhouse to add to the bill the words: *"Provided,* That the several States shall assent thereto, or an amendment to the Constitution of the United States shall authorize Congress to admit said Territory of Orleans into the Union, on the footing of the original States."* This was defeated,[6] and the bill was passed on April 27.[7]

Closely connected with the question of the admission of the territory of Orleans into the Union as a state was that of the status of West Florida. In 1810 an uprising took place in which the people of West Florida threw off the control of Spain

---

sufficiently secured, was given that the negroes would be produced on due notice. If the owner could not give the necessary security the negroes were hired out to citizens who could, and the money so obtained was turned over to the owners. Gayarré, *History of Louisiana,* IV, 214–220.

[2] *Claiborne Papers,* ''Claiborne's Correspondence, Orleans Territory,'' V; Gayarré, *History of Louisiana,* IV, 211–214.

[3] *Annals of Congress,* 11 Cong., Part 1 (1809–1810), 596. The memorial is given in full in the *American State Papers, Miscellaneous,* II, 51–52, and in *Annals of Congress,* 11 Cong., Part 2 (1810), Appendix, 2269–2273.

[4] *Annals of Congress,* 11 Cong., Part I (1809–1810), 596.

[5] *Ibid.,* 646.

[6] *Ibid.,* 670.

[7] *Ibid.,* 674.

and declared themselves free and independent.[8] The declaration
of independence was adopted September 26, 1810, and on October 10, John Rhea, president of the convention, wrote to Robert
Smith, secretary of state of the United States, asking for the
admission of West Florida as a state into the Union. Should
it be thought best to annex West Florida to one of the neighboring territories, or a part of one of them, a preference for
annexation to the island of Orleans was stipulated.[9]

The ''legality'' of the course pursued with regard to West
Florida had been carefully considered by Madison and had
troubled him somewhat. The crisis in West Florida, he confided
to Jefferson, October 19, 1810, presented ''serious questions, as
to the Authority of the Executive, and the adequecy of the existing laws of the U. S. for territorial administration.'' He feared,
also, that the short time intervening before the assembling of
Congress ''might subject any intermediate interposition of the
Ex. to the charge of being premature & disrespectful, if not of
being illegal.'' On the other hand, considering the country to
the River Perdido as belonging to the United States, it ''may be
fairly taken possession of, if it can be done without violence,
above all if there be danger of its passing into the hands of a
third & dangerous party,''[10] a contingency which Madison at that
moment greatly feared. A few days later, October 30, Madison,
writing to William Pinkney, said that his action was ''understood to be within the authority of the Executive.''[11]

---

[8] For the text of the declaration see *Annals of Congress*, 11 Cong., 3
Sess. (1810–1811), Appendix, 1254–1255; also Gayarré, *History of Louisiana*, IV, 231–233; Fuller, *Purchase of Florida*, Chapters IV–VI, for an
extended account of the boundary dispute; Isaac J. Cox, ''The American
Intervention in West Florida,'' in *American Historical Review*, XVII,
290–311.

[9] *Annals of Congress*, 11 Cong., 3 Sess. (1810–1811), Appendix, 1252–
1253; Gayarré, *History of Louisiana*, IV, 233–236.

[10] Madison, *Writings* (Hunt, ed.), VIII, 110.

[11] *Ibid.*, VIII, 121.

What followed is best summed up in President Madison's message to Congress, December 5, 1810:

Among the events growing out of the state of the Spanish Monarchy, our attention was imperiously attracted to the change developing itself in that portion of West Florida which, though of right appertaining to the United States, had remained in the possession of Spain, awaiting the result of negotiations for its actual delivery to them.[12] The Spanish authority was subverted, and a situation produced exposing the country to ulterior events which might essentially affect the rights and welfare of the Union. In such a conjuncture I did not delay the interposition required for the occupancy of the territory west of the river Perdido, to which the title of the United States extends, and to which the laws provided for the Territory of Orleans are applicable. With this view, the proclamation, of which a copy is laid before you was confided to the Governor of that Territory to be carried into effect. The legality and necessity of the course pursued assure me of the favorable light in which it will present itself to the Legislature, and of the promptitude with which they will supply whatever provisions may be due to the essential rights and equitable interests of the people, thus brought into the bosom of the American family.[13]

An inkling of the attitude of the United States Government towards the West Florida revolutionists was given in the statement of Secretary of State Smith, ''that the President could not recognize in the Convention of West Florida any independent authority whatever to propose, or to form a compact with the United States.''[14]

Claiborne, as ordered, marched with the militia to St. Francisville in West Florida and on December 7, 1810, hoisted the flag of the United States and took possession of the country.

---

[12] For a clear-cut statement of the basis for the claims of the United States in the dispute over the eastern and western boundaries of Louisiana, see Gallatin, *Writings* (Adams, ed.), I, 241–243 (Letter to Jefferson, September 12, 1805). The weakness of the claims of the United States is there shown.

[13] Richardson, *Messages and Papers of the Presidents*, I, 484; *Annals of Congress*, 11 Cong., 3 Sess. (1810–1811), 12–13. For the text of the proclamation referred to see *ibid.*, Appendix, 1257–1258. For instructions to Claiborne, *ibid.*, 1256–1257.

[14] Smith to Governor Holmes of Mississippi Territory, November 15, 1810, *ibid.*, 1259; Gayarré, *History of Louisiana*, IV, 240.

The so-called State of West Florida was annexed to the territory of Orleans, and organized into parishes.[15]

On December 10, 1810, the Senate took up the President's message of December 5, and Senators Giles of Virginia, Pope of Kentucky, Crawford of Georgia, Anderson of Tennessee, and Bradley of Vermont were appointed a committee to examine and report on the part of the President's message which referred to West Florida.[16] Giles for the committee reported, December 18, on a bill declaring the laws in force in the territory of Orleans to extend and to have full force and effect to the River Perdido, pursuant to the treaty of April 30, 1803.[17] The question came up on the bill's passage to a third reading December 27, and caused another debate which brought out further interpretation of the constitutional functions of the various branches of the Federal Government.

The issues under the bill were stated by Senator Horsey of Delaware to be, first, in effect, the incorporation with the territory of Orleans of the province of West Florida east of the Mississippi, as far as the Perdido; and, second, the extension to that part of the province thus incorporated of the laws in force in the territory of Orleans. Did the United States have a good title to the province, and was it expedient for the Government to take possession by force, were questions which Horsey proposed for discussion. An examination of the authority of the President to issue the proclamation and orders of August 27, 1810, directing the forcible occupation of West Florida introduced certain constitutional problems. Horsey contended that if the proclamation had been unauthorized, Congress was not committed by it, nor bound to sanction it. The President's authority must have been derived either from the Constitution, or from some act

---

[15] Gayarré, *History of Louisiana*, IV, 243.

[16] *Annals of Congress*, 11 Cong., 3 Sess. (1810–1811), 17.

[17] *Ibid.*, 25–26.

or acts of Congress. The Constitution gave to Congress the exclusive power of declaring and making war; to the President the power of executing the laws of the Union. The powers of the former are legislative, of the latter executive. The President in issuing his proclamation transcended the limits of his powers, the proclamation being a matter of legislation and war—war because it directed the occupation of the territory by a military force. It was true that the troops were ordered not to molest the Spaniards, but if they should be attacked by Spaniards a conflict was inevitable.[18] The same would be true if the revolutionists should attack the troops.

The proclamation was also an act of legislation, continued Horsey, because it annexed the territory in question to the territory of Orleans, created a governor, enacted laws and appropriated money. For all this there had been no authority under the Constitution or by act of Congress. The act, therefore, was an unwarrantable assumption of power and a violation of the Constitution.

Horsey argued, also, that the title of the United States to West Florida was not a good one, and even if it were, to assert it by force was opposed to the equitable and pacific policy of the United States.[19]

Henry Clay rose to answer Horsey. After asserting the clear right of the United States to West Florida, he took up the question of the constitutional powers of the Executive. By one section of the Act of October, 1803, the President had been authorized to occupy the territories ceded by France to the United States; by another, he had been empowered to establish a provisional government there. The first was unlimited in duration; the second was restricted to the expiration of the then

---

[18] Just such a conflict actually occurred at a later date between American and Mexican troops and precipitated the Mexican War.

[19] *Annals of Congress*, 11 Cong., 3 Sess. (1810–1811), 37–55.

session of Congress. The Act of March, 1804 [the Breckinridge Bill], which declared that the previous act of October should continue in force until October 1, 1804, was applicable, said Clay, to the second and not to the first section, and was intended to continue the provisional government which had been established by the President. By the Act of February 24, 1804, for laying duties on goods imported into the ceded territories, the President had been empowered *whenever he should deem it expedient,* to erect the bay and river Mobile, etc., into a separate district, and to establish therein a port of entry and delivery. By the same act Orleans Territory had been laid off and its boundaries so defined as to include West Florida. By other acts the President had been authorized to remove by force, under certain circumstances, persons settling or taking possession of lands ceded to the United States. These laws had vested in the Executive an indisputable power to take possession of the country whenever, in his opinion, it might be proper. Therefore, held Clay, the President had not violated the Constitution and usurped the war-making power; on the contrary, he would have violated the Constitution had he neglected to see that the laws of the land were faithfully executed. Nor was it any more true that he had assumed powers belonging to Congress when he undertook to annex West Florida to the territory of Orleans, inasmuch as Congress had already made this annexation the limits of that territory. The President had not made law but had merely declared to the people of West Florida what the law was.[20]

---

[20] *Annals of Congress,* 11 Cong., 3 Sess. (1810–1811), 55–62. It is interesting to note in this connection Clay's idea of the attitude the Government should take toward a colony of another Power in disorder on the American border: ''I have no hesitation in saying, that if a parent country will not or cannot maintain its authority in a colony adjacent to us, and there exists in it a state of misrule and disorder, menacing our peace, and if moreover such colony, by passing into the hands of any other power, would become dangerous to the integrity of the Union, and manifestly tend to the subversion of our laws; we have a right, upon eternal principles of self-preservation, to lay hold of it.'' *Ibid.,* 63.

An interruption to the Senate debate on this particular question came in the form of a message from the House of Representatives on January 16, 1811, informing the Senate of the passage by the House of a bill entitled, "An act to enable the people of the Territory of Orleans to form a Constitution and State Government, and for the admission of such State into the Union on an equal footing with the original States, and for other purposes"; in which bill they desired the concurrence of the Senate.[21]

On January 25, the House bill, with amendments, was reported by Charles Tait of Georgia, from the Senate committee to whom this bill had been referred. Another discussion of the West Florida question resulted. In arranging for the boundaries of the proposed state, the following stipulation was made: "Provided nevertheless, that the Government of the United States hereby retains the power of altering, in any manner it may hereafter deem proper, the limits of all that portion of the said prescribed territory, which lies east of the river Mississippi and the island of New Orleans."[22]

This proviso was struck out on January 29, after an attempt to amend it had failed. The defeated amendment proposed the retention of power by the United States to attach to the proposed State any part of the territory lying east of the Mississippi River, south of the Mississippi Territory, and west of the river Mobile.[23]

The old partnership-compact theory once more raised its head when Dana of Connecticut proposed an amendment which provided:

That this act shall not be understood to admit such State into the Union as aforesaid, unless each of the original States shall consent to the same,

---

21 *Ibid.*, 97.
22 *Ibid.*, 103.
23 *Ibid.*, 107.

or there shall be a constitutional amendment empowering the Congress to admit into the Union new States formed beyond the boundaries of the United States, as known and understood at the time of establishing the Constitution for the United States.[24]

When this amendment was taken up, January 30, on motion of Clay, it was divided. The first division, providing for the consent of each state to the passage of the act admitting the new state, was determined in the negative, nays eighteen, yeas ten, those voting in its favor being Bradley of Vermont, Champlin of Rhode Island, Dana and Goodrich of Connecticut, German of New York, Gilman of New Hampshire, Horsey of Delaware, Lloyd and Pickering of Massachusetts, and Reed of Maryland. The second division was then voted down, seventeen to eight.[25]

After several other attempts at amendment and postponement the Enabling Act passed the Senate, February 7, by a vote of twenty-two to ten.[26] The next day the Senate turned its attention to the bill declaring the laws in force in the territory of Orleans to extend to the River Perdido, and recommitted it to the original committee to which this part of the President's message had been first referred.[27]

The petition of the legislature of Orleans Territory for admission into the Union as a state, with the same privileges and immunities enjoyed by the other states, was presented to the House on December 17, 1810, by Julian Poydras, delegate from Orleans Territory.[28] Being referred in the usual way to a committee, it was reported December 27, and taken up in the Committee of the Whole, January 2, 1811. Poydras said that the territory contained at least sixty thousand inhabitants and

---

[24] *Annals of Congress*, 11 Cong., 3 Sess. (1810-1811), 108.
[25] *Ibid.*, 110.
[26] *Ibid.*, 127.
[27] *Ibid.*, 129.
[28] *Ibid.*, 413–414.

had a right to become a state. It was left to Congress, however, to act as it saw fit. Troup of Georgia said the House was not prepared to act on the subject. He also alluded to the difficulty arising from including within a state the territory between the Mississippi and the Perdido, which was still in dispute and subject to negotiation. Willis Alston of North Carolina presented the view occasionally heard, although it never had a large following, ''that there was no question of the propriety of admitting the Territory as a State, whilst it was in the power of Congress to make conditions with them. After the population was ascertained to amount to 60,000, they would become a State without asking the leave of Congress.'' Bibb of Georgia favored the bill but thought it wise to postpone decision because of the pending negotiations over the eastern boundary of the territory. ''If it became a State,'' he inquired, ''would not all right of negotiation of the subject be taken from the President?''

Barry of Kentucky claimed the need for state government to be urgent, and answered the objection respecting the boundary question by saying that a modification of the bill could be made, reserving to Congress the power of changing the boundary of the territory. He urged action on the bill while Congress yet had the power to impose conditions on the territory. He agreed with Alston in declaring that if Congress should wait until the population reached sixty thousand, the demands of the people could not be refused. Passing this bill, however, would admit of imposing conditions on them.

Barry appears to have lost sight of the fact that an act of one Congress was not necessarily binding. According to his interpretation, Congress, having set at sixty thousand the number of inhabitants necessary for the admission of Orleans Territory into the Union as a state, was bound as though by compact to allow the admission. While this might be the fair thing to do, there was nothing to prevent Congress from imposing other conditions, even to the extent of delaying the admission of the proposed state by increasing the number of inhabitants required for that act.

Another possible dilemma was pointed out by Sheffey of Virginia, who also took up the question of the extension of the limits of the state to the Perdido. He called to mind the fact that when the Executive had directed the occupation of West Florida a pledge had been given that it should be subject to future negotiation. Would anyone say that the Executive· could convey away any part of a state? What would he be bound to do if it should be proved that the territory was not ceded? Would the doctrine be established that the treaty-making power has a right to cede a state or any part of a state? Sheffey thought it wise to move slowly in this affair. Bibb said that when the bill came up again, he would move to strike out the proviso relating to the inclusion of the territory east to the Perdido. To make it a state would forever preclude negotiation on the subject. A resolution, moved by him, providing for the appointment of a committee to inquire into the expediency of annexing to the Mississippi Territory or creating into a separate territorial government, the territory under dispute, was being discussed when a confidential message was received from the President and further debate was postponed.[29]

The bill for admitting the territory of Orleans into the Union as a state was taken up in Committee of the Whole the next day, January 4. Long and earnest interpretations of constitutional rights were made. Wheaton of Massachusetts reiterated the claim that the Constitution, as shown by its ''enacting clause,'' was ordained and established for the *then* United States of America, implying the exclusion of all others. Failure to set a boundary to extension would ultimately result in the relative

---

[29] *Annals of Congress,* 11 Cong., 3 Sess. (1810–1811), 482–486.

unimportance of the original parties to the compact. He introduced another novel interpretation by remarking that the admission of the people of the territory of Orleans into the Union as a
state would carry with it the right to send representatives and
senators to Congress; yet the Constitution had set as a qualification for senators, citizenship in the United States for at
least nine years, a period longer than any of the people of the
territory had belonged to the United States, unless they happened to be emigrants and had not lost their citizenship.

Miller of Tennessee sided with those who opposed the bill
because it included extension of the limits of the territory to the
Perdido. There was no power, he said, to negotiate concerning
the territory of any state, and this problem would be presented
if the bill passed as drawn up. Miller's colleague, Rhea, favored
the bill, and protested against the doctrine that no territory
could be admitted into the Union as a state which did not belong
to the original states. The United States, a sovereign, had
power to purchase adjacent territory and to admit it into the
Union. In this theory, Gholson of Virginia and Macon of North
Carolina acquiesced.[30]

When discussion of the bill was resumed on January 9,
Sheffey moved to insert in place of the part of the bill which
prescribed the boundaries of the future state the words: "All
that territory now contained within the limits of the Territory
of Orleans, except that part lying east of the river Iberville and
a line drawn along the middle of the lakes Maurepas and Pontchartrain to the ocean." This amendment was opposed by
Wright of Maryland and Rhea on the ground that the Treaty
of 1803 with France guaranteed to the undivided territory of
Orleans a right to become a state on the same conditions with
other states. Bibb and Ely of Massachusetts supported the
amendment, believing it expedient to leave that part of the

---

[30] *Ibid.*, 493–505.

territory in such a position as would enable the United States to negotiate respecting it. Sheffey's motion was agreed to, sixty-three voting in favor of it.[31]

The bill was read the third time on Saturday, January 10, but discussion being interrupted by the receipt of a confidential message from the Senate, it was postponed until the following Monday.[32] The boundary question arose once more to plague the House, but this time from a different angle, when Timothy Pitkin of Connecticut rehearsed at length the problems of the western boundary. The boundary could not be changed after the admission of the territory as a state; therefore, declared Pitkin, conditions ought to be attached giving the United States control of the boundary question.[33] Johnson of Kentucky did not recognize any insurmountable difficulty in the matter. First asserting that "the principles of every State constitution in the Union, the political creed so often professed on this floor, the sentiments of freedom so often expressed, and the articles of the Federal Constitution which circumscribed our powers, all unite to enforce the claims of this Territory to State sovereignty," he added that by the treaty the United States was bound to admit the territory as soon as possible. The boundary question was not a new one. A similar dispute over the northeastern boundary had been settled peaceably with Great Britain, according to provisions of the Jay Treaty of 1794. Similarly the boundary between the state of Georgia and the Spanish provinces of East and West Florida had been established by the Treaty of 1795 between the United States and Spain. There was no reason, said Johnson, why the boundaries of the proposed state might not be settled in the same way.[34]

---

[31] *Annals of Congress*, 11 Cong., 3 Sess. (1810–1811), 513.

[32] *Ibid.*, 516.

[33] *Ibid.*, 518–519.

[34] *Ibid.*, 520–524.

Josiah Quincy then took the floor, and assuming an extremely radical point of view in opposition to the passage of the bill, delivered what is perhaps the most widely known speech on the entire subject, in the course of which he asserted:

...I am compelled to declare it as my deliberate opinion, that, if this bill passes, the bonds of this Union are virtually dissolved; that the States which compose it are free from their moral obligations, and that, as it will be the right of all, so it will be the duty of some, to prepare definitely for a separation—amicably if they can, violently if they must.

Quincy was here called to order by Poindexter, territorial delegate from Mississippi. The Speaker upheld Poindexter but the House, on appeal, voted against the Speaker's decision and Quincy's observations were declared to be in order. Quincy then resumed his speech. He held it to be a usurpation of power, without sanction of the Constitution, for the three branches of the National Government, without recurrence to conventions of the people, in the states, or to the legislatures of the states, to authorize the admission of new partners to a share of the political power, in countries outside the original limits of the United States. The provision that "new States may be admitted, by the Congress, into the Union," referred only to new political sovereignties to be formed within the original limits of the United States. No mention of new territory was to be found in the debates in the period of the adoption of the Federal Constitution. This fact, according to Quincy, would go to show that the people had no idea of territorial expansion on the part of their successors. One of the arguments used against the success of the new Government of the United States had been that the territory was too extensive for a republican form of government. Yet ambitious hopes were already looking far beyond any limits. Quincy pessimistically prophesied what has since come to pass when he said: "We are now about to cross the Mississippi. The Missouri and Red rivers are but roads on which our imagination travels to new lands and new States to be raised and admitted (under the power, now first usurped) into this Union, among undiscovered lands, in the west.'' In like vein a little later in the same speech he added: ''There is no limit to men's imaginations, on this subject, short of California and Columbia river.''

The real motive back of Quincy's fierce denunciation of the principles of the bill was stated clearly and emphatically—that of the political balance of power: ''Whether the proprietors of the good old United States shall manage their own affairs in their own way; or whether they, and their Constitution, and their political rights, shall be trampled under foot by foreigners introduced through a breach of the Constitution.'' The relation between state and federal government was laid down by Quincy in a manner to satisfy the most radical advocate of states' rights:

I hold my life, liberty, and property, and the people of the State, from which I have the honor to be a Representative, hold theirs by a better tenure than any this National Government can give.... We hold these by the laws, customs, and principles of the Commonwealth of Massachusetts. Behind her ample shield we find refuge, and feel safety.... Sir, I confess it, the first public love of my heart is the Commonwealth of Massachusetts. ... The love of this Union grows out of this attachment to my native soil, and is rooted in it. I cherish it, because it affords the best external hope of her peace, her prosperity, her independence.

In conclusion, Quincy claimed that the bill, if passed, would be a deathblow to the Constitution.[35]

---

[35] *Annals of Congress*, 11 Cong., 3 Sess. (1810–1811), 524–542. An idea of the impression made by Quincy's speech is found in William Plumer's letter to John Quincy Adams, February 7, 1811, in which he wrote: ''The Orleans territory is to be admitted as a State into the Union. On this question Josiah Quincy made a long speech in the house, & avowed sentiments more hostile to the integrity of the union of the States, than, I believe, any federalist ever had the hardihood to avow. His political friends in New England tax him with imprudence, & his enemies with folly and rashness;'' *Plumer MSS.* See also John Quincy Adams, *Writings* (Ford, ed.), IV, 207–209, for Adams' opinion of Quincy's speech.

Compare the reply of the House committee of Massachusetts to which was referred Governor Strong's speech at the opening of the spring session

Poindexter's reply to Quincy is also of considerable interest when viewed in the light of constitutional interpretation. He maintained that the provision of the Constitution authorizing Congress "to dispose of and make all needful rules and regulations respecting the territory of the United States" contained an express recognition of the right to possess territory. The right to acquire followed as an indispensable attribute of sovereignty. A nation may extend its territorial limits either by conquest or treaty. No prohibition of the right to acquire territory, either by war or compact, was contained in the Constitution.

The treaty-making power, continued Poindexter, is composed of the President and two-thirds of the senators present. Whenever appropriations of money are necessary to carry a treaty into effect, the House of Representatives has a check on the other branches. A treaty once ratified by each coördinate department of the Government becomes the supreme law of the land, and is as binding on the House as an article in the Constitution itself. A distinction existed between laws and treaties; laws being made in pursuance of the Constitution, treaties "under the authority of the United States." If an article in a treaty contravened an express provision of the Constitution it would not be binding. Who is to be arbiter between the treaty-making power and the Constitution? Poindexter considered it ridiculous that this great power should be given to the Supreme

---

of 1813: "We are duly impressed by your Excellency's suggestion, that the extension of territorial limits was never contemplated by the framers of the Constitution. If the President and Senate may purchase land, and Congress may plant States in *Louisiana,* they may with equal right establish them on the *North-West Coast,* or in *South-America.* It may be questioned hereafter, whether after this formation of new States, the adherence of the old ones which dissented from the measure, is the result of obligation or expediency. And it is evident, that this multiplication of new States, not parties to the original compact, must soon be regarded as fatal to the rights and liberties of some of the present members of the confederacy, and consequently as an insuperable grievance." S. E. Morison, *The Life and Letters of Harrison Gray Otis,* II, 68–69.

Court. Should the other three[36] branches of the General Government determine a treaty to be constitutional, by passing laws to carry it into effect, it becomes at once the supreme law of the land, and so far as its stipulations secure personal privileges and the rights of property, they must be fulfilled. Such an agreement he found in the third article of the treaty of cession of Louisiana.

To Quincy's fear of loss of New England's political power in the Union if the bill should pass, Poindexter gave a more rational answer than his interpretation of the force of treaties:

It results from the very nature of our Government that political influence fluctuates in proportion to the augmentation or diminution of population in the various sections of the country.... If as the gentleman [Quincy] has alleged, the proportions of political power in the several States, is an 'inalienable, essential, intangible right,' it must forever remain the same, like a chartered privilege, let the weight of population rest where it may. Such a principle is inconsistent with the genius of a free Government, and incompatible with the sovereign authority of the people.[37]

As might have been expected, Poindexter's statement of the binding force of treaties did not pass unchallenged. Thomas R. Gold of New York denied that the treaty-making power was free from all restriction of the Constitution. If it were true, as had been asserted, said Gold, that since the admission of Louisiana into the Union had been stipulated by the treaty of purchase, no provision of the Constitution could arrest a bill providing for the admission, the very foundations of the Constitution would be subverted.[38]

Bibb and Wright both spoke in favor of the bill, justifying it on constitutional grounds. Key of Maryland opposed it and was answered by Macon. The indefinite postponement of the

---

[36] Presumably counting the Senate and House as separate branches.

[37] *Annals of Congress*, 11 Cong., 3 Sess. (1810–1811), 555–570. John Adams thought Poindexter and others had offered arguments of "great weight" in answer to Quincy (John Adams, *Works*, IX, 632).

[38] *Annals of Congress*, 11 Cong., 3 Sess. (1810–1811), 570.

bill which had been moved by Quincy was defeated, and the main question that the bill do pass was taken, January 15, and decided in the affirmative, seventy-seven to thirty-six.[39]

On February 9, the House took up the Senate amendment to the bill to make the Sabine River the boundary from the ocean to the thirty-second degree of north latitude and thence due north until it intersected the northern boundary line of Orleans Territory. It was agreed to without opposition.

Another amendment of the Senate proposing to change the part of the bill declaring that the convention should be chosen by free male inhabitants, by adding the word ''white'' so as to exclude free colored people of mixed blood from voting, caused some debate. Smilie of Pennsylvania opposed it. The bill, he pointed out, provided only for the election of a convention to form a constitution; after which the people could settle the matter for themselves as to who should vote for members of Congress, etc. Mitchill of New York thought the convention and legislature better able to decide the question than the House. The amendment was negatived,[40] but the Senate adhering to it, the House again took up the question and receded from its determination to reject the amendment.[41]

The way was now open for Louisiana to enter the Union as a state.

---

[39] *Ibid.*, 573–577.
[40] *Ibid.*, 936–937.
[41] *Ibid.*, 963–964.

CHAPTER XI

ADMISSION TO STATEHOOD

The act enabling the people of the territory of Orleans to form a constitution and a state government, and providing for the admission of the state into the Union was approved by the President February 20, 1811. Section two authorized all free white male citizens of the United States, twenty-one years of age, residing within the territory at least one year previous to the day of election and who had paid a territorial, county, district, or parish tax; and all other persons having in other respects the legal qualifications to vote for representatives in the general assembly of the territory, to choose representatives to form a convention. These representatives were to be apportioned among the several counties, districts, and parishes in such manner as the territorial legislature should direct. The number of representatives was not to exceed sixty. The date of elections for the representatives was set for the third Monday in the September following. The elections were to be conducted in the same manner as provided by the laws of the territory for the election of members of the house of representatives.

Certain conditions were laid down in section three. The convention, upon deciding to form a constitution and state government, must first declare, in behalf of the people, that it adopted the Constitution of the United States; which having been done, the convention was authorized to proceed with the formation of a constitution and state government. It was stipulated that this constitution must be republican in character, and consistent with the Federal Constitution; that it must contain the fundamental principles of civil and religious liberty; that it should secure to the citizens trial by jury in all criminal cases, and the privilege of the writ of habeas corpus, conformable to the Constitution of the United States; and that all legislative and judicial proceedings and records must be in the English language. All waste or unappropriated lands were to belong to the United States; and all such tracts of land sold by Congress were to be exempt from state taxation for the term of five years following the sales. Lands belonging to citizens of the United States, resident outside the state, were never to be taxed higher than lands of persons residing therein. Lands of the United States were not to be taxed. The Mississippi and navigable waters leading into it or the Gulf of Mexico were to be common highways to the inhabitants of the proposed state and all other citizens of the United States, and free from state taxation.

Section four provided that if the convention should frame a state constitution which was not disapproved by Congress at its next session, the state should be admitted into the Union, upon the same footing with the original states.

The last section enacted that five per cent of the net proceeds from the sale of the lands of the United States, after January 1, should be used as the state legislature might direct in the building of public roads and levees in the state.[1]

The territorial legislature of Orleans Territory made the necessary arrangements for the election of members of the constitutional convention, leaving out of consideration, however, the part of West Florida which had recently been taken possession of, because Congress had not yet annexed this district to the Territory of Orleans.

On May 31, 1811, Claiborne wrote to Secretary of State Monroe, enclosing a copy of his proclamation directing the election of members of a constitutional convention. He gave it as his belief that the formation of a state government and admis-

---

[1] *Annals of Congress*, 11 Cong., 3 Sess. (1810–1811), Appendix, 1326–1328; *Laws of U. States*, IV, 328–330.

sion into the Union would strengthen the Union. It would discourage foreign intrigues and internal discontent. A state government might not run smoothly at first but would improve as the people gained experience.[2]

The convention met November 4, but its real work began on November 18, 1811. A constitution was drawn up and adopted, the stipulations made by the Federal Government having first been assented to; and a memorial to Congress requesting the annexation of West Florida to the new state about to be erected was also adopted. The convention, after making all provisions deemed necessary for the carrying of the constitution into effect provided it received the approval of Congress, adjourned January 28, 1812.[3]

A letter from Claiborne to Monroe on January 31, 1812, introduced to him Messrs. E. Fromentin and Allan B. Magruder, who had been appointed by the convention as agents to convey to the President of the United States the constitution proposed for the new state. Once again Claiborne remarked that the general welfare seemed to require that the state government should soon be established. A majority of the people were well disposed toward the Government of the United States and admission as a state would strengthen this feeling.

Claiborne reported also that the agents carried with them a memorial to Congress asking for annexation of a part of West Florida to the new state. The bearing such an act might have on foreign relations Claiborne thought to be outside his province to discuss. He felt that the interests of the new state strongly advised an enlargement of its limits. The annexation would not only conduce to the convenience and prosperity of the people more immediately interested, but to the national good.[4]

---

[2] *Claiborne Papers*, "Claiborne's Correspondence, Orleans Territory," VI, 1809–1812.

[3] For a fuller account of local details, see Gayarré, *History of Louisiana*, IV, 266–275; *Louisiana Gazette*, November 19 and following issues.

[4] *Claiborne Papers*, "Orleans Territory, Miscellaneous Papers."

The proceedings of the constitutional convention were transmitted to Congress by President Madison in a special message on March 4, 1812.[5] The question of the admission of Louisiana into the Union, and of the extension of the laws of the United States thereto was taken up in both Houses of Congress. The chief difficulty, as shown by the report of the debates in the House on March 18 and March 19, was the disposal of West Florida. Poindexter offered an amendment providing that as soon as the consent of the state legislature should be given, this area should be incorporated into, and made a part of the state, and governed as if included within the original boundaries of the state; provided, nevertheless, that the title of the United States to the tract should remain subject to future negotiation. A difficulty was here perceived by Johnson of Kentucky who said that the people of the Florida district, although to be included within the new state, would nevertheless be deprived of a voice in the passage of the first laws, and in the choice of senators in Congress. He therefore moved an amendment to the bill dividing the territory under question into two counties, each to send one senator and one representative to the state legislature. Poindexter asked how Congress could say that those people should form a part of the new state as soon as its consent could be given, and then declare that though by the terms of the law they were not a part of the people of the state, yet they were to be represented in the legislature of the state. Clay cut this Gordian knot temporarily by remarking that it being understood that a memorial would be presented at the earliest opportunity from the convention of Orleans asking for the annexation of the West Florida territory, it would be wise to wait for it, as there might then be a clearer understanding of the subject. His suggestion was adopted.[6]

---

[5] Richardson, *Messages and Papers of the Presidents,* I, 498; *Annals of Congress,* 12 Cong., Part I (1811–1812), 1155, message dated March 3.

[6] *Annals of Congress,* 12 Cong., Part 2 (1811–1812), 1216–1218.

The memorial here referred to was presented to the House on the next day.[7] Johnson's amendment was then taken up. Calhoun was not in favor of incorporating in the law a principle of representation different from that feature in the constitution of the new state which arranged for a different apportionment. To do this the convention which alone could make the change would have to be reassembled. During the same debate he said that the people in question would be unrepresented only until the organization of the state government. This interval was unavoidable and not important because so short. The proposed amendment, he declared, would be engrafting the principle of territorial government on a state government, to which it was wholly inapplicable. It was "assuming to make a constitution for the people of a State, whose inalienable right it was to form a constitution for themselves."

Nelson of Virginia could not see that the proposed amendment was incompatible with the Constitution, or inexpedient. The error lay in considering Louisiana a state, which it would not be until the bill before the House passed. Congress still had the right to impose conditions in the instrument which was to make Louisiana a state. He felt that the people of West Florida could not be constitutionally deprived of representation in the state legislature. In answer to Poindexter's doubts of how a territory could be represented in the first legislature of the state to which it was not annexed until the consent of the legislature should be obtained, Nelson replied that there was not in existence a legislature of Louisiana, nor would there be until the bill had passed raising the territory to statehood. In admitting the state into the Union, having already imposed conditions, Congress could impose the condition proposed by the amendment. Gholson of Virginia considered the amendment, in its present form, to be incompatible with the constitution offered

---

[7] *Annals of Congress,* 12 Cong., Part 2 (1811–1812), 1219.

for the consideration of Congress. He read an amendment which he proposed to offer if the one under consideration was not agreed to. Johnson's amendment was then negatived by the close vote of thirty-nine to thirty-seven.

The amendment which Gholson offered provided:

That the people of that portion of West Florida hereby proposed to be made a part of the State of Louisiana shall, before the election of Senators and a Representative to the Congress of the United States, be invested with, and enjoy equal rights of representation and equal privileges in every respect, with the people of the residue of the said State.

After a brief debate the amendment was agreed to without a division.[8]

The next day, March 20, the bill for the admission of the state of Louisiana into the Union, and for the extension of the laws of the United States thereto was read a third time and passed without debate by a vote of seventy-nine to twenty-three.[9]

The Senate had taken up the same question,[10] but on March 30, had turned to a consideration of the bill passed by the House.[11] The Senate did not accept the House bill as framed,[12] and offered amendments to it, the principal one being that which separated from the bill the provision for extending the limits of the new state to include a portion of the Florida territory. To this the House agreed.[13] Having passed both Houses, the bill was approved by the President April 8. After specifying the territory included within the limits of the new state, and stating that the conditions stipulated by Congress had been fulfilled, it was enacted that the new state was admitted into the Union on an equal footing with the original states, under the name of the state of Louisiana. As a condition of incorporation

---

[8] *Ibid.*, 1224–1226.
[9] *Ibid.*, 1227.
[10] *Ibid.*, Part I, 171.
[11] *Ibid.*, 176.
[12] *Ibid.*, 179, 184, 186.

into the Union it was further enacted that the Mississippi and the navigable waters leading into it and into the Gulf of Mexico must remain free open highways to the citizens of the United States. The other conditions of the Enabling Act were considered binding in like manner.

Section two provided that until the next census and apportionment of representatives, Louisiana was entitled to one representative; and all laws of the United States not locally inapplicable were extended to the state with the same force and effect as in the rest of the United States.

The third section made arrangements for a judicial district, and the fourth for an United States attorney and a marshal.

Section five laid down customs regulations; and by the last section it was enacted that the act should be in force from and after April 30, 1812.[14]

Although the Senate had refused to pass a bill combining with the admission of Louisiana into the Union, a provision to annex to that state the disputed district of West Florida, this did not mean that the Senate was opposed to the annexation. While the discussion over the Statehood Bill was going on, another bill was reported in the Senate, March 27, to enlarge the limits of the state of Louisiana to include the territory aforementioned.[15] Having passed the Senate,[16] it was sent to the House,[17] and passed.[18]

This act, approved by the President, April 14, 1812, provided, in case the legislature of the state of Louisiana should consent, for the inclusion, as if within the original boundaries of the state, of the territory bounded as follows:

---

13 *Annals of Congress,* 12 Cong., Part 2, 1254.

14 *Ibid.,* Part 2, Appendix, 2264–2265; *Laws of U. States,* IV, 402–403.

15 *Annals of Congress,* 12 Cong., Part 1 (1811–1812), 186.

16 *Ibid.,* 194.

17 *Ibid.,* Part 2, 1278.

18 *Ibid.,* 1298.

Beginning at the junction of the Iberville with the river Mississippi; thence, along the middle of the Iberville, the river Amite, and of the lakes Maurepas and Pontchartrain to the eastern mouth of the Pearl river; thence, up the eastern branch of Pearl river to the thirty-first degree of north latitude; thence along the said degree of latitude to the river Mississippi; thence, down the said river to the place of beginning.

It was further enacted that it should be incumbent upon the legislature of the state, having consented to the incorporation, to make provision by law at their first session for the representation of the territory in the state legislature, upon principles of the Constitution, and for securing to the people of the territory, equal rights, privileges, benefits, and advantages, with those enjoyed by the people of the other parts of the state. The law so providing would be liable to revision, modification or amendment by Congress but not by the legislature of the state.[19]

These provisions were assented to by the legislature of Louisiana, August 4, 1812.[20]

On July 30, Claiborne had entered upon the duties of the office of governor of the state of Louisiana;[21] with the passage of the law above referred to annexing West Florida to Louisiana, the immediate constitutional questions arising from the Louisiana Purchase came to an end. What those questions were and in what manner they were decided has been pointed out. Although no definite authority to do so was contained in the Constitution, the United States had acquired territory. That territory had been divided and governed as Congress and the President dictated, and part of it had after a lapse of years been received into the union of the states by act of Congress and the President, without the consent of the individual states. The

---

[19] *Ibid.*, Appendix, 2270; *Laws of U. States*, IV, 409.

[20] Gayarré, *History of Louisiana*, IV, 281. For the annexation question, see *ibid.*, IV, 276–281; Henry Adams, *History of the United States*, V, 319–326.

[21] Claiborne to Madison, August 2, 1812, in *Madison Papers*, ''Writings to Madison,'' XLVI.

significance of all these constitutional precedents can only be realized by a study of the debates in Congress over each new acquisition of territory, and by a careful survey of the cases decided by the Supreme Court where the rights of the inhabitants of the acquired territories have been at issue. With each new extension of the limits of the United States, the interpretations of the Constitution made at the time of the Louisiana Purchase have been reviewed in argument for and against various provisions of the new annexations. During the controversy over Texas, and, a little later, over the territory acquired from Mexico, opposing statesmen like Webster and Calhoun found support for their arguments in the Louisiana precedents; while a survey of the voluminous report of the Insular Cases of 1900 discloses the fact that so numerous are the references to the contemporary writings and debates on the acquisition of Louisiana that the report might almost serve as a source book of constitutional documents for that subject.

The Louisiana Purchase is not a dead issue, therefore, but lives on in the constitutional history of the present day. It serves as the corner stone for all interpretations of the constitutional right of the United States to acquire and govern foreign territory; and such acquisitions have been one of the most significant features in the history of the United States.

BIBLIOGRAPHY

MANUSCRIPTS

Claiborne Papers. Bureau of Rolls and Library of the State Department, Washington, D. C.

"Claiborne's Correspondence relative to Louisiana." 6 vols.

"Claiborne's Correspondence, Orleans Territory, Miscellaneous." 1 vol.

Jefferson Papers. Manuscripts Division, Library of Congress, Washington, D. C.

"Letters from Jefferson, 1st Series." Vols. IX, XI.

"Letters received at Washington, 2d Series." Vols. XVII, XIX, XXVI, LII, LXXVI.

"Letters received at Paris and Philadelphia, 2d Series." Vol. LXV.

"Letters to Jefferson, 2d Series." Vol. LXIII.

Jefferson Papers. Massachusetts Historical Society Library, Boston, Massachusetts.

"The Coolidge Collection." This collection pertains almost exclusively to private matters and contains little of direct political importance. A selection of letters from this collection is printed in the Massachusetts Historical Society, *Collections*, Seventh series, I (*Jefferson Papers*).

Madison Papers. Manuscripts Division, Library of Congress, Washington, D. C.

"Writings to Madison." Vols. XXVI, XLVI.

Monroe Papers. Manuscripts Division, Library of Congress, Washington, D. C.

"Writings to Monroe." Vol. IX.

"Writings of Monroe." Vol. II.

Pickering Papers. Massachusetts Historical Society Library, Boston, Massachusetts.

"Letters from Correspondents, 1800–1803." Vol. XXVI.

"Letters to his Correspondents, 1801–1813." Vol. XIV.

Plumer Manuscripts. Manuscripts Division, Library of Congress, Washington, D. C.; State Library, Concord, New Hampshire.

A large collection of the letters and papers of Senator William Plumer of New Hampshire. Part of this collection is in the Library of Congress, and part in the State Library, Concord, New

Hampshire. Of Plumer's writings, the most valuable for the purposes of this monograph were the three volumes of a journal of the debates in the Senate from October, 1803, to April, 1807. The first volume is entitled, ''Memorandum of the Proceedings of Congress, Particularly of the Senate, from October 17, 1803, to March 27, 1804''; the second, ''Memorandum of the Proceedings of the second Session of the Eight Congress commencing Nov. 5th 1804 and ending March 3d 1805''; and the third, ''William Plumer's Register, Vol. 1,'' which, despite its title, is merely a continuation of the two former volumes, extending the journal from May 2, 1805, to April 21, 1807. All of these volumes are now in the Manuscripts Division of the Library of Congress.

Robbins Papers. Massachusetts Historical Society Library, Boston, Massachusetts.

Vol. VIII, 1800–1838.

CONTEMPORARY PAMPHLETS, 1803–1812

An Address to the Government of the United States, on the Cession of Louisiana to the French; and on the Late Breach of Treaty by the Spaniards: including the translation of a Memorial, on the war of St. Domingo, and cession of the Mississippi to France, drawn up by a French Counsellor of State. Philadelphia, Baltimore, and Washington City, 1803.

Analysis of the third article of the treaty of cession of Louisiana. [Washington? 1803?]

Appendix to an Account of Louisiana, being an abstract of Documents in the Offices of the Departments of State, and of the Treasury. Philadelphia, 1803.

BISHOP, ABRAHAM.

Oration, in honor of the election of President Jefferson, and the peaceable acquisition of Louisiana, delivered at the National Festival, in Hartford, on the 11th of May, 1804. [Hartford.] For the General Committee of Republicans, 1804.

BRAZER, SAMUEL, Jr.

Address, pronounced at Worcester, on May 12th, 1804, in commemoration of the Cession of Louisiana to the United States. Worcester, 1804.

BROWN, JEREMIAH.

A Short Letter to a Member of Congress concerning the Territory of Orleans. Washington City, 1806.

COLVIN, JOHN B.

Republican Policy; or, The Superiority of the Principles of the present Administration over those of its enemies, who call themselves Federalists; exemplified in the late Cession of Louisiana. Fredericktown, Md., 1802.

COMMON SENSE [THOMAS PAINE].

To the French Inhabitants of Louisiana, September 24, 1804, in *The Writings of Thomas Paine* (Moncure Daniel Conway, ed., New York, 1894–1896), III, 430–436.

DUANE, WILLIAM.

Mississippi Question. A Debate in the Senate of the United States on the 23rd, 24th, and 25th February, 1803, on certain resolutions concerning the Violation of the Right of Deposit. Philadelphia, 1803. [Cf. *Annals of Congress,* 7 Cong., 2 Sess. (1803–1804), 105–256.]

Esquisse de la situation politique et civile de la Louisiane depuis le 30 Novembre 1803 jusqu'au 1er Octobre 1804. Par un Louisianais à la Nouvelle-Orleans. New Orleans, 1804.

FESSENDEN, WILLIAM.

The Political Farrago, or a Miscellaneous Review of Politics in the United States; from the Administration of Washington to that of Mr. Jefferson, in 1806. Brattleboro, January, 1807.

FREEMAN, THOMAS, and CUSTIS, PETER.

An account of the Red River, in Louisiana, drawn up from the returns of Messrs. Freeman & Custis to the War Office of the United States, who explored the Same, in the year 1806. [Washington, 1806?]

JEFFERSON, THOMAS.

An account of Louisiana, being an abstract of documents in the office of the Departments of State, and of the Treasury. [Washington?] Duane, printer [1803?]. [Cf. *Am. State Papers, Misc.,* I, 344–356].

LEONARD, DAVID A.

An Oration, delivered at Raynham (Massachusetts), Friday, May 11th, 1804, on the late acquisition of Louisiana, at the unanimous request of the Republican Citizens of the County of Bristol. Newport (R. I.), 1804.

Lois Décrétées par le Congres des Etats-Unis d'Amerique, pour le Gouvernement, pro tempore, de la Province de la Louisiane. Nouvelle-Orleans, 1804.

MAGRUDER, ALLAN BOWIE.

Political, Commercial and Moral Reflections, on the late cession of Louisiana to the United States. Lexington, Ky., 1803.

PIKE, ZEBULON MONTGOMERY.

An Account of a Voyage up the Mississippi River, from St. Louis to its Source; made under the orders of the War Department, by Lieut. Pike, of the United States Army, in the years 1805 and 1806. Compiled from Mr. Pike's Journal. [Washington, 1807?]

RAMSAY, DAVID.

An Oration on the Cession of Louisiana to the United States, delivered on the 12th May, 1804, in St. Michael's Church, Charleston, South Carolina, at the request of a number of the inhabitants, and published by their desire. Charleston, 1804.

RANDOLPH, THOMAS MANN.

Letter of Thomas M. Randolph to his Constituents. (Dated) City of Washington, April 27, 1806.

Representation and petition of the representatives elected by the freemen of the territory of Louisiana, 4th January, 1805. Washington, 1805.

SIBLEY, JOHN, Dr.

A Letter from Dr. John Sibley of Fayetteville (now of Louisiana) to J. Gales, printer, in Raleigh, Louisiana, August 15, 1803. Published, December 14, 1803.

SYLVESTRIS, pseud.

Reflections on the Cession of Louisiana to the United States. Washington City, 1803.

View of the political and civil situation of Louisiana from November 30, 1803 to the first of October, 1804; by A native. Translated from the French. Philadelphia, 1804.

CONTEMPORARY NEWSPAPERS, 1803–1812

Aurora, Philadelphia.
Charleston Courier.
Columbian Sentinel, Boston.
Federal Gazette & Baltimore Daily Advertiser.
The Independent Chronicle, Boston.
Louisiana Gazette, New Orleans.
National Intelligencer, and Washington Advertiser, Washington.
New England Repertory, Newburyport (Boston from 1804).
New York Evening Post.
New York Herald.
Niles' Weekly Register, Baltimore.
Relfs Philadelphia Gazette and Daily Advertiser.
The Spectator, New York.
Thomas's Massachusetts Spy, or Worcester Gazette.

CONTEMPORARY LITERATURE, 1803–1812

BERQUIN–DUVALLON.
Travels in Louisiana and the Floridas, in the year, 1802, giving a correct picture of those countries. Translated from the French, with notes . . . by John Davis. New York, 1806.
Vue de la colonie espagnole du Mississippi, ou des provinces de Louisiane et Floride Occidentale; en l'année 1802, par un observauteur résident sur les lieux . . . B. . . . Duvallon, éditeur. Paris, 1803.

BRECKINRIDGE, HENRY MARIE.
Views of Louisiana; together with a journal of a voyage up the Missouri River, in 1811. Pittsburgh, 1814.

CRAMER, ZADOK.
The navigator; or, The traders' useful guide in navigating the Monongahela, Allegheny, Ohio, and Mississippi rivers; containing an ample account of these much admired waters . . . *a concise description of their towns, villages, harbours, settlements, etc.; with particular direction how to navigate them, in all stages of the water* . . . *5th edition, much improved and enlarged. To which is added, an account of Louisiana.* Pittsburgh, 1806.

JACQUEMIN [NICHOLAS].
Memoire sur la Louisiane, contenant la description du sol et des productions de cette île, et les moyens de la rendre florissante en peu de temps; avec un vocabulaire et un abrégé de la grammaire de la langue des sauvages. Paris, 1803.
Mémoires sur la Louisiane et la Nouvelle-Orleans, accompagnés d'une dissertation sur les avantages que le commerce de l'empire doit tirer de la stipulation faite par l'article VII du traité de cession, du 30 avril 1803, par M . . .; *suivis d'une traduction de diverses notes sur cette colonie publiés aux Etats-Unis peu de temps après la ratification du traité; terminés par un écrit traitant cette question: Est-il avantageux à la France de prendre possession de la Louisiane?* Paris, 1804.

MORSE, JEDEDIAH [Compiler].
The American gazeteer, exhibiting a full account of the civil divisions, rivers, harbors, Indian tribes, etc., of the American continent . . . *with a particular description of Louisiana.* 3d edition, revised and corrected. Boston, 1810.

ORR, GEORGE.
The possession of Louisiana by the French, considered as it affects the interests of those nations more immediately concerned, viz. Great Britain, America, Spain, and Portugal. London, 1803.

PENDERGAST, GARRETT ELLIOTT.
A physical and topographical sketch of the Mississippi territory, lower Louisiana, and a part of West Florida. Philadelphia, 1803.

PERRIN DU LAC, FRANÇOIS MARIE.
Travels through the two Louisianas, and among the savage nations of the Missouri; also in the United States, along the Ohio, and the adjacent provinces, in 1801, 1802, and 1803. Translated from the French. London, 1807.

Voyage dans les deux Louisianes et chez les nations sauvages du Missouri, par les Etats-Unis, l'Ohio et les provinces qui le bordent, en 1801, 1802 et 1803. Paris, 1805.

ROBIN, CLAUDE C.
Voyages dans l'intérieur de la Louisiane de la Floride Occidentale, et dans les îles de la Martinique et de Saint-Domingue, pendant les années 1802, 1803, 1804, 1805 et 1806. 3 vols. Paris, 1807.

STODDARD, AMOS, Major.
Sketches, historical and descriptive of Louisiana. Philadelphia, 1812.

UNITED STATES GOVERNMENT PUBLICATIONS

American State Papers, Foreign Relations. 6 vols. Washington, 1833–1859.

American State Papers, Miscellaneous. 2 vols. Washington, 1834.

Annals of Congress. 7 Cong., 2 Sess. (1802–1803), to 12 Cong., 1 Sess., II (1811–1812). Washington, 1851–1853.

Insular Cases, comprising the records, briefs, and arguments of counsel in the Insular Cases of the October term, 1900, in the Supreme Court of the United States, including the Appendix thereto. Washington, 1901.

Laws of the United States. Laws from 4th of March, 1789, to 4th March, 1815.... 5 vols. Philadelphia and Washington, 1815.

MAGOON, CHARLES E.
Report on the Legal Status of the Territory and inhabitants of the islands acquired by the United States during the war with Spain, considered with reference to the territorial boundaries, the constitution, and laws of the United States, in Senate Documents, 56 Cong., 1 Sess., XVI (serial no. 3858), Doc. 234. Washington, 1900.

MALLOY, WILLIAM M., Compiler.
Treaties, Conventions, International Acts, Protocols, and Agreements between the United States and Other Powers, 1776–1902. 2 vols. Washington, 1910.

Organic Acts for the Territories of the United States, with notes thereon.
... *Also appendixes comprising other matters relating to the government of the territories,* in *Senate Documents,* 56 Cong., 1 Sess., X
(serial no. 3852), Doc. 148. Washington, 1900.

RICHARDSON, JAMES DANIEL, Compiler.
Compilation of the Messages and Papers of the Presidents, 1789–1897.
10 vols. Washington, 1896–1899.

*State Papers and Correspondence bearing upon the Purchase of the Terri-
tory of Louisiana,* in *House Documents,* 57 Cong., 2 Sess., XCII (serial
no. 4531), Doc. 431. Washington, 1903.

Statutes at Large of the United States of America. Boston and Washington, 1850–

*United States Supreme Court Reports. Reports of Cases argued and
adjudged in the Supreme Court of the United States.* New York, 1882–
1916.

GENERAL AUTHORITIES

Primary

ADAMS, HENRY, ed.
Documents relating to New England Federalism, 1800–1815. Boston,
1877.

ADAMS, JOHN.
The Works of. 10 vols. Boston, 1850–1856. Charles Francis Adams, ed.

ADAMS, JOHN QUINCY.
Memoirs of. 12 vols. Philadelphia, 1874–1877. Charles Francis Adams,
ed.
Writings of. 6 vols. New York, 1913–1916. Worthington Chauncey
Ford, ed.

AMES, FISHER.
Works of. 2 vols. Boston, 1854. Seth Ames, ed.

BARBÉ-MARBOIS, FRANÇOIS, MARQUIS DE.
*Histoire de la Louisiane et de la cession de cette colonie, par la France
aux États-Unis de l'Amerique septrionale; précédée d'un discours
sur la constitution et le gouvernement des États-Unis.* Paris, 1829.
*The History of Louisiana, particularly of the Cession of that Colony
to the United States of America.* Translated from French by an
American Citizen. Philadelphia, 1830.

CUTLER, WILLIAM PARKER, and CUTLER, JULIA PERKINS.
   Life, Journals and Correspondence of Rev. Manasseh Cutler. 2 vols.
   Cincinnati, 1888.

ELLIOT, JONATHAN, ed.
   *The Debates in the several State Conventions on the adoption of the
   Federal Constitution.* 2d ed. 5 vols. Philadelphia, 1888.

FARRAND, MAX, ed.
   Records of the Federal Convention of 1787. 3 vols. New Haven, 1911.

The Federalist. New York, 1898. Paul Leicester Ford, ed.

GALLATIN, ALBERT.
   The Writings of. 3 vols. Philadelphia, 1879. Henry Adams, ed.

JEFFERSON, THOMAS.
   Memoirs, Correspondence, and Miscellaneous. 4 vols. Charlottesville,
   1829. Thomas Jefferson Randolph, ed.
   The Writings of. 9 vols. Washington, 1853–1854. H. A. Washington,
   ed.
   The Writings of. 10 vols. New York, 1892–1899. Paul Leicester Ford,
   ed.
   The Writings of. 20 vols. Washington, 1903–1904. Memorial ed.
   [Andrew A. Lipscomb, ed.]
   The Works of. 12 vols. New York and London, 1904–1905. Federal
   ed. [Paul Leicester Ford, ed.]

KING, RUFUS.
   The Life and Correspondence of. 6 vols. New York, 1894–1900.
   Charles R. King, ed.

MADISON, JAMES.
   Letters and other Writings of. 4 vols. Philadelphia, 1865. Published
   by order of Congress.
   The Writings of. 9 vols. New York, 1900–1910. Gaillard Hunt, ed.

MONROE, JAMES.
   Writings of. 7 vols. New York, 1898–1903. Stanislaus Murray Hamilton, ed.

MORRIS, GOUVERNEUR.
   The Diary and Letters of. 2 vols. New York, 188. Anne Cary Morris, ed.

ROBERTSON, JAMES ALEXANDER.
   *Louisiana under the Rule of Spain, France, and the United States,
   1785–1807.* 2 vols. Cleveland, 1911.

SPARKS, JARED.
   The Life of Gouverneur Morris. 3 vols. Boston, 1832.

SECONDARY AUTHORITIES

ABEL, ANNIE HELOISE.
''The History of Events resulting in Indian Consolidation West of the Mississippi,'' in American Historical Association, *Annual Report, 1906*, I, 233–450. Washington, 1908.

ADAMS, HENRY.
History of the United States [1801–1817]. 9 vols. New York, 1909–1911.
John Randolph. Boston, 1882.
Life of Albert Gallatin. Philadelphia, 1879.

AMES, HERMAN VANDENBURG.
The Proposed Amendments to the Constitution of the United States during the First Century of its History. American Historical Association, *Annual Report, 1896*, II. Washington, 1897.

BIKLÉ, HENRY WOLF.
The Constitutional Power of Congress over the Territory of the United States. University of Pennsylvania, *Publications of the Department of Law [1901]*. Philadelphia, 1901.

BUTLER, CHARLES HENRY.
The Treaty-Making Power of the United States. 2 vols. New York, 1902.

CHAMBERS, HENRY E.
''West Florida and its Relation to the Historical Cartography of the United States,'' in Johns Hopkins University, *Studies in Historical and Political Science*, XVI, no. 5, pp. 201–259. Baltimore, 1898.

CHANNING, EDWARD.
The Jeffersonian System, 1801–1811. New York, 1906.
A History of the United States, Volume IV : Federalists and Republicans, 1789–1815. New York, 1917.

CLAIBORNE, JOHN FRANCIS HAMTRAMCK.
Mississippi as a Province, Territory and State. Jackson, Miss., 1880.

COOLEY, THOMAS MCINTYRE.
''The Acquisition of Louisiana,'' in Indiana Historical Society, *Publications*, II, no. 3. Indianapolis, 1887.

COX, ISAAC JOSLIN.
''The American Intervention in West Florida,'' in *American Historical Review*, XVII, 290–311. New York, 1912.

CRANDALL, SAMUEL BENJAMIN.
Treaties, Their Making and Enforcement. 2d ed. Washington, 1916.

CURTIS, GEORGE TICKNOR.
  Constitutional History of the United States. 2 vols. New York, 1896–1897.

DAVIS, SAMUEL M.
  ''Some of the Consequences of the Louisiana Purchase,'' in American Historical Association, *Annual Report, 1897,* 151–160. Washington, 1898.
  Documents relating to the Purchase and Exploration of Louisiana. I. The Limits and Bounds of Louisiana. By Thomas Jefferson. *II. The Exploration of the Red, the Black, and the Washita Rivers.* By William Dunbar. Printed by direction of the Committee on Historical Documents of the American Philosophical Society. Boston and New York, 1904.

DUBOIS, WILLIAM EDWARD BURGHARDT.
  The Suppression of the African Slave-Trade to the United States of America, 1638–1879. New York, 1896.

FARRAND, MAX.
  ''The Commercial Privileges of the Treaty of 1803,'' in *American Historical Review,* VII, 494–499. New York, 1902.
  The Legislation of Congress for the Government of the Organized Territories of the United States, 1789–1895. Newark, N. J., 1896.
  ''Territory and District,'' in *American Historical Review,* V, 676–681. New York, 1900.

FORMAN, SAMUEL EAGLE.
  The Life and Writings of Thomas Jefferson. 2d ed. Indianapolis, 1900.

FORTIER, ALCÉE.
  History of Louisiana. 4 vols. New York, 1904.

FULLER, HUBERT BRUCE.
  The Purchase of Florida. Cleveland, 1906.

GAYARRÉ, CHARLES.
  History of Louisiana. 4th ed. 4 vols. New Orleans, 1903.

GEER, CURTIS MANNING.
  The Louisiana Purchase and the Westward Movement. Philadelphia, 1904.

GILMAN, DANIEL COIT.
  James Monroe in his relations to the public service during half a century, 1776–1826. Boston, 1883.

HAMILTON, JOHN CHURCH.
  History of the Republic of the United States of America. 7 vols. Philadelphia, 1857–1864.

HERMANN, BINGER.
The Louisiana Purchase and our Title west of the Rocky Mountains, with a Review of Annexation by the United States. Washington, 1900. Reprinted in *House Documents,* 56 Cong., 1 Sess., CV (serial no. 4002), Doc. 708.

HILDRETH, RICHARD.
History of the United States of America from the discovery of the continent to the end of the sixteenth congress, 1497–1821. 6 vols. New York, 1863.

HOLST, HERMANN EDUARD VON.
The Constitutional and Political History of the United States. Translated from the German by John J. Lalor ... 8 vols. Chicago, 1876–1892.

HUNT, GAILLARD.
The American Passport. Washington, 1898.

KING, GRACE.
New Orleans, the Place and the People. New York, 1907.

LOCKE, MARY S.
Anti-Slavery in America, 1619–1808. Boston, 1901.

LODGE, HENRY CABOT.
Life and Letters of George Cabot. Boston, 1877.

McCALEB, WALTER FLAVIUS.
The Aaron Burr Conspiracy. New York, 1903.

McMASTER, JOHN BACH.
A History of the People of the United States from the Revolution to the Civil War. 8 vols. New York, 1907–1913.

MARSHALL, JOHN.
John Marshall, Complete Constitutional Decisions, edited with Annotations Historical, Critical and Legal, by John Dillon. Chicago, 1903.

MARSHALL, THOMAS MAITLAND.
A History of the Western Boundary of the Louisiana Purchase, 1819–1841. Berkeley, 1914.

MARTIN, FRANÇOIS-XAVIER.
History of Louisiana from the Earliest Period. New Orleans, 1882.

MEYERHOLZ, CHARLES.
Federal Supervision over the Territories of the United States. Beiträge zur Kultur- und Universalgeschichte, herausgegeben von Karl Lamprecht. Heft 5–7. Leipzig, 1908.

MONETTE, JOHN W.
  History of the Discovery and Settlement of the Valley of the Missis-
    sippi, by the three great European powers, France, Spain, and Great
    Britain, and the subsequent occupation, settlement, and extension of
    civil government by the United States, until the year 1846. 2 vols.
    New York, 1848.

MOORE, JOHN BASSETT.
  Digest of International Law. 8 vols. Washington, 1906.

MORISON, SAMUEL ELIOT.
  The Life and Letters of Harrison Gray Otis. 2 vols. Boston and
    New York, 1913.

MORSE, JOHN TORREY, Jr.
  Thomas Jefferson. Boston, 1898.

OGG, FREDERICK AUSTIN.
  The Opening of the Mississippi. New York, 1904.

PARTON, JAMES.
  Life of Andrew Jackson. 3 vols. Boston, 1870.
  Life of Thomas Jefferson. Boston, 1874.

PHELPS, ALBERT.
  Louisiana. Boston and New York, 1905.

PLUMER, WILLIAM, Jr.
  Life of William Plumer. Boston, 1857.

QUINCY, EDMUND.
  Life of Josiah Quincy. Boston, 1867.

QUINCY, JOSIAH PHILLIPS.
  The Louisiana purchase and the appeal to posterity, in Massachusetts
    Historical Society, *Proceedings,* second series, XVIII, 48–59. Cam-
    bridge, 1903.

RANDALL, HENRY STEPHENS.
  The Life of Thomas Jefferson. 3 vols. Philadelphia, 1888.

ROBERTSON, C. F.
  The Louisiana Purchase and its Influence upon the American System, in
    American Historical Association, *Papers,* I, no. 4, pp. 249–290. New
    York, 1886.

ROBINSON, WILLIAM A.
  Jeffersonian Democracy in New England. New Haven, 1916.

ROOSEVELT, THEODORE.
  The Winning of the West. 6 vols. New York and London, 1900.

SCHOULER, JAMES.
History of the United States under the Constitution. 7 vols. New York, 1880–1913.

SLOANE, WILLIAM MILLIGAN.
''The World Aspects of the Louisiana Purchase,'' in American Historical Association, *Annual Report, 1903,* I, 87–103. Washington, 1904.

STORY, JOSEPH.
Commentaries on the Constitution of the United States. 5th ed. 2 vols. Boston, 1891.

THAYER, JAMES BRADLEY.
Cases on Constitutional Law. 2 vols. Cambridge, 1895.

THOMAS, DAVID YANCEY.
A History of Military Government in Newly Acquired Territory of the United States, in Columbia University *Studies in History, Economics and Public Law,* XX, no. 2. New York, 1904.

THORPE, FRANCIS NEWTON.
The Constitutional History of the United States. 3 vols. Chicago, 1901.

TUCKER, GEORGE.
The Life of Thomas Jefferson, third president of the United States. 2 vols. London, 1837.

TURNER, FREDERICK JACKSON.
''Significance of the Frontier in American History,'' in American Historical Association, *Annual Report, 1893,* 199–227. Washington, 1894.
''Significance of the Louisiana Purchase,'' in *Review of Reviews,* XXVII, 578–584. New York, 1903.

VILLERS DU TERRAGE, MARC DE, BARON.
Les derniers années de la Louisiane française. Paris, 1903.

WEBSTER, SIDNEY.
Two Treaties of Paris and the Supreme Court. New York and London, 1901.

WILLOUGHBY, WESTEL WOODBURY.
The Constitutional Law of the United States. 2 vols. New York, 1910.

WINSOR, JUSTIN, ed.
Narrative and Critical History of America. 8 vols. Boston, 1889.

APPENDIX[1]

THE SENATE DEBATE ON THE BRECKINRIDGE BILL FOR THE GOVERNMENT OF LOUISIANA, 1804, AS REPORTED BY SENATOR WILLIAM PLUMER OF NEW HAMPSHIRE

1804, Monday, Jany. 16th.

THE BILL ERECTING LOUISIANA INTO TWO TERRITORIES

Mr. Worthington.[2] Moved to amend the 4th section so as that the Legislative Council should be authorized to elect a delegate to Congress with the right to debate but not vote.[3]

Mr. Brackenridge.[4] I approve of the motion—it will be the means of conveying useful knowledge to Congress.

Mr. Saml. Smith.[5] This is going as far as we can at present to' satisfy the third article of the treaty.[6] This will be placing that country on the same footing as the other territorial governments[7]—and from this delegate we shall derive much information.

Mr. Dayton.[8] I am opposed. The legislative Council itself will be better able by their memorials to represent the actual state and wants of that country than their agent.

Mr. Jn. Smith.[9] I think the amendment is necessary and important.

---

[1] Reprinted from *The American Historical Review*, vol. XXII, no. 2, January, 1917, through the courtesy of Dr. J. Franklin Jameson, managing editor.

[2] Thomas Worthington, senator from Ohio.

[3] The fourth section of the bill was that providing as to the appointment and powers of the legislative council. It is quoted in the *Journal* of the Senate for this day (III, 340 of the reprint of 1821). It is in almost every particular identical with the fourth section of the act as finally passed. The act made no provision for a territorial delegate.

[4] John Breckinridge, senator from Kentucky.

[5] Samuel Smith, senator from Maryland.

[6] The third article of the Louisiana Treaty provided that the inhabitants of the ceded territory should be incorporated in the Union of the United States and admitted as soon as possible to the enjoyment of the privileges of citizenship, and that in the meantime they should be protected in the free enjoyment of their liberty, property, and religion.

[7] At this time there was statutory provision for delegates from the Mississippi and Indiana territories.

[8] Jonathan Dayton, senator from New Jersey.

[9] John Smith, senator from Ohio.

Mr. Pickering.[10] No man will undertake to say, Louisiana is incorporated into the Union, it is therefore absurd to admit a delegate from that country to debate in our national councils. That is a purchased province and as such we must govern it.

Mr. White.[11] I cannot consider that territory as a part of the Union. The legislative council are to be created by the President and shall they be vested with the power of choosing a delegate to Congress, and who will in fact be the representative of the President. 'Tis wrong.

Mr. Jackson.[12] I am opposed to the motion. The people of that country ought not to be represented in Congress. It is too soon.

Mr. Anderson.[13] If this amendment does not obtain, I must vote agt. the section. What, tax that people without their being represented!

Mr. Worthington. What danger can arise from this measure—the delegate can only debate not vote.

Mr. Bradley.[14] This delegate will be the representative of your President not of that people. I am surprised to find an advocate for such doctrine. Is the Executive to be represented in the other House? If he can have one delegate to represent him, why not fifty?

Mr. Dayton. The motion is unconstitutional. The constitution has provided only for the representation of States, and no man will pretend that Louisiana is a State. It is true by the confederation[15] provision was made for delegates from territories—and our constitution has provided *that all contracts and engagements entered into before its adoption shall be valid* (Art. 6th) but no man will have the hardihood to say that Louisiana was included in that engagement.

Mr. Adams.[16] I was pleased with this motion—but the objections arising from the Constitution, and from the Delegate's being the representative of the Executive and not of that people—compels me *reluctantly* to decide against it.

Mr. Cocke.[17] Gentlemen confound things—this man will not be a representative but a delegate. The government of Louisiana has been compared to other territorial governments, as Mississippi—but this is wrong.

[10] Timothy Pickering, senator from Massachusetts.

[11] Samuel White, senator from Delaware.

[12] James Jackson, senator from Georgia.

[13] Joseph Anderson, senator from Tennessee.

[14] Stephen R. Bradley, senator from Vermont.

[15] Rather, by the ordinance for the government of the Northwest Territory, sec. 12.

[16] John Quincy Adams, senator from Massachusetts. Some account of the proceedings and debates upon this bill will be found in his *Memoirs*, I, 290–295.

[17] William Cocke, senator from Tennessee.

This is an original system, founded on new principles—it is unlike anything in Heaven, in earth or under it—we must therefore reason from itself and not compare it with others—for myself I admire it. What part of the Constitution shall we violate by this amendment—none. This delegate will not be a constitutional representative, the objection therefore is not solid. I know *that* people are ignorant, but ignorant people will always elect learned and wise men to represent them, they know the necessity of it. I love and venerate these people—*they live in the west.*

Mr. Brackenridge. This amendment is no infringement of the constitution. This officer will not be a representative, for he cannot vote—he will be a delegate, and can only deliberate. He will have no legislative power.

Mr. S. Smith. There is nothing in the constitution that precludes the senate from admitting delegates on this floor from the old territories and what is there that can restrain us from admitting Louisiana to send a delegate to the other House? There can be no danger that the delegate will mislead or impose upon the House.

The motion failed yeas 12 nays 18.

1804, Tuesday, Jany. 17th.

The motion to extend the trial by jury in all criminal prosecutions in that territory[18] was lost yeas 11, nays 16.

1804, Tuesday, 24th. Jany.

The Bill for the Government of Louisiana

Mr. Jackson. The inhabitants of Louisiana are not citizens of the United States—they are now in a state of probation. They are too ignorant to elect a legislature[19]—they would consider jurors as a curse to them.

Mr. McClay.[20] Those people are men and capable of happiness—they ought to elect a legislature and have jurors.

Mr. Saml Smith. Those people are absolutely incapable of governing themselves, of electing their rulers or appointing jurors. As soon as they are capable and fit to enjoy liberty and a free government I shall be for giving it to them.

---

[18] The bill provided for trial by jury ''in all cases which are capital''; the motion was to strike out the words ''which are capital.'' *Journal*, III, 343–344.

[19] The amendment under discussion provided for popular election of the legislative council.

[20] Samuel Maclay, senator from Pennsylvania.

Mr. Cocke. The people of that country are free—let them have liberty and a free government. This bill I hope will not pass—it is tyrannical.

Mr. Nicholas.[21] I approve of the bill as it is. I am opposed to giving them the rights of election, or the power of having jurors. We oug'.it not *yet* to give that people *self-government.* As soon as it is necessary I will give my assent to that Country's being admitted as a state into the Union.

Mr. Anderson. Several gentlemen of the Senate, I am sorry to say it, appear to have no regard for the third article of the treaty—they seem opposed to freedom. This bill has not a single feature of our government in it—it is a system of tyranny, destructive of elective rights. We are bound by treaty, and must give that people a free elective government.

Mr. Pickering. That people are incapable of performing the duties or enjoying the blessings of a free government. They are too ignorant to elect suitable men.

Mr. Jackson.[22] Slaves must be admitted into that territory, it cannot be cultivated without them.

Mr. Brackenridge. I am against slavery. I hope the time is not far distant when not a slave will exist in this Union. I fear our slaves in the south will produce another St. Domingo.

Mr. Franklin.[23] I am wholly opposed to slavery.

Mr. Dayton. Slavery must be tolerated, it must be established in that country, or it can never be inhabited. White people cannot cultivate it— your men cannot bear the burning sun and the damp dews of that country —I have traversed a large portion of it. If you permit slaves to go there only from your States, you will soon find there the very worst species of slaves. The slave holders in the United States will collect and send into that country their slaves of the worst description.

Mr. John Smith. I know that country. I have spent considerable time there—white men can cultivate it. And if you introduce slaves from foreign Countries into that territory, they will soon become so numerous as to endanger the government and ruin that country. I wish slaves may be admitted there from the United States. I wish our negroes were scattered more equally, not only through the United States, but through our territories—that their power might be lost. I can never too much admire the deep policy of New England in excluding slavery. I thank God we have no slaves in Ohio.

21 William Cary Nicholas, senator from Virginia.

22 Comparison of the original bill, amendments, and amended bills preserved in the Senate files shows that the Senate at this point began the consideration of an amendment which extended to the new territory the act of February 28, 1803, forbidding importation of slaves into states which prohibited their importation.

23 Jesse Franklin, senator from North Carolina.

Mr. Franklin. Slavery is in every respect an evil to the States in the south and in the west, it will, I fear, soon become a dreadful one—negro insurrections have already been frequent—they are alarming. Look in the laws of Virginia and North Carolina made for the purpose of guarding against and suppressing these rebellions, and you will learn our dangers.[24]

1804, Wednesday, Jany. 25.

BILL FOR THE GOVERNMENT OF LOUISIANA.
QUESTION RELATIVE TO SLAVERY

Mr. Bradley. I am in favor of extending slavery to that country, because it is a right they claim, and by the treaty we are bound to grant it to them—but I think that in this bill we had better say nothing on that subject.

Mr. Hillhouse.[25] Negroes are rapidly increasing in this country—there encrease for the ten years ending with the last census was near two hundred thousand. I consider slavery as a serious evil, and wish to check it wherever I have authority. Will not your slaves, even in the southern states, in case of a war, endanger the peace and security of those states? Encrease the number of slaves in Louisiana, they will in due time rebel—their numbers in the district of Orleans, are now equal to the whites[26]—why add fuel to this tinder box, which when it takes fire will assuredly extend to some of your states. Why encrease the evil at a distant part of your territory—which must necessarily require a standing army to protect it? If that country cannot be cultivated without slaves, it will instead of being a paradise prove a curse to this country, particularly to some of the states in its vicinity.

Mr. Bradley. I am in favor of establishing a form of a general, not particular, government—we ought not to descend to particulars. We are incompetent to that—they are too distant from us, and we are ignorant of their wants, their habits and manners. Congress is an improper body to make municipal laws—we have abundant proof of this in our legislation for this district in which we sit—our laws here are very imperfect and insufficient.

---

[24] Here Senator Plumer gives a summary of a letter of Governor Claiborne, describing conditions in New Orleans, which the Senate at this point received from President Jefferson, covered by his brief message of this date, given in the *Journal* and in Richardson, I, 367.

[25] James Hillhouse, senator from Connecticut.

[26] Hillhouse probably meant the district consisting of the island of New Orleans with its immediate dependencies. In that case the numbers, according to the statistics which had been furnished by Jefferson (*American State Papers, Miscellaneous*, I, 384), were, 25,000 whites, 25,000 blacks.

Mr. Adams. Slavery in a normal sense is an evil; but as connected with commerce it has important uses. The regulations offered to prevent slavery are insufficient, I shall therefore vote against them.

Mr. Dayton. I do not wonder at the sentiments of the gentleman from Connecticut (Mr. Hillhouse), for he has been opposed to everything that relates to Louisiana—he appears to me to wish to render this bill as bad as possible; but I am surprised that gentlemen who are friendly to that country, wish to prohibit slavery—it will barr the cultivation and improvement of that extensive territory. The lives of white people are shorter there than in any of our states, and the labour of slaves more necessary. An elective government and trial by jury would be a curse to that people; but slavery is essential to their existence.

Mr. Hillhouse. I do not understand the doctrine nor censures of the gentleman from New Jersey (Mr. Dayton). The constitution is by him winked out of sight—that admits of a republican government and no other. We must apply the constitution to that people in all cases or in none. We must consider that country as being within the Union or without it—there is no alternative. I think myself they are not a part or parcel of the United States.

Mr. John Smith. I have traversed many of the settlements in that country. I know that white men labour there—they are capable of cultivating it. Slaves ought not to be permitted to set their feet there. Introduce slaves there, and they will rebel. That country is full of swamps—negroes can retire to them after they have slain their masters. This was in fact the case not eighteen years since—they rose, slew many, and fled to the morasses.[27] Will you encrease there number, and lay the necessary foundation for the horrors of another St. Domingo? If slaves are admitted there, I fear, we shall have cause to lament the acquisition of that country—it will prove a curse.

Mr. Jackson. The treaty forbids this regulation. It will depreciate your lands there fifty pr cent. I am a Rice-planter—my negroes tend three acres each pr man—I never work them hard, they finish their stint by one or two o'clock, and then make three shillings pr diem to themselves. I know that a white man cannot cultivate three acres of rice, and yet Georgia is not so warm as Louisiana. You cannot prevent slavery—neither laws moral or human can do it. Men will be governed by their interest, not the law. We must keep the third article of the treaty always in view.

Mr. Anderson. On the ground of the interest of the western states, the admission of slaves into Louisiana ought to be opposed—it will prove a

---

[27] Possibly the reference is to the abortive attempt at insurrection in Pointe Coupée parish in 1795, *eight* years before.

curse to us. By the constitution slavery is criminal. All the States, except South Carolina, have passed laws against the importation of slaves.[28]

Mr. White. I think it unfortunate that whenever this question is stirred, feelings should be excited that are calculated to lead us astray. I have entertained the hope that Congress would on all occasions avail themselves of every mean in their power to prevent this disgraceful traffick in *human flesh*. There is nothing in the treaty that guarantees to the people of that Country the *power*, I will not say *right*, of holding slaves. 'Tis our duty to prevent, as far as possible, the horrid evil of slavery—and thereby avoid the fate of St. Domingo. Nothing but the interposition of Heaven, an unusual thunder-storm, prevented the slaves, only two years since, from destroying Richmond in Virginia.[29] That, and other states are obliged annually to make many severe and expensive provisions to protect and guard the lives of the masters and their families against the violence of the slaves.

It is said that Louisiana cannot be cultivated by *white men*. May not this proceed from the very circumstance of their having slaves. Let white men be accustomed to the culture of that country, and they will, I believe, find they are able to bear the fatigue of it. We may by use, by long habit, be brought to bear heat and fatigue as well as blacks. We boast of liberty and yet in the very bosom of our Country, establish slavery by law. Examine the state of this Union. In the Eastern States where slavery is not suffered, their lands are highly cultivated—their buildings neat, useful and elegant—and the people are strong, powerful and wealthy. But as you travel south, the instant you arrive to where slavery is, you find the lands uncultivated, the building decaying and falling into ruins and the people poor weak, and feeble. This is not the effect of climate—for our southern climates are more favorable than the eastern and the northern.

Mr. Bradley. I am opposed to slavery in the eastern states; but the resolution under consideration admits the principle of slavery, and therefore I shall vote against it.

Mr. White. I shall vote for it not because I wholly approve of it, but because I think it as favorable toward people of colour as anything we can now obtain.

Mr. Saml Smith. I am at a loss to know why the gentleman from Massachusetts (Mr. Adams) has so often considered and declared himself as the exclusive advocate for constitutional rights. I am against this motion. The people of that country wish for African slaves, and we ought to let them have a supply—we have a constitutional right to prohibit slavery in that

---

[28] By successive enactments, from 1787 to 1803, South Carolina had, like the other states, forbidden the importation of slaves, but these laws had just been repealed, December 17, 1803, and the trade reopened.

[29] The reference is to Gabriel's Insurrection, September, 1800.

country, but I doubt as to the policy of it—I shall vote against the motion. We are bound to provide for the support of the clergy of that country.

Mr. Hillhouse. The gentleman from Vermont (Mr. Bradley) is opposed to slavery. To prove his opposition he declares he will vote against this resolution, which is designed to limit slavery to those who are in the country —and if he prevails in his opposition, the consequence will be that the people of Louisiana will have the liberty of importing slaves not only from the United States, *but also directly from Africa.* If that country cannot be cultivated without slaves, let slaves hold it—or let it remain a wilderness forever. Those are the real friends of liberty who extend it to others, as well as to themselves.

Mr. Israel Smith.[30] The provision proposed, is insufficient—it will rather encrease than prevent slavery. I am opposed to slavery but as Congress cannot prohibit it effectually till 1808—and as there are many slaves in Louisiana I think the change proposed will be too sudden—that it will operate as an encouragement to South Carolina to import slaves.[31] I am therefore opposed to doing anything upon the subject at the present.

No vote taken on the subject.

1804, Thursday, Jany. 26.

GOVERNMENT OF LOUISIANA—SLAVERY

Mr. Hillhouse. I have been accused of being unfriendly to this territory —and of having made the motion now under discussion not from a regard to that country or its inhabitants but to embarrass the measures of government. I was opposed to the ratification of the treaty, but as that is past, I am bound to act in relation to that country upon such principles as to me appear correct and calculated to promote the general interest of the Nation. And I hope I shall never find it necessary to adduce evidence to prove the sincerity of my disposition or the truth of my declaration. It has been said on this floor that I am an *Eastern man.* I am so, but *while* I am the representative of a State which is *yet* a member of the *Union,* I hope I shall have as much influence as if I was a *southern man.* I did not expect *so soon* to hear on this floor the distinction of *eastern and northern, and southern, men.* Has it indeed come to this—are we to be designated by a geographical line?

The question was on the following motion, to wit.

"That it shall not be lawful for any persons or persons, to import or bring into the said territory, from any port or place without the limits of the United States, or to cause or procure to be so imported or brought, or

---

[30] Israel Smith, senator from Vermont.
[31] See note 28 above.

knowingly to aid or assist in so importing or bringing, any slave or slaves; and every person so offending and being thereof convicted, before any court within the said territory, having competent jurisdiction, shall forfeit and pay, for each and every slave, so imported or brought the sum of...................
dollars, one moiety for the use of the United States, and the other moiety, for the use of the person or persons who shall sue for the same; and every slave so imported or brought, shall thereupon become entitled to and receive his or her freedom.''

Note, This amendment was presented by Mr. Hillhouse.[32]

Mr. Jackson. Slavery must be established in that country or it must be abandoned. Without the aid of slaves neither coffee or cotton can be raised. My interest is to prevent slavery in that country, because that will prevent its settlement, and thereby raise the value of estates in Georgia—but my duty is in this opposed to my interest, and that of my State.

I think it would be for the real interest of the United States to have an end to slavery in this country; but we cannot get rid of them.

I am against the prohibition—let those people judge for themselves—the treaty is obligatory upon us.

I dislike the traffic in human flesh—but we must decide not on the morality but policy of the case.

The present time is an improper time to prohibit the importation of slaves into that country—our government is not yet established there.

Slaves in America are generally well fed clothed and taken care of—our interest obliges us to do it—they live better than if they were free—they are incapable of liberty.

Mr. Dayton. These very debates will encrease the *hopes* of slaves. You are about to prohibit African slaves from that country—and to admit the worst of slaves—such as the southern planters wish to sell:—I say admit slaves for slaves must cultivate Louisiana—white people cannot subsist there without them.

The faith of the nation, is by the treaty, pledged to that people, that their rights shall be secured to them—one of ther rights is slavery.

It is of importance that we should raise our own sugar—that we can do if we have slaves.

Mr. Bradley. The prohibiting slaves in that territory from Africa, and admitting them from the States, will encrease, not lessen, slavery. Each State can till 1808 import slaves from Africa, and by this law the slave states may send their vicious slaves to Louisiana.

Mr. Brackenridge. I have no hesitation in saying, That the treaty does not in the smallest degree authorize that people to hold slaves—much less

---

[32] This amendment of Hillhouse, preserved in manuscript in the Senate files, is that which appears in the printed *Journal*, III, 345.

does it pledge the faith of the Union to support this unjust, unnatural traffic. When I look at the Census, I am alarmed at the encrease of slaves in the southern states. I consider slavery as an evil—and am for confining it within as small a compass as possible.

Mr. Bradley. I am against slavery—but this provision is insufficient, and I shall vote against it. If the States holding slaves, require it, I will go as far as they wish in abolishing slavery, for I am an enemy to it. But that time is not yet come—the public mind is not ready for it—and I think we had now better do nothing upon the subject.

Mr. Samuel Smith. I am sorry this proposition is brought before the Senate—I am against slavery—but I shall vote against this proposition— and I fear it will thereby appear that I am in favor of slavery. Yet let it be remembered, that although I am a slave holder, I declare I disapprove of slavery.

Mr. Franklin. My wish is to prohibit slaves altogether from that coun- try, except those carried thither by actual settlers from the United States— but I dispair of obtaining such a vote in Senate—I will vote for such a prohibition as I can obtain.

I have no objection to sending a frigate to Charlestown to prevent the landing of slaves from Africa imported by South Carolina—and *frittering those nefarious traders to pieces.*

Mr. Jackson. Gentlemen from the north and the east do not know that *white men* cannot indure the heat of a vertical sun—they cannot cultivate and raise a crop of rice—negroes are necessary for that country. It is as impossible to prevent the importation of them into that country as to move the sun into the moon. Human power and invention cannot prevent it. Within less than a year 10,000 slaves have against law been imported into South Carolina and Georgia.[33] 'Tis in vain to make laws upon this subject. Slaves directly from Africa are preferable to those who have been long in this country or even to those born here. I am sorry that the constitution of Georgia prohibits slavery.[34]

Mr. Pickering. When this subject was first brought up I was favorably inclined to the admission of slavery in that territory—but the discussion has convinced me that it will be bad policy indeed to admit slaves there—that it will entail upon their posterity a burthen they will be unable to bear or remove—and that slaves are unnecessary there—white people can cultivate it. I therefore approve of the resolution.

---

[33] See the statements of Lowndes of South Carolina and Mitchell of New York in the House debate of February 14, 1804. *Annals of Congress,* 8 Cong., 1 Sess., pp. 992, 1000.

[34] The constitution of Georgia, 1798, art. IV, sec. 11, prohibited, not slavery, but the future importation of slaves into that state from Africa or any foreign place.

Mr. Bradley. This resolution supports slavery. I shall therefore vote against it, although it is bro't forward by those who wish to destroy slavery. The Constitution of Vermont declares all men free—I have sworn to support it, and I will.

Mr. Israel Smith. I am opposed to this resolution, because it will not prevent slavery—I am opposed to slavery; but I think no law can prevent or destroy it—the law will be useless and therefore I shall vote against it. If a law was made to prohibit the use of cyder in New England, where it is now being used in every family, could you carry it into effect. This is the case of slaves in that country. We cannot till 1808 pass any effectual law against slavery. South Carolina has opened its ports for the importation of slaves from Africa, and this she has a *right* to do.

The people of Louisiana ought not to be subject to much change in government, laws, or habits at present. They are not yet bound to us by any ties. This resolution will estrange them from us—it will oppress them. It cannot be carried into effect. It will give encouragement to the States in 1808 to resist any laws that we may then constitutionally make to abolish slavery. I therefore hope we shall *now* do nothing relative to slavery.

Mr. Samuel Smith. I wish I could prevent the taking of the yeas and nays when the Senate are sitting in Committee of the whole—I dislike it—it is absurd.

Mr. Jackson. It is now more than half past three P.M. and I move for an adjournment. Refused. He then said, It is unfair for a *majority* thus to press the subject.

The question was then taken on the amendment (page 316)[36] and prevailed, yeas 21, nays 6.

Mr. Bradley. As tomorrow is to be a day of festivity on account of the acquisition of Louisiana,[37] I move that the Senate adjourn to Monday next.

Negatived.

After the Senate was adjourned, he said with great passion that he would not on the morrow either attend the Senate or the feast. He kept his word.

1804, Monday, Jany. 30.

Mr. Hillhouse moved the following amendment, to the Louisiana bill.

"That no male person bro't into said territory of Louisiana, from any part of the United States, or territories thereof, or from any province or

---

35 See J. Q. Adams, *Memoirs,* I, 292–293.

36 Of the manuscript. Hillhouse's amendment, see note 36.

37 J. Q. Adams, *Memoirs,* I, 293.

colony in America belonging to any foreign prince or state, after the ....
day of .... next, ought or can be holden by law to serve for more than
the term of one year, any person as a servant, slave, or apprentice, after
he attains the age of 21 years; nor female in like manner, after she attains
the age of 18 years, unless they are bound by their own voluntary act, after
they arrive to such age, or bound by law for the payment of debts, damages,
fines, or costs. Provided, that no person held to service or labor in either
of the States or territories aforesaid, under the laws thereof, escaping into
said territory of Louisiana, shall by anything contained herein, be discharged
from such service or labor, but shall be delivered up in the manner prescribed by law.''[38]

Mr. Hillhouse. I am in favor of excluding slavery from that Country
altogether. Every slave increases the necessity of a standing army. Every
slave weakens the power of the militia. The *distance* from the States
encreases the necessity of excluding slavery there.

Mr. Bradley, made a few observations in support of the amendment.

It was rejected yeas 11, nays 17.

Mr. Hillhouse then offered the following amendment,

''That it shall not be lawful for any person or persons, to import or
bring into the said territory, from any port or place within the limits of
the United States, or cause to, or procure to be so imported or bro't, or
knowingly to aid or assist in so importing or bringing, any slave or slaves,
which shall have been imported, since the day —————— into any port or
place within the limits of the United States, from any port or place without
the limits of the United States; and every person so offending and being
thereof convicted, before any court within the said territory, having competent jurisdiction, shall forfeit and pay for each and every such slave, so
imported or bro't, the sum of .... dollars: one moiety for the
use of the person or persons who shall sue for the same.''[39]

Mr. Hillhouse, observed this was but a part of the system necessary to
be adopted.

Mr. Dayton. South Carolina has now a constitutional right to import
slaves from Africa—she is in the exercise of that right—and this amendment
impairs it.

Mr. Hillhouse. It does, and *justly.*

Mr. Jackson. It is unfortunate that we have slaves; but having them
we cannot with safety or policy free them. A very few *free negroes* in
Louisiana would revolutionize that country. In Georgia we prohibit men

---

[38] *Journal,* III, 346–347.

[39] The amendment presented at this time by Hillhouse (*Journal,* III,
347) embraces both this text and that which appears at the beginning of
the next day's proceedings in this record, and of p. 353.

from manumitting their slaves[40]—one free negro is more dangerous where there are slaves than a 100 slaves. I will join to *export* all the slaves.

Mr. Hillhouse. I believe slavery is a real evil; but I am sensible we must extinguish it by degrees. It will not do to attempt to manumit all the slaves at once. Such a measure would be attended with serious evils. These slaves are men—they have the passions and feelings of men. And I believe if we were slaves, we should not be more docile, more submissive, or virtuous than the negroes are.

Mr. Nicholas. Free men of *colour* have a very ill effect upon slaves— they do much more mischief than strangers conceive of.

Mr. Adams. The general complaint against gentlemen from the eastern States has been that they have discovered too much opposition to slavery. I am opposed to slavery; but I have in this bill voted against the provisions introduced to prohibit and lessen it. I have done this upon two principles, 1. That I am opposed to legislating at all for that country. 2. I think we are proceeding with too much haste on such an important question.

Mr. Bradley. I abhor slavery. I am opposed to it in every shape. *He that steals a man and sells him ought to die.*[41] I will on every occasion vote against slavery. I am very sorry the question is *now* called up. I have done everything I could to prevent it—but since gentlemen, (and many of them from Slave States) will stir the question, I am prepared and will on all occasions vote against slavery.

The amendment was adopted, yeas 21, nays 7.

1804, Tuesday, Jany. 31.

BILL RELATING TO LOUISIANA

Motion to strike out the following words, from the amendment to the bill.

"And no slave or slaves shall directly or indirectly be introduced into said territory, except by a person or persons removing into said territory for actual settlement, and being at the same time of such removal *bona fide* owner of such slave or slaves; and every slave imported or bro't into the said territory, contrary to the provisions of this act, shall thereupon be entitled to, and receive his or her freedom."[42]

Mr. Bradley. I am opposed to this paragraph, because it admits the doctrine of slavery to be just—it is like a law regulating theft or any other crime, I shall therefore vote to expunge it. I really consider slavery as a moral evil—as a violation of the laws of God—of nature—of Vermont.

---

[40] A Georgia act of 1801 made manumission illegal unless accomplished by act of the legislature. Cobb, *Digest*, p. 983.

[41] Exodus XXI, 16.

[42] See note 39 above. The motion also provided a substitute with slight modifications. *Journal*, I, 348.

Mr. Nicholas. The gentleman from Vermont (Mr. Bradley) has surprised me by his extraordinary conduct—for several days he spoke and
voted with his friends who advocated slavery—but yesterday and today he
has avowed other sentiments and changed his vote. He is now become
vociferous for emancipation. Is he apprehensive the restriction will prevail. Is he afraid of finding his name on the journal against the vote. Why
this unaccountable change?

Mr. Bradley. I have not changed my sentiments. I am unwilling to
have the question stirred. I was desirous of shutting my eyes against the
subject—but since I am compelled to act, I will vote in favor of *liberty*.

Mr. Jackson. If this law with these amendments passes you destroy
that country—you render it useless—you will excite alarms in the mind of
Frenchmen—you will render a standing army necessary. I again say that
country cannot be cultivated without slaves—it never will.

Mr. John Smith. I am willing to admit slaves into that country from
the U.S., because slaves are already there, but I am unwilling to admit them
from Africa. You cannot prevent slaves going there from the United States.
I know this is an evil, but it is an evil they will have.

Mr. Saml Smith. When the prohibition of slavery was first introduced
into this bill I was much alarmed. I foresaw it would take up time—that
it would create alarm and even endanger the peace and security of these
States holding slaves—especially when the subject is debated in the other
House—and those debates published in Newspapers. God knows that I
am not friendly to slavery, although I own slaves and live in a state where
slavery is established by law. I am unwilling to think much less to speak
on this subject. This bill if passed into a law cannot be carried into effect
—the people of that country will not submit to it. I will render a standing
army necessary. In the year 1808 we may then effectually legislate on the
subject—the constitution will then admit of it, and our navy will then enable
us to carry it into effect. American slaves carried to Louisiana will prove
adders that will sting that people to the heart. The report of your debate
in this Senate on this subject will reach that country in twelve days, and
I fear will produce a rebellion—our troops there are few and feeble, and
will be unable to prevent it.

Mr. John Smith. If the slaves now in the southern States continue to
encrease, in 20 or 30 years those States will be compelled to call on the
eastern and western states to aid them against their rebellious slaves.

Mr. Franklin. We cannot wink this subject out of sight—if we leave
it, it will follow us. We must make laws against slavery, unless we mean
to aid the destruction of our southern States, by laying the foundation for
another St. Domingo. Slavery is a dredful evil—we *feel* it in North Carolina—we can emancipate. I am for restraining foreign importation, but
to proceed no further.

Mr. Brackenridge. We can make laws to prevent slaves, and we can carry those laws into effect—if we cannot do this our power is too feeble to govern this nation. We must not despair—we must act. We are legislating for a great country—for an important section of the nation. In doing this I will not for a moment attend to its immediate effects, whether it will lessen or encrease sugar, or other articles. No Sir, I extend my views to posterity. It is of importance that our first acts of Legislation should be correct. Can it be right to extend and foister slavery into that country?

I think it good policy to permit slaves to be sent there from the United States. This will disperse and weaken that race—and free the southern states from a part of its black population, and of its danger. If you do not permit slaves from the United States to go there, you will thereby prohibit men of wealth from the southern States going to settle in that country.

It has been said by the gentleman from Vermont (Mr. Bradley) *that liberty cannot exist with slavery.* This is not correct—it exists in these states who have slaves. Our constitution recognizes *slavery*—it does more—it expresly *protects it.*

Mr. Nicholas. One State only, South Carolina, can now import Slaves—and that is a *right* derived not from Congress, but from the constitution—it is a mere temporary right. The people of Louisiana cannot therefore complain of partiality in Congress because we deny them the liberty of importing foreign slaves. It is no more than what we long since denied to the Mississippi and Ohio territories. We are now making a form of government for Louisiana, not establishing a common and ordinary law. I am for prohibiting the people of that country from importing slaves from foreign countries, and leave it optional with the government of Louisiana, when they have one, to prohibit it from the United States also, if they should think best.

Mr. Adams. I do not like either of the amendments that have been offered, but if I must vote for either it will be to retain the word moved to be struck out. If I must vote it will be in favor of liberty. The Constitution does not recognize slavery—it contains no such *word*—a great circumlocution of words is used merely to avoid the term *slaves.*

Mr. Venable.[43] I know the constitution does not contain the *word* slave—but it admits the *thing* and protects it—and Congress have uniformly acted accordingly.

The question for striking out was lost, yeas 13, nays 15.*

---

[43] Abraham B. Venable, senator from Virginia.

* It is obvious that the zeal displayed by the Senators from the Slave States, to prohibit the foreign importation of Slaves into Louisiana, proceeds from the motive to raise the price of their own slaves in the market—and to encrease the means of dispersing of those who are most turbulent and dangerous to them.

1804, Wednesday, Feby. 1.

BILL FOR THE GOVERNMENT OF LOUISIANA

It was moved by *Mr. Hillhouse* to amend it by adding the following,—
"And no slave or slaves shall directly or indirectly be introduced into the said territory, except by *a citizen of the United States*,[44] removing into said territory, for actual settlement, and being at the time of such removal *bona fide* owner of such slave or slaves; and every slave imported or brought into the said territory, contrary to the provisions of this act, shall thereupon be enttled to, and receive his or her freedom.''

Mr. Jackson. I move to postpone the further consideration of this amendment to September.

Mr. Hillhouse. This being an amendment to a bill it cannot be postponed unless the bill is postponed with it.

The President.[45] The motion is not in order—it cannot be recd.

Mr. Wright.[46] The owners of land in that country who do not live there ought to have liberty of sending their slaves to cultivate their own land but not to sell their slaves there.

It is wrong to reproach us with the *immorality* of *slavery*—that is a crime we must answer at the bar of God—we ought not therefore to answer it here—for it would be unjust that we should be punished twice for the same offence.

I am against admitting *foreign slaves,* because the State of Maryland has declared it *wrong.*[47]

Mr. Jackson. This amendment does not authorize foreigners who may go to settle in that country to carry their slaves with them, I am therefore on this ground opposed to the amendment. The great object we should have in view should be the settlement of that country. Our interest is to admit Englishmen there as soon and as fast as possible.

Mr. Hillhouse. I hope foreigners will not be permitted to settle in that *distant* country. It is seldom, that any but the *worst* of men leave their own to settle in a foreign country.

Mr. Jackson. I am not afraid of such evils. The *friends of liberty only will come*—let us encourage the settlement of that country as much

---

[44] The words which Plumer has underlined are the new matter, substituted for ''person or persons,'' as is shown by the amendments in the Senate files, as well as by the *Journal.*

[45] On January 23, Vice-president Burr being absent on account of illness, Senator John Brown of Kentucky had been chosen president of the Senate *pro tempore.*

[46] Robert Wright, senator from Maryland.

[47] Maryland act of 1796, c. 67.

as possible. It is dangerous to exclude foreigners. The very best of men will flee from Europe—for liberty exists only in this country. Bad men are afraid to come here—they are encouraged to stay at home. *I trust the present Congress are not apprehensive of having too many Jacobins in this country.* The government and the Congress were five years ago afraid of Jacobins—I hope we are not like them.

Mr. Pickering. I am very willing that foreigners should be admitted to settle in that country—for I believe before we purchased that we had territory in the United States sufficient for *us* and *our* posterity to the thousandth generation. I am willing that in Louisiana oppressed humanity should find an assylum, and that the patriots of no country should there find a country in which no restraints should be imposed upon them.

It was then moved to strike out of the amendment the words *citizen of the United States* and insert *person.*

The motion was lost yeas 13 nays 14.[48]

The question was then carried on the amendment, yeas 18, nays 11.

Mr. Jackson. If you establish a regular government there, you will destroy the western States, by the strong inducements you will hold out to people to settle Louisiana. The cession will prove a curse—why invite people to settle it now—it is too soon—50 or 100 years hence will be soon enough. By exposing these immense tracts of uncultivated lands to sale you will encourage bribery. I was offered half a million of acres to hold my tongue in the Georgia speculation. *I* had *virtue* to resist the temptation.[49]

The settlement of Louisiana will destroy the value of our lands. It will effect what I very much deprecate, a *separation* of this Union.

How great, how powerful, was Spain before she acquired South America. Her wealth has debased and enervated her strength. If you establish a regular government in Louisiana, that will be settled—you cannot then prevent it—and if settled, such is the enterprizing spirit and avaricious disposition of Americans that they will then soon conquer South America, and the rich mines of that country will prove our ruin. A military government ought to be established in upper Louisiana—that would prevent settlement. I would pay those Americans who are now there for their lands if they would quit them.

Mr. Cocke. I am glad Georgia has one uncorrupt man, and I rejoice that he is a senator. I trust we have many such in the nation. I am ready to vote. The debate on this bill has been so long that I have already lost

---

[48] This motion does not appear in the *Journal.*

[49] In 1796 Jackson was the leader of the ''Anti-Yazoo Party'' in the Georgia House of Representatives, having resigned his seat in the United States Senate in order to conduct the contest.

the benefit of much of it, for I have really forgotten it. I can throw no new light. I call for the question. We must give that people a rational government.

Mr. Worthington. The government contemplated by this bill is a military despotism, and I am surprised that it finds an advocate in this enlightened Senate. The gentleman from Georgia (Mr. Jackson) talks of a *separation*—Sir, the *western states* will not *separate* unless the *eastern States* by their conduct render it absolutely *necessary.*

1804, Thursday, Feby. 2nd.

GOVERNMENT OF LOUISIANA. MOTION TO STRIKE OUT THE 8TH SECTION OF THE BILL.[50]

Mr. Hillhouse. I am against the establishment of an arbitrary government in that country. It has been said it is best to establish such a government in that country as will prevent its settlement. I wish gentlemen to consider, that by the treaty the rights of the inhabitants of that country are guaranteed to them. Look at documents now on your tables, by them it appears that much of those vacant or uncultivated lands are granted to Spaniards. And you must give to them such a government as they can live under, or you will not protect them in the enjoyment of their rights as you have by your treaty stipulated. You must give that people a practical government—not like our own, for they are unacquainted with it—a military government would be too arbitrary. I would not give them a trial by jury, because they are not used to it—but I would give them the liberty of having trials by jury whenever they are able to express their desire of it by their own legis[la]ture and to make laws regulating that mode of trial.

Mr. John Smith. The establishment of a military government is at war with the third article of the treaty—with the letter and spirit of your constitution—which knows no other government than that of republicanism. That country is now ours—and it will be utterly impossible, by any law you can pass, to prevent people from emigrating to and settling in that country. Reference is frequently made to the documents that the President has sent us respecting that country. Those documents are incorrect. I know of three large settlements in that country that are not even named in these papers. We know but little of that Country.

---

[50] The eight section of the original bill, with slight modifications, is quoted in the Journal, III, 349. It relates to the government of the portion of the Louisiana cession north of the territory of Orleans, and provides for rule by a governor having the executive and judicial powers (''paramount powers'' in the original bill) exercised by the former governors of the province.

Mr. Cocke. Give that country a Jury. I know we can prevent its settlement. I would not give them a *good* government. I prefer a *bad* one to a good one *for them*—because a bad one will make them contented, they have been used to it. The only way to govern that country safely is to govern it justly. Let them have their old laws and ancient customs, except a trial by jury and that they *should have*. Too much wisdom is painful— it conjures up too many evils. I fear we are too wise to do good. Our way is plain, it is the old way—but I am really afraid we are fond of projects—novelties. Our fears are chimerical. We should be bold and resolute. Tell that people you shall have justice, but you shall obey the laws. I have taken up much of your time, but coming from the westward, I have frequently been urged to tell my opinion—no arbitrary—no military government will do—we must give them a free government. We talk too much of the ignorance of that people they know more than what you think they do—they are not so plagay ignorant.

Mr. Jackson. Rome flourished while she confined herself within proper bounds—but she extended her limits too far—when she gratified her insatiable thirst for lands—the northern hordes overwhelmed and destroyed her. I fear this will be our case in the *south.* I never wish to see our people go beyond the Mississippi. We ought not to give them such a government as will afford them protection in their settlements. If you permit the settle- ment of that country, you will depreciate the value of your public lands and destroy the western states. I know the President approves of this eight[h] section.

Mr. Anderson. This 8th. section is a military despotism—its unconsti- titional—its opposed to the spirit and genius of our constitution. The only power we have to legislate for that country is derived from the constitution —and we must give them a republican government—we can give them no other.

There never existed on earth a free Republican Government untill the present government of the United States.

This section establishes the former laws and government of Spain in that Country—and what those are we know not.

I know the settlement of Louisiana will materially injure Tennessee—it will injure all the western states—still we must give them a constitutional government. I am for preventing the settlement of that country by law, and I think our laws may be executed.

There is now about 8000 inhabitants in upper Louisiana—more than two thirds of them are Americans—most of them have emigrated from Virginia. They understand and will demand their rights.

If the President of the United States now approves of this 8th section— and should it be adopted, I will venture to say he will soon have cause to repent of it.

Mr. Dayton. I ask the gentleman (Mr. Anderson) where, and in what part of the Constitution does he find any authority to legislate for that Country. The constitution gives us no authority on the subject. We derive our power and right from the nature of government. That Country is a purchased territory and we may govern it as a conquered one.

A military government is the best and the only government you can prudently and safely establish in Upper Louisiana. A strong efficient government is essential. I hope we shall prevent the settlement of Upper Louisiana, not only for the present, but forever. If that country is settled, the people will separate from us—they will form a new empire—and become our enemies.

I believe we may induce the Indians on this side to remove to the other side of the Mississippi—and this will be a great and useful thing to us.[51]

This section of the bill is important and will I hope be retained.

Mr. Wright. I am in favor of the section. The constitution requires that the governments of States should be republican, but not so of territorial governments. The Territorial governments in this Country are not, or is it necessary they should be, republican—none of them have the power to elect representatives. To extend the trial by jury to that country would be a denial of Justice—they live too remote from each other to derive any benefit from it.

Mr. Samuel Smith. This 8th section embraces a country in which there are settlements 800 miles distant from each other. A governor and three Judges cannot regular their affairs. This section of the bill is in principle republican—we ourserves are their Legislators and the Commandants are only our agents.

Mr. Pickering. I think we are in an error in applying the Constitution to that country—it does not extend there. But we are bound by the treaty to extend protection to the people of that country, and secure to them their rights and priveledges. We must consider and govern them as a colony.

Laws will never be sufficient to prevent the settlement of that country. If people find their interest in settling it, your prohibitions will prove unavailing.

Mr. Brackenridge. I do not feel any constitutional difficulty as to the form of government. I am for giving them such a system as to me appears best. The provisions contained in this 8th section are arbitary. There is no legislative authority given to that people. I am opposed to the section.

Mr. Nicholas. I am glad the section gives no legislative authority—that country needs none. I am inimical to change. Do as little for that people as possible. Let them have and enjoy their old laws and customs.

---

[51] See Miss Abel in *Annual Report* of the American Historical Association for 1906, I, 241–249. Sec. 9 of the original bill in Breckinridge's manuscript provides for exchange of land by Indian tribes.

Mr. Wright. I would have such a despotic government in the territory of Upper Louisiana as should absolutely prevent people from settling it. I would remove those who are now settled there, if I could—but at all events I would let no more go there.

Mr. Cocke. I will always give a good government when I can. I will not do evil meerly because I have the power of doing so. The question.

The question was then taken and the 8th section was struck out—yeas 16, nays 9.

See Journal of Senate, p. 174.[52]

1804, Friday, Feby. 3d.

THE BILL FOR THE GOVERNMENT OF LOUISIANA UNDER CONSIDERATION[53]

Mr. Jackson. I have high authority for saying it is the intention of our government to take effectual measures to induce all the Indians on this side of the Mississippi to exchange their lands for lands in upper Louisiana.[54] I think it a prudent and practicable measure—and that is one reason why I wish to prevent the establishment of a civil government in that territory. In the name of God have we not land enough for a settlement without this! I would buy up the title of those who have already gone there. The Indians would have gone there before this had not the Spaniards have prevented them. The Indian wars have cost us millions of dollars—and much blood. They are bad dangerous neighbors. There are already many Indians there—if you establish a civil government--if you permit settlers—you will find the expense of that government immense—it will render the purchase a curse.

Mr. Worthington. The Indiana Territory is as good soil and situation as Upper Louisiana. There have been settlers in the former for 100 years, and a civil government established for sometime—that government has not encreased settlers—and in *all* the Indiana Territory there are not now more 7000 souls.

Mr. Nicholas. I hope the Upper Louisiana will not for many, very many years, be admitted as a State or States—New Orleans, perhaps must soon be admitted as such.

Mr. Jackson. I move to annex Upper Louisiana to the Indiana Territory.

Mr. Brackenridge. I have little objections to this.

---

[52] Page 174 of the original edition; page 349 of vol. III of the reprint of 1821.

[53] Debate was apparently on an amendment not mentioned in the *Journal* but preserved in manuscript in the Senate files, giving Upper Louisiana a territorial government of the simplest form, with its own governor, secretary, and judges, and with legislative power vested in the governor and judges. This amendment is endorsed "Breckinridge."

[54] For Jefferson's course in this matter see Miss Abel, *loc. cit.*

Mr. Hillhouse. The government, laws, customs, manners and habits of the two countries are in direct opposition to each other. The regulations of the one cannot be established in the other. You cannot immediately effect such a change.

Mr. Saml. Smith. I approve of the measure. It will lessen the number of offices and of course expence. I know it will estop slavery there, and to that I agree.

Mr. Wright. This is a new proposition, but I am in favor of it—it will lessen expence. I would unite the two territories governmentally but not territorially.

Mr. Hillhouse. Both of those Countries have separate *rights,* and by this regulation you will impair them both. The ordinance establishing the Indiana Territory created certain rights which are vested in the inhabitants of that territory. The people in Louisiana have their *rights* and we have by treaty guaranteed to them the enjoyment of those rights. If these territories are united who will legislate for them—must they be governed by different laws. This union will make one of the territories a mere colony to the other.

Mr. Wright. They must be governed by different laws.

Mr. John Smith. I cannot wholly approve of the motion. I think there is weight in the argument of the gentleman from Connecticut (Mr. Hillhouse). But I will accord with the majority. I should be better pleased if a part of Upper Louisiana was annexed to the Mississippi Territory.

Mr. Venable. I approve of the principle, but wish it modified. It is not yet settled that Louisiana is a part of the United States. I would not therefore annex the two territories together; but I would extend the authority of the government of the Indiana territory to the territory of Upper Louisiana.

1804, Tuesday, Feby. 7th

THE BILL FOR THE GOVERNMENT OF LOUISIANA

The debate on this bill was principally confined to the question whether people of colour should be necessarily disqualified and excluded from serving on juries. Excluded. Democrats in general voted in favor of exclusion.

1804, Wednesday, Feby. 8th.

SAME BILL

The amendment to annex the upper Territory of Louisiana to Indiana, was withdrawn. Mr. Nicholas offered an amendment authorizing the officers of the Indiana Territory to govern the Upper District of Louisiana

—and establishing the existing laws of Louisiana in that district.[55] Adopted. Act as amended ordered to be printed.

The democratic senators held a Caucus last evening in which they settled the principles of the bill—and agreed to the same in the Senate without any debate.[56]

1804, Thursday, Feby. 16.

Louisiana Bill. Salaries to the Officers

Governor Orleans

Mr. Jackson, Mr. Dayton } reasoned in favor of $8000 pr
Mr. Saml Smith and Mr. Logan[57] } annum—7 only voted for it.
Mr. Brackenridge and John Smith for $6000. 12 voted for it.
Mr. Olcott,[58] Franklin and Cocke for $5000. 18 voted for it—carried.

The salary to the Secretary	$2000
Three Judges each	2000
District Judge	2000
Attorney	600
Marshall	200

The members of the Legislative Council each to have four dollars per diem while attending the Council.

In the course of this debate, Jackson and Samuel Smith observed ''That the people must be governed more by pomp, parade and shew than by reason —that splendid retinues and armed men are more convincing than arguments.

1804, Friday, Feby. 17.

Louisiana Bill

Mr. Stone.[59] There are near 900,000 slaves in the U.S. and they are worth $200,000,000. Slaves are property. The rights of property are by the Constitution guaranteed and why should the holders of this kind of property be prohibited from sending and selling their slaves in Louisiana?

Mr. McClay. That country was purchased to serve as an *outlet* for the U.S.—to admit slaves there will defeat that object.

Mr. Jackson. It has been proposed to prohibit South Carolina from sending slaves into Louisiana, because she imports slaves from Africa. She

---

[55] This amendment, in manuscript, is in the Senate files, and also appears in the bill as amended (and in the statute) as sec. 12.

[56] Some amendments offered on subsequent days appear in the *Journal,* but Plumer records no debates respecting them.

[57] George Logan, senator from Pennsylvania.

[58] Simeon Olcott, senator from New Hampshire.

[59] David Stone, senator from North Carolina.

has a right to do it. If you pass this prohibition you will offend that State —and I will venture to say very serious consequences will follow. I will speak plain—offend her and she will reject the amendment to the Constitution—and if she rejects it, it will never be ratified.

Some people laugh at the provision that the bill contains authorizing the Presidint to make an exchange of lands in Louisiana with the Indians for their lands on this side of the Mississippi. Let me tell such, That this is a favorite measure of the President's—he has assured me so. He has, this week, informed me that sixteen of the Cherokee Chiefs have already agreed to pass over to Louisiana and relinquish their lands on this side of the Mississippi.

1804, Saturday, Feby. 18.

BILL FOR THE GOVERNMENT OF LOUISIANA

Mr. Adams. This bill is to establish a form of government for the extensive country of Louisiana. I have from the beginning been opposed to it—and I still am. It is forming a government for that people without their consent and against their will.

All power in a republican government is derived from the *people.* We sit here under their authority.

The people of that country have given no power or authority to us to legislate for them. The people of the United States could give us none, because they had none themselves. The treaty has given us none, for they were not parties to it—it was made without their knowledge. To pass this bill is an encroachment on their rights—its a commencement of assumed power—its establishing a precedent for after Congresses destructive of the essential principles of genuine liberty.

The first territorial ordinance under the Confederation was made by the then Congress without any legal authority—but the Constitution afterwards sanctioned it.

This bill contains arbitary principles—principles repugnant to our Constitution. The legislative Council are to be appointed by the Governor, who is a creature of the President's—not elected by the people.

The judges are to legislate—make laws and expound them—this is of the essence of tyranny.

In the other territorial governments, even in the departure from liberty, there is a reverence for it—for it provides that when its inhabitants are encreased to a certain number they shall elect a representative.

This bill provides that the officers shall be appointed by the President *alone* in the recess of the Senate—why this departure from the Constitution.

The Judicial officers are to be appointed for a term of years only, and yet the bill is not limited. The constitutional tenure for judicial officers *is during good behavior.*

The first thing Congress ought to have done in relation to that Country, should have been to propose an amendment to the Constitution, to the several States to authorize Congress to receive that Country into the Union —we ought to have applied to the inhabitants of Louisiana to recognize our right to govern them. This we ought to have done, and there is no doubt that the States and that territory would have given the authority before the next session.

The 3d article of the treaty pledges the faith of the Nation to the inhabitants of that country that we will protect their persons, religion property and rights; but we have taken no measures to ascertain there numbers, religion or rights.

We have not the necessary information to pass a law containing the great fundamental principles of government. We know little of that people or Country. In thus passing this bill we commit an act of practical tyranny.

The bill contains incongruous articles—establishment of courts—juries— numerous laws—prohibition of slavery etc. This is a Colonial system of government. It is the first the United States have established. It is a bad precedent—the U.S. in time will have many colonies—precedents are therefore important.

The governor's appointing and proroguing the Council is an act of tyranny.

Tis too soon to extend the trial by jury to that Country. There are serious inconveniences attending this mode of trial—and those people have not laws, customs or habits to correct those evils. Extending juries to them in their present condition, will, I fear, excite opposition to the institution itself. There present mode of trial is *summary*—no jury—a single judge decides. Trial by jury and delay are synonymous—by introducing it you establish new principles. What is meant by *vicinage* in that country? In law books it has a definite and precise meaning—it is confined to a County. There you have no Counties. Is it to extend thro' the whole country. Will it not give too much power to the judge—and will it not be burthensome and even oppressive to compel people from distant parts of that extended world (for such I may call it) to attend Courts of law as grand and petit jurors! The District court is to sit once in three months, and the Supreme Court once every month—the call for jurors will therefore be frequent.

The governor and judges of the Indiana territory are to govern Louisiana —will they not govern it in an arbitrary manner—will they not consider it as a colony to them?

The bill passed yeas 20 nays 5.

INDEX

Adams, John, defends Louisiana purchase, 34–35.

Adams, J. Q., opinion on need of constitutional amendment for Louisiana purchase, 30–31, 45–47, and for fulfilling engagements of Art. 7 of Louisiana treaty, 75; motion to pass Breckinridge bill, 102; opposition to delegate to Congress from Louisiana Territory, 104; opinion on slavery, 110, 117; comments on slavery provisions in Louisiana government bill, 115, note 27, 117, 121, note 42; interpretation of constitution on slavery, 119; vote against Louisiana government bill and reasons therefor, 129–131.

Alston, W., of North Carolina, on admission of Orleans Territory to statehood, 179.

Ames, F., denunciation of Louisiana Purchase, 29.

American Insurance Co. vs. Canter, interpretation by Supreme Court of status of territorial courts, 130, note 60, 140, note 23.

Anderson, of Tennessee, opinion on government for Louisiana, 107, on slavery, 111; motion against prescribing a government for Upper Louisiana, 121, 126, note 49; opposition to section 8 of Louisiana government bill, 123; amendment to Louisiana government bill, 127.

"Anti-Yazoo Party," 121, note 43.

Articles of Confederation, article 11, bearing on constitutional right to acquire territory, 14.

Bedinger, of Kentucky, support of bill providing for registry of vessels, 132.

Barry, of Kentucky, on admission of Orleans Territory, 179.

Bibb, of Georgia, on admission of Orleans Territory, 179, 180, 186, on division of Orleans Territory, 181.

Boré, E. de, resignation as mayor of New Orleans, 149; report against Claiborne, 154.

Boyle, of Kentucky, opposed to Breckinridge bill, 138.

Bradley, of Vermont, opposition to delegate to Congress from Louisiana Territory, 103; opinion on slavery, 109, 112, 114, 119, on form of government for Louisiana, 110, on government of District of Columbia, 110; opposed first Hillhouse amendment, 114, favored second Hillhouse amendment, 116.

Breckinridge, J., opinion on limitation of area of a republic, 62; denial of unconstitutionality of Art. 3 of Louisiana Treaty, 69, 70; cited on confining Americans to east side of Mississippi, 99; opinion on slavery, 108, 114, 118–119, on annexation of Upper Louisiana to Indiana Territory, 126. *See also* Breckinridge Bill.

[235]

Index

Lucas, of Pennsylvania, opinion on Breckinridge bill, 136.

Lyon, of Kentucky, opinion on Breckinridge bill, 136–137.

McKinley, President, 42, *note* 14.

Maclay, of Pennsylvania, opinion on formation of legislative council for Louisiana, 107, on slavery in Louisiana, 129.

McLemore resolutions, 5, *note* 13.

Macon, of North Carolina, opinion on form of government for Louisiana, 137; on admission of new territory to Union, 181, on Orleans Territory statehood bill, 186.

Madison, James, cited on admission of Missouri into the Union, 48; comment on President's message announcing ratification of the treaty, 49; instructions regarding rights of inhabitants of acquired territory, 66–67; quoted on provision concerning commercial privileges in Louisiana Treaty, 79–80, on form of government for Louisiana, 100; action regarding West Florida, 172–173.

Magruder, A. B., opinion on expansion of territory, 37, *note* 1, 62, *note* 2; agent bearing Louisiana State Constitution and West Florida memorial to President, 190.

Marbois, B., expression of French apprehension for French West Indies, 33.

Marbury vs. Madison, significance of decision of Supreme Court, 61.

Marshall, Chief Justice, approval of Constitutional right to acquire territory, 35; opinion concerning writ of habeas corpus, 169.

Mason, S. T., cited on Ross resolutions, 12.

Memorial to Congress against Claiborne, 153–162; bearers of, to Washington, 155, 156, 161, 162; resolution submitted in the House, 160; bill passed in the Senate, 160–161.

Mexican War, 175, *note* 18.

Mexico, 196.

Miller, of Tennessee, opposed to admission of Orleans Territory, 181.

Mississippi, The, efforts ot Executive and Congress toward securing of rights of Americans on, and of establishment of as boundary line between United States and Louisiana, 9–11; the Ross resolutions, 11; plan of Attorney General Lincoln, 17.

Mississippi Territory, introduction of slaves forbidden, from without the United States, 102, *note* 6; annexation to, of Upper Louisiana, 126.

Mitchell, N., of Massachusetts, review of the Louisiana question, 144–146.

Mitchell, of New York, opinion on resolution requesting documents from President, 51, on right to acquire territory, 64–65; on preparation of people of territories for statehood, 72, on power to make citizens under Louisiana Treaty, 73, on constitutionality of Art. 7 of Louisiana Treaty, 78, on power of the Executive, 87; on amendment of Orleans Territory Statehood bill, 187.

DATE DUE